T0185507

Lecture Notes of the Institute for Computer Sciences, Social Informatics and Telecommunications Engineering　355

More information about this series at http://www.springer.com/series/8197

Honghao Gao · Ramón J. Durán Barroso ·
Pang Shanchen · Rui Li (Eds.)

Broadband Communications, Networks, and Systems

11th EAI International Conference, BROADNETS 2020
Qingdao, China, December 11–12, 2020
Proceedings

 Springer

Editors
Honghao Gao
Shanghai University
Shanghai, China

Pang Shanchen
China University of Petroleum
Hangzhou, China

Ramón J. Durán Barroso
University of Valladolid
Valladolid, Spain

Rui Li
Xidian University
Xi'an, China

ISSN 1867-8211   ISSN 1867-822X (electronic)
Lecture Notes of the Institute for Computer Sciences, Social Informatics
and Telecommunications Engineering
ISBN 978-3-030-68736-6   ISBN 978-3-030-68737-3 (eBook)
https://doi.org/10.1007/978-3-030-68737-3

This Springer imprint is published by the registered company Springer Nature Switzerland AG
The registered company address is: Gewerbestrasse 11, 6330 Cham, Switzerland

Preface

We are delighted to introduce the proceedings of the 11th European Alliance for Innovation (EAI) International Conference on Broadband Communications, Networks, and Systems (Broadnets 2020). This conference brought together researchers, developers, and practitioners around the world who are interested in 5G/6G technologies, internet of everything, security in communication, cloud, and so on.

The technical program of Broadnets 2020 consisted of 13 papers, including 7 full papers and 6 workshop papers in oral presentation sessions at the main conference tracks. The conference sessions were: Session 1 - Wireless Network and Security; Session 2 - Communication Quality. Apart from high-quality technical paper presentations, the technical program also featured two technical workshops. The organized workshops were Edge Computing Networks, Systems and Services Workshop (Go2Edge). The aim of Go2Edge is to encourage academic researchers and industry practitioners to explore different computing and network technologies to develop future edge computing technologies.

Coordination with the steering chair, Imrich Chlamtac, was essential for the success of the conference. We sincerely appreciate his constant support and guidance. It was also a great pleasure to work with such an excellent organizing committee team for their hard work in organizing and supporting the conference. In particular, the Technical Program Committee, led by our General Chairs, General Co-Chairs and TPC Co-Chairs, Prof. Shanchen Pang, Prof. Rui Li, Prof. Yushen Xu, and Prof. Xiangwei Zheng have completed the peer-review process of technical papers and made a high-quality technical program. We are also grateful to the Conference Manager, Natasha Onofrei, for her support and to all the authors who submitted their papers to the Broadnets 2020 conference and workshops.

We strongly believe that the Broadnets conference provides a good forum for all researchers, developers, and practitioners to discuss all scientific and technological aspects that are relevant to broadband communications and networking. We also expect that future Broadnets conferences will be as successful and stimulating, as indicated by the contributions presented in this volume.

Gao Honghao
Ramón J. Durán Barroso
Pang Shanchen
Li Rui

Conference Organization

Steering Committee

Chair

Imrich Chlamtac   University of Trento, Italy

Members

Jizhong Zhao   Xi'an Jiaotong University
Honghao Gao   Shanghai University
Victor Sucasas   Technology Innovation Institute
Faming Gong   China University of Petroleum

Organizing Committee

General Chair

Shanchen Pang   China University of Petroleum

General Co-chair

Rui Li   Xi'dian University

Technical Program Committee Chairs

Yushen Xu   Xi'dian University
Xiangwei Zheng   Shandong Normal University

Web Chair

Xiaoxian Yang   Shanghai Polytechnic University

Publicity and Social Media Chairs

Yukun Dong   China University of Petroleum
Rossi Kamal   Xaria ICT

Workshops Chair

Yuanyuan Zhang   Qingdao University of Technology

Sponsorship and Exhibits Chair

Yulin Zhang   Shandong University of Science and Technology

Publications Chair

Xinzeng Wang   Shandong University of Science and Technology

Local Chair

Tao Song   China University of Petroleum

Technical Program Committee

Shijun Liu   Shandong University
Shaohua Wan   Zhongnan University of Economics and Law
Yirui Wu   Hohai University
Haiyan Wang   Nanjing University of Posts and Telecommunications
Qi Li   Nanjing University of Posts and Telecommunications
Qingsong Yao   Xidian University
Lin Wang   Yanshan University
Pablo Fondo-Ferreiro   University of Vigo
Abdullah Alhasanat   Al-Hussein Bin Talal University
Alvaro Barradas   University of Algarve
Jaime Martins   University of Algarve
Mohammad Abu Shattal   The Ohio State University

Contents

Wireless Network and Security

Possibility of Using Existed WLAN Infrastructure as an Emergency Network for Air-to-Ground Transmissions: The Case of WebRTC-Based Flying IoT System

Agnieszka Chodorek[1]($\boxtimes$) , Robert R. Chodorek[2] , and Krzysztof Wajda[2]

[1] Kielce University of Technology, Al. 1000-lecia P.P. 7, Kielce 25-314, Poland
a.chodorek@tu.kielce.pl
[2] The AGH University of Science and Technology, Al. Mickiewicza 30,
Krakow 30-059, Poland
chodorek@agh.edu.pl, wajda@kt.agh.edu.pl
http://www.kt.agh.edu.pl

Abstract. In many urban and industrial areas, there exist wireless network infrastructures - usually complex, covering large public buildings (often with adjacent parking lots and green areas). In the case of emergency situations, such infrastructure could be used as a production network (i.e. a network dedicated to the transmission of user data) for creating ad-hoc flying monitoring systems, composed of one or more air stations (drones equipped with specialized sensors and detectors, as well as a high resolution camera), and corresponding ground station(s). This paper proves that the existing network architecture is able to play a significant role in the casual assurance of suitable air-to-ground transmission of monitoring data. Transmissions are carried out between two WebRTC applications of IoT brokers, placed on the air station, and on the ground one. The stations are connected through the IEEE 802.11ac (Wi-Fi) production network. During experiments, two different wireless local area networks were used as a production network. The first one was dedicated to transmissions coming from the flying monitoring system. The second one was the private network of the AGH University of Science and Technology, available for the academic community. Results of experiments show that although a dedicated network better fits the needs of the flying monitoring system, a well-dimensioned public network that has good coverage of the monitored area is able to effectively replace it in an emergency.

Keywords: Internet of Things · Performance evaluation · Real-time multimedia · Unmanned aerial vehicle · WebRTC

This work was supported by the Polish Ministry of Science and Higher Education with the subvention funds of the Faculty of Computer Science, Electronics and Telecommunications of AGH University.

H. Gao et al. (Eds.): BROADNETS 2020, LNICST 355, pp. 3–21, 2021.
https://doi.org/10.1007/978-3-030-68737-3_1

1   Introduction

In many places, especially in strongly urbanized environments, there exist complex network infrastructures. In urban areas extensive local network infrastructures have been built, based on cellular telephony (LTE[1], GSM[2]/EDGE[3] or UMTS[4]/HSPA[5]) and (or) IEEE[6] 802.11 wireless local area network (wireless LAN, or WLAN) technology (also known as Wireless Fidelity, or Wi-Fi). Large companies and institutions have built complex IEEE 802.11 networks, which include anything from a few to a large number of access points. Complex IEEE 802.11 networks have also been created by network service providers. In many cities, there are large public IEEE 802.11 networks available to a large group of users.

All these networks are usually designed considering the local propagation of radio signals to obtain full coverage of a given area. As a result, they could be used, in emergency situations, as data transmission networks for the purpose of ad-hoc installed flying monitoring systems. Such systems consist of one or more air station(s), i.e., flying drones equipped with high resolution cameras and specialized sensors and detectors, and corresponding ground station(s), connected with the air one through a wireless local area network.

The Authors believed that the use of existing network infrastructure could facilitate and accelerate the process of the construction of flying monitoring systems, although there are some unknowns, such as the behaviour of flying monitoring systems when non-dedicated, not-optimized (in terms of a flying monitoring system), typically configured user channel will be used for the transmission of monitoring data. This paper sheds a light on these aspects through the experimental evaluation of the air-to-ground transmission of environmental data from sensors and video from a 4K UAV camera.

1.1   WebRTC and WebRTC-Based Flying Monitoring System

The World Wide Web real-time communications (WebRTC) [15,24,32] is a novel technology, not fully standardized yet [25], which assures real-time transmission of media (audio and/or video) in a non-real-time Web environment. The media are streamed using the Real-time Transport Protocol (RTP) version 2 [34], which uses the classic Audio Video Profile (RTP/AVP) [35] and the security extension to this profile, namely RTP/SAVP [3] (Secure RTP, or SRTP). Cryptographical protection of the SRTP is performed with the use of the Advanced Encryption Standard (AES) algorithm. The WebRTC technology also offers data transmission, which uses symmetric Data Channels [19], enabling transmissions of non-real-time data flows with the use of the Stream Control Transmission Protocol

---

[1] Long-Term Evolution.
[2] Global System for Mobile Communications.
[3] Enhanced Data rates for GSM Evolution.
[4] Universal Mobile Telecommunications System.
[5] High Speed Packet Access.
[6] Institute of Electrical and Electronics Engineers.

(SCTP) [37]. SCTP transmissions are secured using the Datagram Transport Layer Security (DTLS) protocol [31,38].

Both audio/video streams and data flows are congestion controlled. The SCTP congestion control is a slightly modified TCP Congestion Control [1]. Streaming media congestion control is mainly based on the TCP-friendly Rate Control (TFRC) [14] and the Google Congestion Control (GCC) [17] (both used as sender-side congestion control). Additionally, stream replication simulcast and layered simulcast can be used as node-side congestion control. Performance evaluation of the sender-side congestion control is presented in [7,36], and the node-side one in [8,16].

One of the possible applications of the WebRTC technology is the Internet of Things (IoT) broker [9,10], which was one of the main parts of the flying IoT system, designed to monitor parking lots.

The flying IoT system consists of an air station and a ground station. The air station is composed of the IoT carrier, which is an Unmanned Aerial Vehicle (UAV), and the flying IoT system, which is composed of a 4K video camera, a set of environmental sensors, and a single-board computer, on which the WebRTC application of an IoT broker is run. Streaming media from the camera and non-media data from sensors are aggregated into one stream and transmitted to the ground, where they are received by the other WebRTC application of an IoT broker, run at the ground station. The ground station also is composed of the two parts (as the air station is): the WebRTC multimedia and monitoring station (WMMS), and the command and control console (CCC). The WMMS is the WebRTC-based IoT broker run on a computer device (e.g.. desktop computer, laptop or even smartphone on which WebRTC-capable web browser is run). The CCC is used for piloting the UAV.

Due to reliability and quality of service (QoS) issues, the network connecting the air station and the ground station has been physically divided into two separate parts: the production network, used for the communication between the IoT system on board the UAV and the WMMS, and the management and control network, used for communication between the UAV and the CCC.

1.2   Complex Infrastructure-Based Production Network

The example of a complex infrastructure-based variant, based on an IEEE 802.11 network, is shown in Fig. 1. The flying IoT system uses a set of available access points AP1, AP2, AP3, which are connected to a central controller to authorize future clients of the successive access points and to allow for fast roaming between access points. In practice, in a given instant of time, usually only a subset of this set is being used. Which available access points belong to the subset of currently used access points varies in time.

In contrast to the simple infrastructure-based variant, where a single access point is a kind of relay station that receives application data and resends them directly to the WMMS, the solution shown in Fig. 1 allows the data transmission

In the case of a simple infrastructure-based variant, a single intermediate device (access point) is used. It acts as a kind of relay station that receives

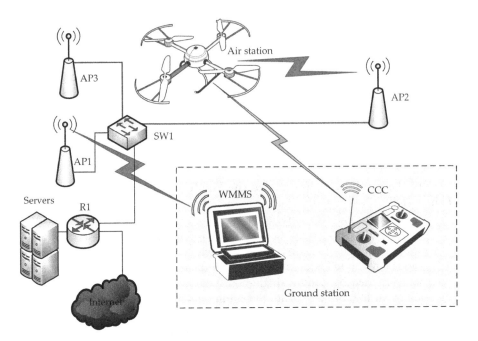

Fig. 1. General architecture of the flying IoT system: infrastructure-based variant with multiple APs (red - production network, yellow - management and control network). (Color figure online)

application data and resends them directly to the WMMS. The complex infrastructure-based variant extends the simple one with multiple (two or more) intermediate devices. Example of such a solution is shown in Fig. 1. In contrast to the simple infrastructure-based variant, the complex one allows the data transmission path to travel through a set of access points.

In the situation depicted in Fig. 1, one access point (AP2) receives the application data from the IoT system mounted on the UAV, and sends them using the infrastructure of the distribution network (the so-called Distribution System, or DS, which can be implemented as a wired or wireless one) to the other access point (AP1), which broadcasts data directly to the WebRTC multimedia and monitoring station. AP1 and AP2 belong to the subset of currently used access points.

This situation may change over time. The range of an average drone is greater than the range of an average IEEE 802.11 connection. Areas monitored by flying IoT systems will often be large enough to display a significant deterioration of the signal-to-noise ratio when IoT systems are connected to single access points. In the case of the availability of multiple access points, if the quality of connections between IoT systems and the currently connected access points become poor, the current points of attachment to the IEEE 802.11 network will be changed (e.g.. from AP2 to AP3). Thus, the subset of currently used access points will change (here: from {AP1, AP2} to {AP1, AP3}).

An essential condition of the IEEE 802.11 network connectivity is that all access points connected to a given network (and so belonging to a given set of available access points) must provide the same extended set of services. They must create an Extended Service Set (ESS) and be identified by the same identifier (the same ESSID). In practice it means that classic roaming consists of several steps, which take time and causes some more or less serious breaks in transmission. This is usually unnoticeable during reliable data transfer, but can be seen during media streaming.

The use of a seamless handover allows streaming media to be transferred during the changing of their point of attachment from one access point to another, without significant degradation of the quality of the transmission service (QoS parameters should not fall below a level acceptable by a streaming application). So, in the case depicted in Fig. 1, fast roaming (standardized as the IEEE 802.11r) is recommended. For purposes of the flying IoT system, both the IEEE 802.11r over-air roaming and the IEEE 802.11r over-ds (over Distribution System) roaming can be used.

Large companies and institutions build IEEE 802.11 networks working in so-called enterprise mode, in which central databases based on the 802.1x protocol and RADIUS servers are used for authentication. The use of this infrastructure for the flying IoT system requires registration of all used network devices (here: network adapters of IoT systems and of WMMSs) within the authentication server.

The complex infrastructure-based variant of the flying IoT system has two general advantages, common for both infrastructure-based variants: easy access to additional services provided by the external infrastructure, and the ability for transmissions between a WMMS and multiple UAVs. However, the main advantages of the complex infrastructure-based variant are the increased range of communication within large areas, and the high performance of the communication, which is optimized to a given area.

The main disadvantages of the complex infrastructure-based variant is a complex setup and a longer time to start gathering data, when compared with the simple infrastructure-based variant. Additionally, if the production network is attached to the public Internet, cyber threats that are coming from any site of this global network may appear in the production network nodes.

The complex infrastructure-based variant of the flying IoT system assumes that the production networks may or may not be dedicated. In particular, it may be built in whole as a dedicated network, or it may be constructed (partially or in whole) using fragments of existing network infrastructures.

1.3 Motivations, Main Contributions and Organization of This Paper

In the paper [9] a WebRTC-based flying Internet of Things system to monitor a parking lot was introduced. The presented system consists of an air station, a ground station, and two wireless local area networks that connect stations. The first WLAN is a management and control network, intended for the pilotage of a UAV, which serves as the carrier of a WebRTC-based IoT. The second is a production network, used for WebRTC transmissions of video from the UAV camera and environmental data from sensors.

The aim of this paper is to discuss performance of the flying IoT system, when the production network has a relatively complex topology, i.e. transmission paths lead through more than one intermediate node. The question is: must such a network be built as a dedicated one, or is possible to use existing infrastructure, covering the whole monitoring area but not being under the administrative control of the owners of the flying IoT system? The latter is especially important in the case of emergency situations, where there is no time for the ad-hoc building of complex networks, and in the case of occasional events, where the building of complex networks may not be economically feasible. The main contributions of this paper are:

- Discussion of the architectural issues of the flying monitoring system in the context of the building of a complex production network.
- Evaluation of the prototype flying monitoring system in terms of the performance of air-to-ground communication carried out in a dedicated 802.11ac WLAN.
- Evaluation of the prototype flying monitoring system in terms of the performance of air-to-ground communication using an existing, general-purpose 802.11ac WLAN infrastructure, which is a functional equivalent of the dedicated one.

The rest of this paper is as follows. The next, second Section describes related work. The third Section briefly describes the analyzed system and the test environment. The fourth Section presents the results of the experiments that were carried out. The last, fifth Section summarizes our experiences and concludes this paper.

2   Related Work

Several aspects of communication (routing, various communications technologies) in the context of UAVs were presented in paper [2]. Literature reearch carried out in the paper [39] shows that advanced high-bandwidth UAV communication can be carried out mainly with the use of the IEEE 802.11 technology.

The transmission from a drone to a ground station using LTE was analyzed in [6, 27, 29]. In [6] is presented a system in which the mobile phone supporting LTE was installed on the drone. Only data generated by the application which runs on the mobile phone are sent to the ground station using the LTE network. The transmission of both the video live stream and the control data between the drone and the ground station using the LTE network was presented in [27]. The LTE network used for the video transmission from the UAV for the surveillance a crowd of people was presented in [29]. It is worth remarking that experiments were carried out only in private LTE network, fully administrated by persons which conducted experiments.

In [5] usage of a Narrow Band IoT (NB-IoT) for collecting data from underground sensors in potato crops was presented. The base station of the NB-IoT using the 716 MHz band was mounted on a UAV.

Analysis of the usage of a UAV as a gateway between IoT devices which uses LoRaWAN technology and a LTE network was presented in [4].

Very small drones with only a few sensors onboard (humidity, temperature, light intensity) were analyzed in [18]. For communication dedicated RF working in the 900 MHz ISM band was used. Data are sent using ON-OFF keying modulation.

In [28] the integration of a UAV IoT communication platform which minimized both energy consumption and the time to handle events was analyzed. The performance of the presented system was validated using simulation.

In several applications, IoT devices are being located not on the drone but on the ground. In those solutions drones work as a communication relay [11–13]. In the paper [12] the performance of air-to-ground communication between the drone and multiple wireless IoT devices in a WiFi 2,4 GHz test environment was analyzed. Paper [13] analyzes two problems of the communication between the drone and multiple wireless IoT devices: different numbers of devices in different areas and potential traffic congestion in those areas. To avoid those problems the concept of load balancing is proposed. The concept was evaluated in a simulator. An analysis of the usage of multiple UAVs in a dynamic environment to cover multiple regions was presented in [11]. The proposed solution was evaluated using the numerical simulations which were performed in the Matlab.

3   Analyzed System and Experimental Environment

This Section outlines a WebRTC-based flying monitoring system, build as reported in [9], describes the environment of experiments that were carried out at a parking lot of the AGH University of Science and Technology, and overviews practical aspects related to these experiments.

3.1   WebRTC-Based Flying Monitoring System

The WebRTC-based flying monitoring system, introduced in the paper [9], includes an air station and a ground one. The air station is composed of a WebRTC-based IoT system, which performs a monitoring service, and a flying carrier (here: a UAV), on which the IoT system is mounted. The ground station is composed of two consoles:

- CCC, which is the remote control console,
- WMMS, which is the IoT console.

The WMMS is also the destination point of the air-to-ground transmissions coming from the IoT system.

The important part of the analyzed system is an emulator of an IoT broker, written as a WebRTC application. This software implements full encapsulation and decapsulation of non-real-time data in/from messages of the Message Queue Telemetry Transport (MQ Telemetry Transport, MQTT) protocol. The MQTT is used as an application layer protocol for the transmission of data coming from sensors. For transmission of video frames no application layer protocol is used.

On the air station, the WebRTC application of the IoT broker is run on the Chromium browser, which, in turn, is run on a single-board computer (SBC) working under the control of the Raspbian operating system. On the ground station, the application of the IoT broker is run on the Chrome browser.

The broker running on the air station collects data from sensors and from a 4K video camera, and then sends that data to the WMMS. Video data are transmitted as a media stream, using the RTP. Environmental data from sensors are transmitted as non-media flow, using the SCTP. The media stream and non-media flow are aggregated before being sent to the WMMS. The broker running on the WMMS disaggregates the received stream, decapsulates video frames from RTP packets and non-media data from SCTP packets and MQTT receivers. Then the broker processes the obtained information (if needed) and displays it on the dashboard. The video is displayed in the form of moving pictures, and the environmental data from sensors are displayed as successive points of time graphs and/or numerical values.

As was mentioned in the Introduction, the air station and the ground station are connected through two networks:

- the management and control network, which connects the IoT carrier and the CCC,
- the production network, which connects the WebRTC-based IoT system and the WMMS.

In the prototype implementation [9], the production network was built according to the IEEE 802.11ac standard. Thus, at least three variants of the production network are possible:

- the infrastructure-less variant, implemented as the simplest Independent Basic Service Set (IBSS), which is composed of only two stations,
- the simple infrastructure-based variant, implemented as two Basic Service Sets (BSSs) connected through a shared access point,
- the complex infrastructure-based variant, implemented as a single Extended Service Set (ESS).

In the case of the infrastructure-less variant, transmissions between the air station and the ground station are carried out using a single, direct path, and no intermediate devices are used. This variant offers high mobility and great simplicity, although it suffers from a limited range of communication.

Both the infrastructure-based variants offers indirect transmissions, which lead through one (the simple infrastructure-based variant) or more (the complex infrastructure-based variant) intermediate access points. The use of infrastructure-based variants results in an increased range of communication when compared to the infrastructure-less one.

3.2   Test Environment

Experiments were carried out at one of the parking lots of the AGH University of Science and Technology. During experiments, the flying IoT system described in the paper [9] and briefly characterized in the previous Section, was used.

Experiments were conducted with the use of a complex infrastructure-based variant of the production network, depicted in the Fig. 2, and according to following scenarios:

- the use of a portable, temporary network infrastructure (scenario S1),
- the use of the existing permanent network infrastructure (scenario S2).

To realize the above scenarios, three access points were used. Devices AP1, AP2 and AP3 (Fig. 2) belonged to the portable infrastructure that was built for the purpose of the experiments described in the next Section. The access points were NETGEAR Nighthawk X4 R7500 AC2350 devices. As the DS, a 1 Gbps Ethernet network was used. The SW1 Ethernet switch, which belonged to the DS, was an HP 3500-24G-PoE+ yl Switch, with 24 ports, 1 Gbps each.

The AP1 was placed in a corner of the rectangular parking lot, at the place marked as the point B. Access points AP2 and AP3 were placed, respectively, 30 meters from point A, and 28,3 m from the point A'. The placement of AP1, AP2 and AP3 was chosen so that:

- the change of the access point location after the scenario changed to S2 was as small as possible,
- access point locations were safe for both access points and users of the parking lot.

Note that the Fig. 2 is an explanatory figure (not shown to scale).

In tests carried out according to the S2 scenario, three access points (AP1', AP2' and AP3') belonging to the permanent infrastructure of the AGH University of Science and Technology were used. The IEEE 802.11 university network covers the entire campus, and connects local IEEE 802.11 networks built by some university departments. The access point chosen to be the AP1' belongs to WLAN administrated by Department of Telecommunications, while AP2' and AP3' are administrated by the University. This allowed the air station to use an account with its transfer rate unlimited administratively.

AP1', AP2' and AP3' were placed in nearby buildings, a bit further from the parking lot than AP1, AP2 and AP3. AP1' was located 16.2 m in a straight line from the point B, AP2' was 37.2 m from point A, and AP3' was 34,4 m from point A'.

The ground station was equipped with a IEEE 802.11 Intel®Dual Band Wireless-AC 7260 network adapter, and the air station was equipped with an IEEE 802.11ac dual band (2.4 GHz and 5 GHz) network adapter embedded in the Raspberry Pi 4 B single-board computer. The ground station was placed about 1 to 1.5 m from point B.

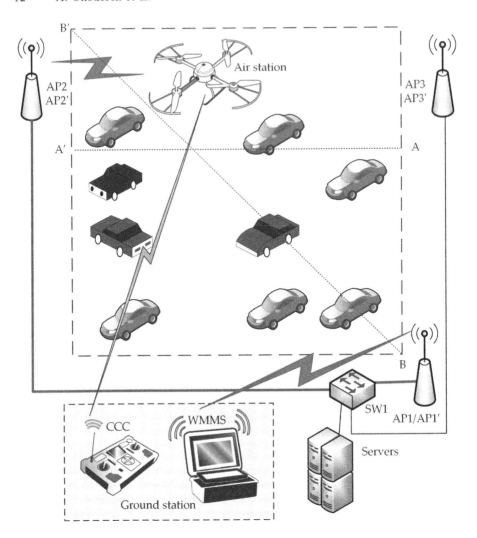

Fig. 2. Test environment.

During the WebRTC session establishment three auxiliary servers must be used (the WWW server, the signalling server, and the NAT traversal server). In both S1 and S2 scenarios, all three servers were run on external machines (see Fig. 2).

3.3   Experiments

During the experiments, the air station flew 15 m over the parking lot on the course shown in Fig. 2 as lines A-A' and B-B'. The line A-A' crosses the parking lot horizontally, in the place where the strength of the signal coming from the ground station becomes small enough to possibly cause transmission problems and the air station should change its point of attachment to the production network. The line B-B' leads diagonally across a rectangular parking lot, passing through expected areas of weak and strong signal. Note that signal strength all time was high enough to keep the air station and the ground station connected. The distance between points A and B was 50 m.

After ascending to the cruising altitude of 15 m (measured with an accuracy of 10 cm by the on-board barometric altimeter), the UAV flew to the measurement starting point, i.e. point A or point B. Then it followed trajectories, respectively, of A-A' or B-B'. Every 5 m the UAV hovered in the air, enabling measurements of total throughput (expressed in megabits per second, or Mbps) and readings of the parameters set by the network adapter mounted on the air station (available data rate, expressed in Mbps, and the Received Signal Strength Indicator, or RSSI, expressed in decibel-milliwatts, or dBm) at fixed positions. The five-meter distances were measured horizontally, using the accuracy of the on-board NSS[7] (up to 0.5 m), in a straight line between the starting point (A or B) and the current position of the air station. The total length of trajectory A-A' was 70 m, and trajectory B-B' was 100 m.

Experiments were carried out over a few days, at approximately the same time and the same weather conditions. The RSSI, the available data rate, and the total throughput were averaged over 5 times. The available data rate was computed as a dominant, and other quantities as an arithmetic mean. Results of experiments are shown and discussed in the next Section.

4 Experimental Results

The results of the experiments are depicted in figures from Fig. 3 to Fig. 5. Quantities shown in these figures are presented as functions of the horizontal distance between the air station and the beginning of a trajectory: point A (d_{aA}) and point B (d_{aB}). During experiments the air station followed trajectories A-A' and B-B', and at about the fortieth meter (A-A') or the fiftieth meter (B-B') from the starting point of each trajectory (A or B, respectively) the air station changed its point of attachment to the DS.

4.1 Received Signal Strength Indicator

The RSSI represents the power of the received signal, and is used by IEEE 802.11 standard as a relative signal strength quantity.

Nearly symmetric placement of access points causes that end-points of each trajectory are characterized by a very good (if the dedicated network was used: S1 scenario) or good (if the public network was used: S2 scenario) relative signal strength. In detail, if the dedicated network was used (S1 scenario, figures Fig. 3a and Fig. 3c), end-points of A-A' trajectory were characterized by the RSSI of −45 dBm (point A) and −46 dBm (point A'). And both end-points of B-B'

---

[7] Navigation Satellite System.

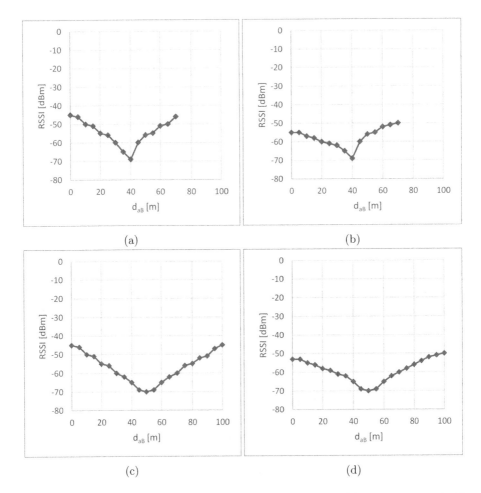

Fig. 3. Relative signal strength (RSSI) measured in scenario: (a) S1, trajectory A-A';
(b) S2, trajectory A-A'; (c) S1, trajectory B-B'; (d) S2, trajectory B-B'.

trajectory were characterized by the RSSI of -45 dBm. The use of the public
network (S2 scenario, figures Fig. 3b and Fig. 3d) allows the RSSI to achieve
-55 dBm (point A), -53 dBm (point B), and -50 dBm (points A' and B').

The closer to the mid-point of each trajectory, the smaller the Received
Signal Strength Indicator. A small asymmetry of the placement of pairs of access
points AP2 and AP3, and AP2' and AP3' causes that the switching of the
point of attachment of the air station to the DS (from AP3/AP3' to AP2/AP2')
occurs 40 m from point A and 30 m from point A'. The placement of pairs of
access points AP1 and AP2, and AP1' and AP2' is more symmetric about the
trajectory B-B', so switching from AP1/AP1' to AP2/AP2' is observed exactly
at the middle of the B-B' (50 m from the point B and 50 m from the point B').
The values of the RSSI observed at the point of switching between access points

are the smallest values of the RSSI read at a given trajectory. In the case of the testbed presented in the Fig. 2, the minimum value of the RSSI did not depend on the type of network (a dedicated one or public), but on the length of trajectory only, and was:

- −69 dBm at the shorter trajectory (A-A'),
- −70 dBm at the longer trajectory (A-A').

Note that in the case of both trajectories, and of both scenarios, the −67 dBm limit for the minimal signal strength required by real-time media streaming was exceeded. The next, −70 dBm limit of applicability of non-real time non-media reliable transmission service was not exceeded, although in the case of the A-A' trajectory the minimum RSSI was equal to this limit. This means that the production network was at the limit of use (in terms of IoT transmissions). However, in the case of both S1 and S2 scenarios, the RSSI never exceeds the limit of basic connectivity (−80 dBm).

Comparative analysis of the RSSI obtained for dedicated and public production networks shows that in the case of both trajectories the RSSI achieved by a well-dimensioned, dedicated network, designed to optimize a flying monitoring system, was larger than or equal to the values of the RSSI observed in the case of the use of an existing, multi-purpose infrastructure. The largest differences were observed at end points of trajectories, and ranges from 22% (point A), through 18% (point B) and 11% (point B') to 9% (point A') in favor of the dedicated network. However, at close to the middle of each trajectory, this difference was smaller. As a result, on the last 20 m of the 70 m of the A-A' trajectory and on the last 35 m of the 100 m of the B-B' trajectory, the RSSI read in the dedicated network equals the RSSI read when the public network was used for transmission of monitoring data.

4.2   Available Data Rate and Total Throughput

The signal strength has an impact on the performance of the wireless communication. In the case of the evaluation of communication between stations of the flying monitoring system, two performance parameters were used:

- available data rate (a parameter of the network card), which is maximum data rate that can be obtained on a given network circumstances; this parameter is read from the settings of network card mounted at the air station,
- total throughput of the aggregated WebRTC stream, measured at the ground station.

Generally, the curve of the available data rate depends on the RSSI curve. In the case of the dedicated production network, at the very beginning and very end of trajectory A-A' (Fig. 4a) and B-B' (Fig. 4c) the maximal available data rate was set at 540 Mbps (points A, A', B, and B'). Then, according to the declining curve of the RSSI, it falls down until the air station changed its point of attachment. Then the curve of the available data rate rises, as does the RSSI curve. The smallest values of the maximal available data rate were observed where the point of attachment changed. They values were 54 Mbps for A-A' trajectory and 26 Mbps for the B-B' trajectory.

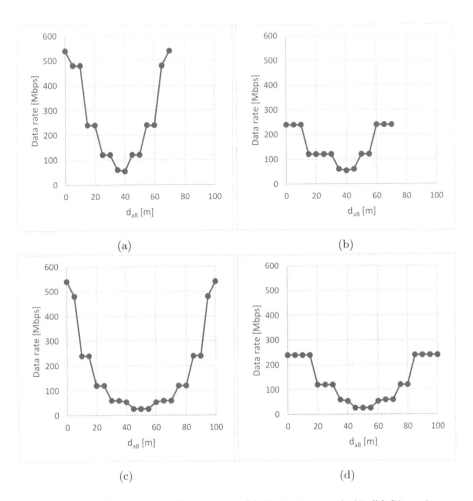

Fig. 4. Available data rate read in scenario: (a) S1, trajectory A-A'; (b) S2, trajectory A-A'; (c) S1, trajectory B-B'; (d) S2, trajectory B-B'.

In the case of a production network that uses an existing infrastructure, the curve of the available data rate is flatter than is drawn for a dedicated production network. At the very beginning of trajectory A-A' (Fig. 4b) and B-B' (Fig. 4d) the maximal available data rate was set at 240 Mbps (points A, A', B, and B'). However, the smallest values of the available data rate are the same as read for the dedicated network: 54 Mbps read when the air station follows the A-A' trajectory and 26 Mbps read for the B-B' trajectory.

The comparative analysis of the available data rate obtained for dedicated and public production networks shows that in the case of the A-A' trajectory, when the air station is close to the end points A and A', the available data rate set for the public network was two times smaller than the available data rate set for the dedicated one. And if the air station was exactly over the points A and A', the available data rate obtained for the public network was a little more than two times smaller. However, at 6 of 15 points of measurements established on this trajectory, there were no difference between the available data rate observed for the dedicated production network and the public one.

In the case of measurement points established along the B-B' trajectory, at almost the entire trajectory the differences between the available data rate read for the dedicated production network and the public one equals zero. Only if the air station was exactly over the points B and B', this difference was more than 100% in favor of the dedicated network. And five meters away towards the middle of the B-B' trajectory it was exactly 100% in favor of the dedicated network. As a curiosity at one of the measurement points this trend has been reversed: the available data rate read for the dedicated production network was two times smaller than read for the public network.

Despite the changes to the RSSI and the maximal available data rate, the curve of the total throughput of the aggregated WebRTC stream (Fig. 5) is almost completely flat whatever the trajectory is followed by the air station and however the production network is used. Almost all the time the throughput is 20 Mbps, and it falls to from 19.8 to 19.4 Mbps only when the air station changes its point of attachment to the DS.

Comparative analysis of the dedicated production network and the production network that uses an existing infrastructure shows that in the majority of the measurement points established along the trajectory A-A' and the trajectory B-B' the total throughput of the aggregated WebRTC stream measured for the dedicated production network was the same as measured for the public one. Only in two points of each trajectory, situated near the middle of this trajectory, were observed differences between total throughput. These differences were in favor of the dedicated network, and were about 1% of measured throughput. As a result, if the public network is well dimensioned, differences in the RSSI and the available data rate do not necessarily entails large differences in total throughput of aggregated WebRTC stream transmitted between the air station of the flying monitoring system and the ground one.

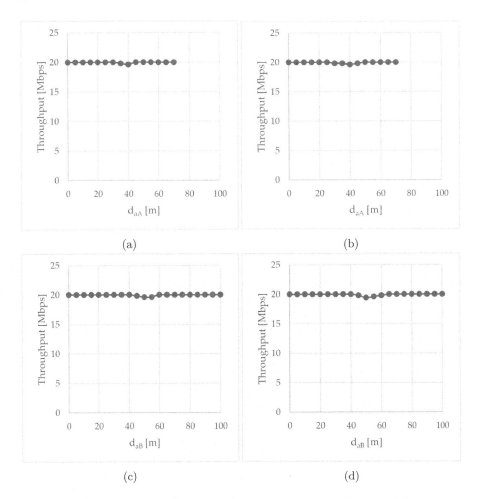

Fig. 5. Total throughput measured in scenario: (a) S1, trajectory A-A'; (b) S2, trajectory A-A'; (c) S1, trajectory B-B'; (d) S2, trajectory B-B'.

5   Conclusions

In the flying monitoring system, introduced in the authors' previous paper [9], to multiplex the data coming from the IoT devices and aggregate it with the video stream WebRTC technology was used. In this paper the performance evaluation of the aggregated WebRTC air-to-ground transmissions was carried out, and two implementations of the IEEE 802.11 network infrastructure connecting the air station and the ground one were taken into consideration.

The first one (S1 scenario) uses a dedicated IEEE 802.11 network infrastructure, which was designed and built especially for this flying monitoring system. The second (S2 scenario) uses an existing infrastructure covering the monitored area.

To analyze the performance of the air-to-ground transmissions the test trial was carried out at one of the parking lots of the AGH University of Science and Technology. Both the measurements of the total throughput of the aggregated WebRTC stream and the readings of the parameters set by the network adapter mounted on the air station (the RSSI and available sending rate) were analyzed.

Experimental results show that a dedicated network gives a little bit better performance at the cost of both the complicated physically building of and setup of the network, and the longer time to reach operational readiness (due to the necessity of performing practical tests of the area coverage). The usage of existing infrastructure, which is designed to work in a given area for ground-to-ground operation (not air-to-ground), gives not as good, but still satisfactory results.

References

1. Allman, M., Paxson, V., Stevens, W.: TCP congestion control. In: RFC2581, IETF (1999). https://doi.org/10.17487/RFC2581

2. Alzahrani, B., Oubbati, O.S., Barnawi, A., Atiquzzaman, M., Alghazzawi, D.: UAV assistance paradigm: state-of-the-art in applications and challenges. J. Netw. Comput. Appl. **166**, 102706 (2020). https://doi.org/10.1016/j.jnca.2020.102706

3. Baugher, M., McGrew, D., Naslund, M., Carrara, E., Norrman, K.: The secure real-time transport protocol (SRTP). In: RFC 3711, IETF (2004). https://doi.org/10.17487/RFC3711

4. Carrillo, D., Seki, J.: Rural area deployment of internet of things connectivity: LTE and LoRaWAN case study. In: 2017 IEEE XXIV International Conference on Electronics, Electrical Engineering and Computing (INTERCON), pp. 1–4. IEEE (2017). https://doi.org/10.1109/INTERCON.2017.8079711

5. Castellanos, G., Deruyck, M., Martens, L., Joseph, W.: System assessment of WUSN Using NB-IoT UAV-aided networks in potato crops. IEEE Access **8**, 56823–56836 (2020). https://doi.org/10.1109/ACCESS.2020.2982086

6. Chen, L., Huang, Z., Liu, Z., Liu, D., Huang, X.: 4G network for air-ground data transmission: a drone based experiment. In: 2018 IEEE International Conference on Industrial Internet (ICII), pp. 167–168 (2018). https://doi.org/10.1109/ICII.2018.00028

7. Chodorek, A., Chodorek, R. R., Wajda, K.: An analysis of sender-driven WebRTC congestion control coexisting with QoS assurance applied in IEEE 802.11 wireless LAN. In: 2019 International Conference on Software, Telecommunications and Computer Networks (SoftCOM), pp. 1–5. IEEE, Split, Croatia (2019). https://doi.org/10.23919/SOFTCOM.2019.8903749

8. Chodorek, A., Chodorek, R.R., Wajda, K.: Comparison study of the adaptability of layered and stream replication variants of the WebRTC simulcast. In: 2019 International Conference on Software, Telecommunications and Computer Networks (SoftCOM), pp. 1–6. IEEE, Split, Croatia (2019). https://doi.org/10.23919/SOFTCOM.2019.8903887

9. Chodorek, A., Chodorek, R.R., Wajda, K.: Media and non-media WebRTC communication between a terrestrial station and a drone: the case of a flying IoT system to monitor parking. In: 2019 IEEE/ACM 23rd International Symposium on Distributed Simulation and Real Time Applications (DS-RT), pp. 1–4. IEEE, Cosenza, Italy (2019). https://doi.org/10.1109/DS-RT47707.2019.8958706

10. Chodorek, R.R., Chodorek, A., Rzym, G., Wajda, K.: A comparison of QoS parameters of WebRTC videoconference with conference bridge placed in private and public cloud. In: 2017 IEEE 26th International Conference on Enabling Technologies: Infrastructure for Collaborative Enterprises (WETICE), pp. 86–91. Poznan, Poland (2017). https://doi.org/10.1109/WETICE.2017.59

11. Dai, H., Zhang, H., Li, C., Wang, B.: Efficient deployment of multiple UAVs for IoT communication in dynamic environment. China Commun. **17**(1), 89–103 (2020). https://doi.org/10.23919/JCC.2020.01.007

12. Duangsuwan, S., Chusongsang, A., Promwong, S.: Performance analysis of power outage probability for drone based IoT connectivity network. In: 2019 International Symposium on Intelligent Signal Processing and Communication Systems (ISPACS), pp. 1–4 (2019). https://doi.org/10.1109/ISPACS48206.2019.8986314

13. Fan, Q., Ansari, N.: Towards traffic load balancing in drone-assisted communications for IoT. IEEE Internet of Things J. **6**(2), 3633–3640 (2018). https://doi.org/10.1109/JIOT.2018.2889503

14. Floyd, S., Handley, M., Padhye, J., Widmer, J.: TCP Friendly Rate Control (TFRC): protocol specification. In: RFC 5348. IETF (2008). https://doi.org/10.17487/RFC5348

15. García, B., Gortázar, F., Gallego, M., Hines, A.: Assessment of QoE for video and audio in WebRTC applications using full-reference models. Electronics **9**(3), 462 (2020). https://doi.org/10.3390/electronics9030462

16. Grozev, B., Politis, G., Ivov, E., Noel, T., Singh, V.: Experimental evaluation of simulcast for WebRTC. IEEE Commun. Stand. Mag. **1**(2), 52–59 (2017). https://doi.org/10.1109/MCOMSTD.2017.1700009

17. Holmer, S., Lundin, H., Carlucci, G., Cicco, L.D., Mascolo, S.: A Google congestion control algorithm for real-time communication. Internet-Draft, draft-ietf-rmcat-gcc-02, IETF (2016)

18. Iyer, V., Nandakumar, R., Wang, A., Fuller, S.B., Gollakota, S.: Living IoT: a flying wireless platform on live insects. In: The 25th Annual International Conference on Mobile Computing and Networking, pp. 1–15 (2019). https://doi.org/10.1145/3300061.3300136

19. Jesup, R., Loreto, S., Tuexen, M.: WebRTC data channels. Internet Draft, draft-ietf-rtcweb-data-channel-13, IETF (2015)

20. Jesup, R., Loreto, S., Tuexen, M.: WebRTC data channel establishment protocol. Internet Draft, draft-ietf-rtcweb-dataprotocol-09, IETF (2015)

21. Kim, J., Yun, J., Choi, S.C., Seed, D.N., Lu, G., Bauer, M., Al-Hezmi, A., Campowsky, K., Song, J.: Standard-based IoT platforms interworking: implementation, experiences, and lessons learned. IEEE Commun. Mag. **54**(7), 48–54 (2016). https://doi.org/10.1109/MCOM.2016.7514163

22. Kobayashi, T., Matsuoka, H., Betsumiya, S.: Flying communication server in case of a largescale disaster. In: 2016 IEEE 40th Annual Computer Software and Applications Conference (COMPSAC), vol. 2, pp. 571–576 (2016). https://doi.org/10.1109/COMPSAC.2016.117

23. Lea, P.: Internet of Things for Architects: Architecting IoT Solutions by Implementing Sensors, Communication Infrastructure, Edge Computing, Analytics, and Security. Packt Publishing Ltd, Birmingham (2018)

24. Loreto, S., Romano, S.P.: Real-Time Communication with WebRTC: Peer-to-Peer in the Browser. O'Reilly Media, Inc., United States (2014)

25. Loreto, S., Romano, S.P.: How far are we from WebRTC-1.0? an update on standards and a look at what's next. IEEE Commun. Mag. **55**(7), 200–207 (2017). https://doi.org/10.1109/MCOM.2017.1600283

26. McGrew, D.: The Use of AES-192 and AES-256 in Secure RTP. RFC 6188. IETF (2011). https://doi.org/10.17487/RFC6188
27. Mohamed, A.M.A., AbuElgasim, A.E.: Controlling drone-using IOT platform. In: 2019 International Conference on Computer, Control, Electrical, and Electronics Engineering (ICCCEEE), pp. 1–4 (2019). https://doi.org/10.1109/ICCCEEE46830.2019.9071087
28. Motlagh, N.H., Bagaa, M., Taleb, T.: UAV selection for a UAV-based integrative IoT platform. In: 2016 IEEE Global Communications Conference (GLOBECOM), pp. 1–6. IEEE (2016). https://doi.org/10.1109/GLOCOM.2016.7842359
29. Motlagh, N.H., Bagaa, M., Taleb, T.: UAV-based IoT platform: a crowd surveillance use case. IEEE Commun. Mag. **55**(2), 128–134 (2017). https://doi.org/10.1109/MCOM.2017.1600587CM
30. Park, J.H., Choi, S.C., Ahn, I.Y., Kim, J.: Multiple UAVs-based surveillance and reconnaissance system utilizing IoT platform. In: 2019 International Conference on Electronics, Information, and Communication (ICEIC), pp. 1–3. IEEE (2019). https://doi.org/10.23919/ELINFOCOM.2019.8706406
31. Rescorla, E., Modadugu, N.: Datagram Transport Layer Security Version 1.2. RFC 6347. IETF (2012). https://doi.org/10.17487/RFC6347
32. Roy, R.R.: Handbook of SDP for Multimedia Session Negotiations: SIP and WebRTC IP Telephony. CRC Press, Boca Raton, FL, United States (2018)
33. Saputro, N., Akkaya, K., Uluagac, S.: Supporting seamless connectivity in drone-assisted intelligent transportation systems. In: 2018 IEEE 43rd Conference on Local Computer Networks Workshops (LCN Workshops), pp. 110–116. IEEE (2018). https://doi.org/10.1109/LCNW.2018.8628496
34. Schulzrinne, H., Casner, S., Frederick, R., Jacobson, V.: RTP: A Transport Protocol for Real-Time Applications. RFC 3550. IETF (2003). https://doi.org/10.17487/RFC3550
35. Schulzrinne, H., Casner, S.: RTP profile for audio and video conferences with minimal control. RFC 3551. IETF (2003). https://doi.org/10.17487/RFC3551
36. Singh, V., Lozano, A.A., Ott, J.: Performance analysis of receive-side real-time congestion control for WebRTC. In: 2013 20th International Packet Video Workshop, pp. 1–8. San Jose, CA, USA (2013). https://doi.org/10.1109/PV.2013.6691454
37. Stewart, R.: Stream control transmission protocol. RFC 4960. IETF (2007). https://doi.org/10.17487/RFC4960
38. Tuexen, M., Seggelmann, R., Rescorla, E.: Datagram Transport Layer Security (DTLS) for Stream Control Transmission Protocol (SCTP). RFC 6083. IETF (2011). https://doi.org/10.17487/RFC6083
39. Van den Bergh, B., Chiumento, A., Pollin, S.: Ultra-reliable IEEE 802.11 for UAV video streaming: from network to application. In: El-Azouzi, R., Menasché, D.S., Sabir, E., Pellegrini, F.D., Benjillali, M. (eds.) Advances in Ubiquitous Networking 2. LNEE, vol. 397, pp. 637–647. Springer, Singapore (2017). https://doi.org/10.1007/978-981-10-1627-1_50

Constructing a Green MPTCP Framework for Industrial Internet of Things Applications

Michał Morawski$^{(\boxtimes)}$ (iD) and Przemysław Ignaciuk (iD)

Lodz University of Technology, Lodz, Poland
michal.morawski@p.lodz.pl

Abstract. In the typical distributed applications, the data exchange between the communicating peers proceeds along the transport path established in the connection initialization phase, even if a better one is discovered during the active session. With the recent advancement in the multipath protocol development, e.g., MPTCP, the peers can benefit from a concurrent use of a few channels, thus improving the transmission quality. However, the present approaches to the multipath transfer organization tend to neglect the energy aspects, crucial for resource-constrained Internet of Things (IoT) devices. In this paper, a framework for MPTCP module tuning, targeting the power expenditure, is developed. A new Scheduler and a new Path Manager promoting a conservative energy economy are designed by adopting a formal optimization approach. Moreover, explicit guidelines regarding the TCP variant selection are provided. As confirmed by numerous experiments involving physical devices and real networks, the proposed configuration scheme allows for several percent energy gain with respect to the default one, thus setting a solid framework for green MPTCP-based Industrial IoT communication.

Keywords: Green networking · Industrial Internet of Things · MPTCP

1 Introduction

Industrial control systems have evolved from centralized, through distributed, to Internet of Things (IoT) installations. These changes reflect the ever more challenging requirements of heterogeneity, multi-vendor equipment integration, and management facility. The IoT and Industry 4.0 applications unify various electronic devices in a joint effort to manage an industrial process. While designed to handle different functional aspects, e.g., monitoring, or dynamic adaptation, and created using different tools and technologies, they recur to a common communication platform to realize the intended goals [1]. The industrial applications expect the network to deliver the data within assumed time bounds, which imposes stringent throughput and robustness constraints. When dedicated links are not available, e.g., when the wireless media need to be incorporated, the streams generated by different system components (and different systems) interfere with each other [2, 3]. Then, neither the time, nor throughput requirements cannot be guaranteed, thus downgrading the quality or even compromising the industrial process objectives.

© ICST Institute for Computer Sciences, Social Informatics and Telecommunications Engineering 2021
Published by Springer Nature Switzerland AG 2021. All Rights Reserved
H. Gao et al. (Eds.): BROADNETS 2020, LNICST 355, pp. 22–32, 2021.
https://doi.org/10.1007/978-3-030-68737-3_2

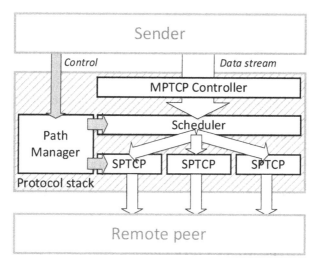

Fig. 1. MPTCP architecture from the sender point of view.

Today, extending the capabilities of a networking device by additional interfaces is relatively inexpensive and easy to perform. Unfortunately, due to the design principles of common communication protocols, the extra interfaces cannot simultaneously direct the data to the same peer.

2 Multipath Communication

A self-imposing solution for obtaining smooth data transfer over the links with variable bandwidth is to simultaneously engage multiple channels. Unfortunately, the most widely network protocol used today – TCP – identify peers using single address-port tuple, thus changing interface leads to the connection break. To overcome this limitation, recently, a multipath version of TCP [4–6] – has become available. The newly standardized Multipath TCP (MPTCP), transparent for the applications and networking devices [4], allows for concurrent data transfer in many channels. From the architectural perspective, MPTCP extends the TCP protocol stack by a few additional modules (Fig. 1). When a client application initiates the transfer of data, the standard TCP handshaking procedure between an arbitrary pair of the logical interfaces at the sender and remote peer is executed. The peers exchange also the information concerning possible paths of data flow. By default, the *Path Manager* module attempts to build as many channels as possible from the pool of available interfaces at the communicating device (*full-mesh* option). As a result of device displacement, noise intensification, or networking failures, a path may need to be closed, or a new one established. The path closure/opening procedure may be executed many times during the communication session, however, the logical MPTCP connection persists until at least one channel is valid. *Path Manager* handles the path creation during the entire MPTCP session.

The data transfer process is managed by a joint effort of three modules: *MPTCP Controller*, *SPTCP Controller(s)*, and *Scheduler*. *MPTCP Controller* dictates the general properties of the data stream, with respect to the throughput, fairness, and buffer allocation objectives. *Scheduler* splits the stream shaped by *MPTCP Controller* over the paths (channels) established by *Path Manager*. Various splitting strategies can be exercised [7–10], however, neither *Scheduler*, nor *Path Manager*, influences the traffic intensity, directly. This task is delegated to *SPTCP Controllers*, acting in each path separately according to the rules of the standard, Singlepath TCP (SPTCP) and the corresponding congestion control algorithms. Those modules, the sender and receiver applications, and the network interact with each other in a complex way, which poses a serious challenge for establishing an efficient communication platform. The design of such a platform, respecting energy and resource constraints of industrial environment, is the focus of this work.

3 Proposed Green MPTCP Framework

The IoT devices are not destined for constant networking activity. They perform actions after a specified time elapses (time-driven systems), or in response to a trigger (event-driven systems). In either case, the application running on the device may power up additional cores, engage accelerators, or increase the clock frequency. Once the processing is finished, the additional components, including the network interfaces, should be powered down to conserve energy. Meanwhile, the MPTCP modules, possibly except *MPTCP Controller*, are typically tuned for maximum throughput, thus for persistent activity. In this work, a systematic tuning methodology of the MPTCP modules so that a low energy profile is achieved is proposed. Each module will be given a separate treatment in latter sections.

Let $k = 0, 1, 2,...$ mark the subsequent instants within the session time t_D when *Scheduler* takes a decision regarding the path selection. k is also a moment of the acquisition of a new segment from *MPTCP Controller*. At that instant, the device processing unit, and other essential components except the network interfaces, e.g., display, or accelerators, are supplied with power $p_D(k)$. In turn, interface $i \in [1, n]$, n – the number of available interfaces at the device, requires power $p_i(k)$ to send (or receive) the data. Both $p_D(k)$ and $p_i(k)$ are measurable, thus, assumed known in the mathematical model. The energy dissipated to handle the MPTCP stream in a single session can be expressed as

$$E = \sum_{i=1}^{n} \sum_{k=0}^{t_i} p_i(k)\Delta\tau(k) + \sum_{k=0}^{t_D} p_D(k)\Delta\tau(k), \tag{1}$$

where t_i is the instant of the last *Scheduler* decision concerning channel i, t_D is the instant of the last decision in the entire session, and $\Delta\tau(k)$ is the time between instants k and $k + 1$. $\tau_i = \sum_{k=0}^{t_i} \Delta\tau(k)$ is the time of sending data through interface i, covering all the link layer activities, and $\tau_D = \max_i \tau_i$ is the overall session time.

The objective is to adjust the MPTCP modules so that E is minimized. A major challenge to overcome is the fact that once the data exchange session is initiated one cannot determine precisely how long it will take to process the data and effectuate the transfer. The session duration depends on the fluctuating networking conditions on the paths, the volume of processed data, and the physical interface specifics.

3.1 Path Manager

The effort necessary to establish multiple paths is not justified when the communicating peers exchange only short messages. However, the decision about setting an additional path needs to be taken in real-time, because the length of the data stream coming from the application in not known in advance by *Path Manager*. In the typical networking scenarios, the initial data burst is limited by the slow-start threshold, set as 10 segments by default. Therefore, if the amount of data in the sender buffer does not exceed this initial burst, additional channels need not be used to avoid energy dissipation for setting or tearing down the paths. In other words, irrespective of the direction of data flow, it is justified to engage a secondary channel only if the data exceeds the initial slow-start threshold. Note that the primary channel (interface) used to establish the MPTCP connection usually promises the best performance. The operation of the proposed green *Path Manager* can thus be summarized as:

Rule 1: Delay opening new channels until the IoT device effectuates the transfer of the initial burst of data (14–15 kB).

3.2 Scheduler

By default, *Scheduler* chooses the path of transmission from the pool created by *Path Manager* using solely the information about the low-pass filtered time between sending a segment and acknowledgement reception – *srtt* (Smoothed Round Trip Time). The power necessary to transfer the data is not taken into account at all. In order to design a green *Scheduler*, in this work, a formal optimization procedure with low computational footprint as a target is conducted. The design basis is set in the following theorem.

Theorem 1: The energy dissipated by the device to handle the application stream (1) is minimum, if all the paths are used simultaneously, i.e., if for every $i, j \in [1, n]$, the time of using the paths $t_i = t_j = t_D$.

Proof: Let us order the transmission times through interfaces 1, 2, …, n as $t_1 \leq t_2 \leq \ldots \leq t_n$. Then, (1) can be written as

$$E = \sum_{i=1}^{n} \sum_{k=0}^{t_1} p_i(k) \Delta\tau(k)$$

$$+ \sum_{k=t_1+1}^{t_2} p_2(k) \Delta\tau(k) + \sum_{k=t_1+1}^{t_3} p_3(k) \Delta\tau(k) + \ldots$$

$$+ \sum_{k=0}^{t_1} p_D(k) \Delta\tau(k) + \sum_{k=t_1+1}^{t_D} p_D(k) \Delta\tau(k). \tag{2}$$

The elements in the second row in (2) reflect the energy dissipation in the time exceeding the transfer through channel 1. Therefore, taking into account the fact that $p_i(k)$ and $p_D(k)$ are non-negative, E is the lowest, if those terms disappear. This conjecture implies $t_1 = t_2 = \ldots = t_n = t_D = \max_i t_i$.   □

In the sequel, using the implications from Theorem 1, a formula for efficient load balancing to be implemented as the green Scheduler will be derived. Let $h_i(k)$ denote the throughput in channel i at instant k, $h_D(k)$ the throughput of the entire MPTCP stream, and $p_i(k) = w_i(k)v_i(k)$, where $w_i(k)$ [W/b] is the power necessary to transfer a unit of data (e.g., a segment) and $v_i(k)$ is the amount of sent data. $w_i(k)$ aggregates the energy expenditures for the MAC procedures and link layer retransmissions. $w_i(k)$ depends on interface manufacturer, engaged technology, distance to the hub, noise level, and it fluctuates. Recall that $p_D(k)$ is the power invested by the device into all the activities not associated directly with the interface procedures, e.g., managing the display. For the sake of consistency, it will be expressed in a similar way as $p_i(k)$: $p_D(k) = w_D(k)v_D(k)$, with $w_D(k)$ determined from the measurements of $p_D(k)$ and $v_D(k)$.

Let $g_i(k) = w_i(k) + w_D(k)/n$, i.e., the power efficiency of channel i augmented by the power dissipation of other components averaged over interfaces. With this notation, after substituting $p_i(k)$, $p_D(k)$, and $h_i(k)$ into (1), one obtains

$$E(k) = \sum_{i=1}^{n} g_i(k) \frac{v_i^2(k)}{h_i(k)}, \tag{3}$$

and for the entire MPTCP stream

$$E = \sum_{k=0}^{t_D} E(k). \tag{4}$$

In the practical implementation, the scheduling decisions need to be taken in real-time. Since at instant k the power profiles are not known for time $l > k$, the minimum energy expenditure is sought by minimizing (3), i.e., by solving $\partial E(k)/\partial v_i(k) = 0$ individually at each moment k. Consequently, the optimal volume of data to be sent through channel i is calculated as $v_i^{opt}(k) = 2g_i(k)/h_i(k)$. As Scheduler is not destined to manipulate the stream intensity, rather the split ratio, the data distribution strategy among the channels follows

$$\frac{v_i^{opt}(k)}{v_j^{opt}(k)} = \frac{g_i(k)/h_i(k)}{g_j(k)/h_j(k)}, \tag{5}$$

with the current throughput of channel determined as

$$h_i(k) = \frac{inflight_i(k)}{srtt_i(k)}, \tag{6}$$

where $inflight_i(k)$ is the amount of data already sent, but not yet acknowledged, and $srtt_i(k)$ is the current srtt of channel i. Both values are readily available in the TCP stack.

The operation of the proposed green Scheduler can be summarized as:

Rule 2: at each instant k, split the MPTCP stream according to (5) with the instantaneous throughput calculated from (6).

3.3 SPTCP Algorithm Selection

In order to satisfy the premises of green networking, one should limit the transfer of superfluous packets. The associated energy expenditure is related both to the direct effort of sending the data, and to the wasted channel bandwidth that could have been used for other purposes. Therefore, green congestion control algorithms, while increasing throughput, should limit the number of transmitted packets.

Unfortunately, by definition, Scheduler does not analyze dropped and retransmitted packets. In the implementation of green Scheduler, this inopportune situation is partly remedied by reading the aggregate in-flight data count $inflight_i(k)$. Nevertheless, the energy economy can further be enhanced by a judicious choice of the SPTCP congestion control algorithm governing the flow rate in the individual channels.

Note that in a common TCP transmission scenario, many packets are dropped, because the internal congestion/bandwidth sensing procedures use loses to shape the transfer profile [11]. There exist, however, TCP variants that incorporate other conges-tion indicators, e.g., Westwood+ (time between acknowledgments) [12], or BBR (probe pattern timing) [13]. Therefore, for green MPTCP implementation, it is proposed to

Rule 3: Employ an SPTCP congestion control algorithm, which evaluates the traffic conditions using methods not based on drops. As the performed experiments indicate, a particularly good candidate is BBR – it is as effective energetically as Westwood, but tends to attain a higher throughput.

3.4 MPTCP Controller

MPTCP Controller shapes the general properties of the data stream. Typically, it is set to maintain fairness at all costs, i.e., to prevent the MPTCP stream from dominating legacy TCP ones [14]. In the industrial IoT applications, other policies might be more appropri-ate, e.g., robust controller [15]. However, while choosing the MPTCP congestion control algorithm, one should also consider its impact on the other entities in the network and their energy profiles. The problem of *MPTCP Controller* selection for green network-ing applications, owing to its multidimensionality, deserves a separate, thorough line of research. In this work, it is left at the default configuration recommended for general networking [5].

4 Experimental Environment

In order to assess the impact of the proposed green MPTCP framework on the actual transmission properties, the test setup illustrated in Fig. 2 has been prepared. It reflects a common scenario in the IoT communication, i.e., agent data collection by a control server [2]. The agent is represented by a low-performance device (here, Raspberry Pi), equipped with two wireless interfaces. As an IIoT data sink, a high-end server placed in the multi-access university data center is considered. Both the client and the server operate under Linux ver. 4.19 with the MPTCP stack ver. 0.95. The agent is modified according to *Rules 1–3*, stipulated in Sect. 3. The uncertain networking conditions of the

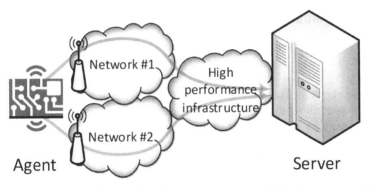

Fig. 2. Experimental setup. Upper path (red) – primary, lower path (blue) – secondary. First mile
– wireless links operating in different bands. (Color figure online)

industrial environment are recreated by using crowded, public Internet Service Provider
(ISP) network. The ISPs are unrelated, thus the corresponding paths have no common
bottleneck – the common infrastructure has capacity ~100 times higher than that of ISPs.
The primary path incorporates 8 hops, with the measured throughput 8.7–8.9 Mbps
and the initial *srtt* 25–60 ms, whereas the secondary one – 19 hops, 6.0–12.5 Mbps
throughput, and 30–120 ms initial *srtt*, respectively. The popular *iperf3* utility is used as
the data source.

Two scenarios – reflecting short message exchange and persistent data transfer –
are considered. The experiments are repeatable in the sense that they provide similar
outcomes in the subsequent runs under a comparable traffic load.

4.1 Scenario 1

The multipath transmission is usually not recommended for short-lived communication
due to the energy expenditure concerns [16]. In the IIoT applications, however, the
agent-server exchange of the measurement and control data proceeds in short bursts.
Therefore, the purpose of the first group of tests is to evaluate the proposed method of
protocol tuning so that MPTCP can be used also in the IIoT systems. Consequently,
the stream (message) length is constrained to 10 kB. As neither *Scheduler*, nor *SPTCP*
congestion control algorithm impact the power efficiency in the case of short streams,
Scenario 1 emphasizes the performance of green *Path Manager*.

4.2 Scenario 2

In order to evaluate the green MPTCP framework in a composite way, in the experiments
conducted under Scenario 2 streaming data transfer is considered. The test time has
been set as 10 s. Such interval is long enough to eliminate measurement bias related
to specific networking events, e.g., a noise surge on a wireless link. The following
cases concerning the device power profiles w_1: w_2: w_D have been considered: a) 1:2:0
– interface 2 requires twice as much power as interface 1, power for other components
disregarded (not measured); b) 1:3:10 – balanced energy dissipation; and c) 1:1:1 – equal

power demands of interfaces and other components – throughput optimization case, i.e., shortening the time of transmission.

The framework settings are the same for either scenario, i.e., the proposed method ensures self-adaptation of the MPTCP components to both short and long-lived transmission in real-time. No *a priori* knowledge of the stream type is required.

Table 1. Measured transmission properties

Parameter	Case	Green setting	Default setting
Throughput [Mbps]	a	15.8–16.3	11.7–14.0
	b	13.6–14.8	10.3–10.9
	c	16.1–18.0	7.28–9.05
Primary path data volume [MB]	a	10.29–10.30	8.19–10.59
	b	10.06–10.25	3.37–7.51
	c	10.11–10.17	5.52–9.52
Secondary path data volume [MB]	a	11.16–12.02	6.44–11.00
	b	8.38–10.11	7.88–11.34
	c	11.83–14.44	2.44–9.54
Primary path drop count	a	4–13	7–70
	b	5–14	7–424
	c	21–41	40–151
Secondary path drop count	a	4–9	108–119
	b	5–11	7–218
	c	16–37	106–366
Dissipated energy [J]	a	4.55–4.67	5.22–6.27
	b	6.79-7-11	8.47–8.60
	c	4.23–4.55	8.42–10.10
Energy gain – green vs. Default [%]	a	11–18	
	b	14–20	
	c	**49–55**	

5   Results and Discussion

The proposed green tuning framework has been compared with the default MPTCP configuration [4] in numerous experiments. Each test was executed 30 times. The results have been summarized in Table 1, with an example case (b) selected for closer examination in Fig. 3.

The measurements obtained in Scenario 1 indicate lower energy dissipation in the range 3–10% of the green MPTCP with respect to the default setting. Although the actual savings depend on the w_i ratio and channel $srtt_i$, and vary according to the current network capabilities, the gain of applying the green MPTCP components, notably the green *Path Manager*, is always observed. On average, it amounts to ~5% when short data exchange in the IIoT environment takes place.

In Scenario 2, a number of additional benefits can be observed, as documented in Table 1. First of all, thanks to the application of a modern congestion control algorithm (BBR), the drop count indeed diminished, which implies no energy expenditure for spurious retransmissions. Secondly, although tuned independently from other modules, the green *Scheduler* happens to cooperate in synergy with the SPTCP algorithms, boosting further the power efficiency. It occurs that using BBR as the SPTCP congestion control algorithm helps the *Scheduler* evaluate the current throughput $h_i(k)$ in a more reliable way and, hence, choose a better channel for data transfer. In the default MPTCP setting, the channel selection is based on the *srtt* value, only, which leads to energetically inefficient load balancing.

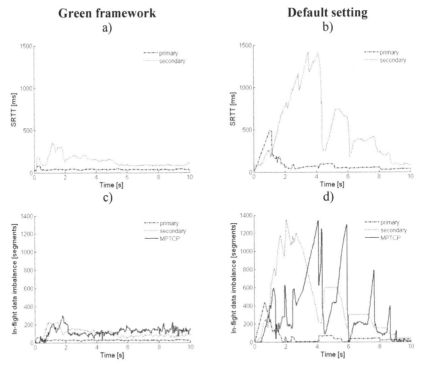

Fig. 3. Transmission properties (Scenario 2, case b): a), b) *srtt* evolution, c), d) *inflight* data.

Probably, the biggest obstacle in achieving the desired power conservation in multipath data transfer is Head-of-Line (HoL) blocking phenomenon, i.e., the situation when the stream reconstruction at the receiver is stalled due to missing segments on certain paths. HoL prolongs the transmission time and might bring down the entire multipath transfer system. A good, quantitative measure of this inopportune phenomenon is flow imbalance, calculated as the difference of the in-flight data seen at the MPTCP level with respect to the path level $inflight_D(k) - \sum_{i=0}^{n} inflight_i(k)$. In a properly operating multipath system it should be as low as possible. As depicted in Fig. 3(c, d), in a typical traffic scenario, the flow imbalance in the green MPTCP setting is nearly an order of magnitude lower than in the case of the default configuration. It relates, again, to the improper (from the energy point of view) estimation of the temporary channel conditions by the MPTCP components in their default setting.

The default MPTCP *Scheduler*, using the initial *srtt* readings (Fig. 3b, 0–1 s), over-estimates the capabilities on the secondary path and directs too many data segments into that channel. It results in a large *srtt* increase (Fig. 3b, 2–4 s). As a consequence, the primary path becomes temporarily suspended, as MPTCP needs to wait for the data sent through the sluggish, secondary channel (though it initially promised a lower *srtt*). The described situation is particularly important for IIoT applications, as the majority of data exchange is likely to be concluded in the first couple of seconds. The green *Scheduler* does not fall for this bait of a "lower-*srtt* channel". Conversely, it quickly corrects the initial erroneous bandwidth estimation, and the data goes through the primary, uncongested channel.

6 Conclusions

MPTCP, intended as a replacement of the single-path TCP, promises better performance and higher reliability in the general networking context. However, which is crucial in the IIoT systems, it does not come up to the energy efficiency expectations of its predecessor. Moreover, if improperly tuned, MPTCP may actually arrive at worse transmission properties due to HoL blocking.

In this paper, a systematic tuning procedure for improving the energy efficiency of MPTCP data transfer is proposed. Precise guidelines for all major components of the protocol stack are provided and verified in strenuous tests involving physical devices and shared networks. For *Path Manager*, contrary to the default full-mesh option, it is recommended to refrain from opening spurious paths. *Scheduler*, in turn, should split the application stream taking into account both the power needed to transfer the data at the interfaces and the power needed to operate the device, as well as the current throughput at each path. The splitting rule for the green *Scheduler* has been established here through a formal optimization procedure. Finally, *SPTCP Controllers* should use the algorithms that minimize the number of drops, e.g., BBR, so that resources are not wasted on retransmissions. Although treated separately, the proposed adjustments happen to reinforce each other in increasing the overall energy gain. As stated in the measurement summary in Table 1, one can achieve an energy boost in the range of several percent in the case of a common IoT scenario. When throughput maximization is the primary objective, the gain from applying the proposed green tuning framework is even bigger – it can be as high as 50% with respect to the default configuration (marked bottom row in Table 1.

All the presented rules are straightforward to implement at a physical device, with minor code complexity and negligible increase of computational power. In this way, the fundamental principles of IIoT system communication are fulfilled.

References

1. Koutsiamanis, R.-A., Papadopoulos, G.Z., Fafoutis, X., Del Fiore, J.M., Thubert, P., Montavont, N.: From best effort to deterministic packet delivery for wireless Industrial IoT networks. IEEE Trans. Ind. Inf. **14**(10), 4468–4480 (2018)
2. Xu, L., He, W., Li, S.: Internet of Things in industries: a survey. IEEE Trans. Ind. Inf. **10**(4), 2233–2243 (2014)
3. Willig, A.: Recent and emerging topics in wireless industrial communications: a selection. IEEE Trans. Ind. Inf. **4**(2), 102–124 (2008)
4. Barré, S., Paasch, C., Bonaventure, O.: MultiPath TCP: from theory to practice. Technical report, Université Catholique de Louvain (2011)
5. Ford, A., Raiciu, C., Handley, M., Bonaventure, O., Paasch, C.: TCP extensions for multipath operation with multiple addresses. RFC 8684 (2020)
6. Barré, S., Paasch, C.: MultiPath TCP – Linux kernel implementation. https://www.multipath-tcp.org
7. Paasch, C., Ferlin, S., Alay, O., Bonaventure, O.: Experimental evaluation of multipath TCP schedulers. In: Proceedings of the ACM SIGCOMM CSWS, Chicago, USA, pp. 27–32 (2014)
8. Ferlin, S., Alay, Ö., Mehani, O., Boreli, R.: BLEST: blocking estimation-based MPTCP scheduler for heterogeneous networks. In: Proceedings of the IFIP Networking Conference Workshops, Vienna, Austria, pp. 431–439 (2016)
9. Frommgen, A., Erbshäußer, T., Buchmann, A., Zimmermann, T., Wehrle, K.: ReMP TCP: low latency multipath TCP. In: 2016 IEEE International Conference on Communications (ICC), Kuala Lumpur, pp. 1–7 (2016)
10. Ferlin, S., Kucera, S., Claussen, H., Alay, Ö.: MPTCP meets FEC: supporting latency-sensitive applications over heterogeneous networks. IEEE/ACM Trans. Netw. **26**(5), 2005–2018 (2018)
11. Afanasyev, A., Tilley, N., Reiher, P., Kleinrock, L.: Host-to-host congestion control for TCP. IEEE Commun. Surv. Tutor. **12**(3), 304–342 (2010). 3Q
12. Mascolo, S., Casetti, C., Gerla, M., Sanadid, M.Y., Wang, R.: TCP westwood: bandwidth estimation for enhanced transport over wireless links. In: Proceedings of the ACM Mobicom, Rome, Italy (2001)
13. Cardwell, N., Cheng, Y., Gunn, C.S., Yeganeh, S.H., Jacobson, V.: BBR: congestion-based congestion control. ACM Queue **14**(5), 20–53 (2016)
14. Xu, C., Zhao, J., Muntean, G.: Congestion control design for multipath transport protocols: a survey. IEEE Commun. Surv. Tutor. **18**(4), 2948–2969 (2016)
15. Ignaciuk, P., Morawski, M.: Discrete-time sliding-mode controllers for MPTCP networks. IEEE Trans. Syst. Man Cybern. Syst. **50**(2) (2020, in press)
16. Deng, S., Netravali, R., Sivaraman, A., Balakrishnan, H.: WiFi, LTE, or both? Measuring multi-homed wireless internet performance. In: Proceedings of the ACM IMC, Vancouver, Canada, pp. 181–194 (2014)

Identification of Significant Permissions for Efficient Android Malware Detection

Hemant Rathore[(✉)], Sanjay K. Sahay, Ritvik Rajvanshi, and Mohit Sewak

Department of CS and IS, Goa Campus, BITS Pilani, Goa, India
{hemantr,ssahay,f20160544,p20150023}@goa.bits-pilani.ac.in

Abstract. Since Google unveiled Android OS for smartphones, malware are thriving with 3Vs, i.e. volume, velocity and variety. A recent report indicates that one out of every five business/industry mobile application leaks sensitive personal data. Traditional signature/heuristic based malware detection systems are unable to cope up with current malware challenges and thus threaten the Android ecosystem. Therefore recently researchers have started exploring machine learning and deep learning based malware detection systems. In this paper, we performed a comprehensive feature analysis to identify the significant Android permissions and propose an efficient Android malware detection system using machine learning and deep neural network. We constructed a set of 16 permissions (8% of the total set) derived from variance threshold, autoencoders, and principal component analysis to build a malware detection engine which consumes less train and test time without significant compromise on the model accuracy. Our experimental results show that the Android malware detection model based on the random forest classifier is most balanced and achieves the highest area under curve score of 97.7%, which is better than the current state-of-art systems. We also observed that deep neural networks attain comparable accuracy to the baseline results but with a massive computational penalty.

Keywords: Android malware · Deep neural network · Machine learning · Malware detection · Static analysis

1 Introduction

Today smartphones have penetrated very deep into our modern society and touch the lives of more than 60% of the world population [9]. There has been an explosive growth in new smartphones sold every year (from 173.5 million in 2009 to 1,474 million in 2017) [17]. Smartphone uses an Operating System (OS) for resource management. Currently, Android OS from Google holds more than 80% of market share, followed by iOS from Apple at 14.9% [9]. The broad acceptance of Android OS is due to its open-ecosystem, large application base, multiple app stores, and customizability. Around 50% of smartphone customers connect to the internet, which is currently the primary attack vector for malware developers [24,28].

© ICST Institute for Computer Sciences, Social Informatics and Telecommunications Engineering 2021
Published by Springer Nature Switzerland AG 2021. All Rights Reserved
H. Gao et al. (Eds.): BROADNETS 2020, LNICST 355, pp. 33–52, 2021.
https://doi.org/10.1007/978-3-030-68737-3_3

Malicious Software (a.k.a. Malware) are not new to the current digital world. The first malware was a worm named *Creeper*[1], an experimental self-replicating program written for fun in 1971 [28]. On mobile devices, *Cabir*[2] (2004) was the first malware designed for Symbian OS, and it used Bluetooth capabilities for infection [28]. Gemini (2010) was the first malware on the Android platform and was part of a mobile botnet system [28]. Since then, there has been an exponential growth of new malicious applications detected on Android OS (from $214,327$ in 2012 to more than $4,000,000$ in 2018) [5]. Recently Symantec reported (February 2019) every one in thirty-six mobile device has a high-risk application installed on it [23]. According to McAfee threat report published in December 2018, the current mobile malware growth is fueled by fake applications with an average infection rate of more than 10% for every quarter in 2017 [13]. Although there has been an aggressive growth of Android malware in the last decade, the dataset (malicious samples) available to the academic research community is limited [24,28].

The primary defence against any malware attack is provided by Antivirus (AV) companies (Symantec, McAfee, Quick Heal, Kaspersky, etc.) and the anti-malware research community [7,18,24,28]. Initially, AV engines were based on signature-based detection mechanism. A signature is a specific pattern (like known malicious instruction/activity sequence) maintained in an AV database [18]. However, the major drawbacks of the signature-based mechanism are that the approach is not scalable and is also suspectable to zero-day attacks [24,28]. Heuristic engines in AV often complement signature-based detection where malware experts define rules to detect malicious activities in an environment. Writing precise rules for such engines to identify malicious activity without increasing the false positive rate is a hard task [28].

Recently researchers have begun exploring ways to develop a cutting edge malware detection system based on machine learning and deep learning [4,7,21,28]. The above process requires data collection, feature extraction, feature engineering and building classification model. For example, Arp et al. constructed the Drebin dataset containing malicious Android applications [1]. They extracted $5,45,000$ features with static analysis and built a support vector machine based malware detection model with an accuracy of 93.90% [1]. Static analysis conducts broad examination and if not performed carefully leads to a large feature vector, which then contributes to the curse of dimensionality and higher false-positive rate [28]. On the other hand, TaintDroid tracked information flow in Android APKs using dynamic analysis of thirty popular applications downloaded from third-party app stores [3]. They found sixty-eight instances of potential misuse of the information in twenty different mobile apps. Dynamic analysis is often hard and infeasible to perform because of inadequate knowledge to trigger the malicious code path. Thus we used Android permissions gathered by static analysis to build the state-of-art malware detection

---

[1] https://www.trendmicro.com/vinfo/us/threat-encyclopedia/archive/malware/creeper.472.b.

[2] https://www.f-secure.com/v-descs/cabir_dropper.shtml.

system using machine learning and deep learning. The extensive list of permissions was handcrafted from the original Android documentation. Firstly we performed exploratory data analysis with correlation grid to gather useful insight about the data. Further, we performed a comprehensive feature vector analysis to reduce attributes using attribute subset selection methods (variance threshold) and also attribute creation methods (principal component analysis and autoencoders). Finally, we used an extensive list of classifiers derived from the traditional set (decision tree, support vector machine, and k-nearest neighbour), ensemble methods (random forest and adaptive boosting) and three deep neural networks (shallow, deep and deeper) to build and compare different classification models. We performed an in-depth analysis to develop an efficient Android malware detection system and made the following contributions:

1. We propose an Android malware detection system based on comprehensive feature engineering (using different attribute reduction techniques) followed by classification models (based on machine learning and deep neural network).
2. Our baseline model built with the random forest classifier was able to achieve the highest accuracy (94%). Our reduced feature models constructed with only 8% Android permissions attained comparable accuracy with appreciable time-saving. To evaluate the efficacy of our approach, we used only 16 Android permissions and achieved an accuracy of 93.3% with random forest classifier (~1% less than the baseline model). The decrease in Android permissions reduced the train and test time by half and tenth, respectively. This pattern of reduction in train and test time was virtually observed in almost all the analyzed classification models.
3. Deep neural network models achieve comparable accuracy against machine learning models but have a massive computational penalty (hundred and ten times more train and test time respectively compared to random forest models). We also found that malicious applications tend to use similar Android permission sets while for benign applications, the set is more scattered.

The rest of the paper is organized as follows. Section 2 presents a literature review of existing work on malware analysis and detection. Section 3 explains the background, broad framework and performance metrics. Section 4 discusses experimental setting and analysis (dataset, feature extraction, feature engineering and classification techniques) followed by experimental results and discussion. The last section concludes the paper by highlighting important points.

2   Related Work

Android malware detection is a rat-race[3] between malware developer and the anti-malware community. Currently, popular detection mechanisms like signature-based and heuristic-based detection have severe limitations [7,24,28].

---

[3] https://attack.mitre.org/.

Thus researchers are trying to develop state-of-the-art malware detection systems using machine learning and deep learning techniques. Building these systems is a two-stage process: attribute extraction and classification/clustering [28]. Android applications can be analyzed using the static or dynamic analysis to generate features for the construction of machine learning models. In static analysis, attributes are generated without running the code. However, in dynamic analysis, the sample application is executed in a sandbox to extract its behaviour. Then the extracted features are used to build models using classification/clustering algorithms for detecting malicious applications.

We have divided the literature review into two sub-areas:

(1) Feature extraction: An Android malware detection system named Droid-Delver was developed by Hou et al. using API call blocks as the feature set on comodo cloud dataset [8]. Lindorfer in Andrubis collected one million android applications from various sources and found that malicious applications tend to request more permissions (12.99) than benign applications (4.5) [12]. In DroidMat, features like application components, intents, permissions, and API calls were extracted for building the detection model [27]. Drebin collected intents, application components, API calls, permissions and network address for malware detection [1]. They concluded that certain combinations of hardware are requested more by malicious applications than benign ones. Sharma et al. grouped apps based on dangerous permissions and then used opcode to generate the feature vector [22]. Harris et al. developed a model for prediction of Android applications requesting excessive permissions. They also suggested changes in the way Android permissions are displayed and explained to the consumers [6]. Nguyen et al. modified the Snapchat application by adding excessive permissions and repacking it. The modified application is then checked using static and dynamic analysis tools simulating a zero-day repacked malware attack [14]. Wang et al. extracted features viz. API calls and permissions from Android apps for DroidDeepLearner [26]. Zhou et al. discovered that 93% of malware applications connect to the malicious source on the internet [26]. Sarma et al. found that malware apps tend to request network access more often than their benign counterparts [19].

(2) Classification model: After constructing the feature vector, various algorithms can be used to build the malware detection system. Arp et al. with benchmark Drebin dataset used support vector machine on the feature set with $5,45,000$ attributes and achieved 93.8% accuracy [1]. However, the model suffers from the curse of dimensionality due to an enormous vector size. Further, Li et al. in 2018 used the Drebin dataset to perform multilevel data pruning to find the 22 most significant permissions and achieved an accuracy of 91.97% [10]. However, the cost of data pruning was not discussed in the paper, which might adversely affect the overall performance of the detection model. In the past, new permission(s) have been added in almost every major Android update. Thus, finding the new significant permissions for effective malware detection is a recursive exercise and should be

cost-efficient. Also, MalPat (2018) combine permissions and API calls on the same dataset to obtain an F1 score of 98.24% [25]. MalPat used the top 50 most sensitive APIs for classification, but again the cost of selection was not discussed in the article. Wang et al. constructed a deep belief network with one hidden layer called DroidDeepLearner and reported the highest accuracy of 92.67% [26]. Sharma et al. used the tree-based classifiers viz. J48, random forest, functional trees, NBTree, & logistic model tree and achieved the accuracy of 79.27% with functional trees on Drebin dataset [22]. Later in 2016, Hou et al. using the same dataset proposed DroidDelver. They analysed models based on support vector machine, deep learning, decision tree, naive bayes and obtained the highest accuracy of 94.04% with decision tree model [8]. Sewak et al. used the random forest classifier and deep neural network of various depths on Malicia project with different feature reduction techniques. They attained the highest detection accuracy of 99.78% with random forest classifier [20]. DroidMat used k-means, naive bayes, k-nearest neighbour algorithms and accomplished the highest f-measure of 91.8% [27]. Patri et al. performed entropy analysis and shapelet-based classification for PE files [15]. Wenjia Li et al. in 2018 used kirin rules on Drebin to achieve a recall of 94.29% [11].

3 Overview and Framework

Machine learning and deep learning are subset of artificial intelligence and are currently used in various applications like email filtering, financial market analysis, information retrieval, computer vision and others. In the last decade, deep learning combined with current computational resources (hardware and software) has provided promising results in various fields like natural language processing, recommendation systems, medical image analysis and others. These models are often developed as a black box, thus have less interpretability. Explainability of any machine learning/deep learning model is a crucial factor for its real-world deployment today [16,28]. In this paper, we performed an empirical investigation to build an Android malware detection system using machine learning and deep learning.

Presently Android OS enjoys the smartphone duopoly with a current market share of than 80%. Principal protection for any user on the Android platform is derived from the Android permission system [2]. An Android application must request for the specific permission needed in order to access user data (SMS, photographs, etc.) or system resources like (storage, wifi, etc.). An application might be allowed to access the data or resource depending on the request. Based on the protection level, Google has classified Android permissions[4] into four different sets normal, dangerous, signature, and signatureOrSystem. We have used Android permissions to build a malware detection system using machine learning and deep neural network. Based on an exhaustive literature review and study of the Android platform, we were motivated to solve the following research questions:

---

[4] https://developer.android.com/guide/topics/permissions/overview.

- **Research Question-1**: Do malware designers use specific Android permission set to perform malicious activities?
- **Research Question-2**: Can a reduced Android permission set be constructed for efficient Android malware detection?
- **Research Question-3**: Do Android malware detection model(s) based on machine learning tend to use less computational resources as compared to the deep learning algorithms?

3.1 Framework Design

This study aims to propose an effective and efficient Android malware detection system. Figure 1 shows the systematic framework used for empirical analysis for malware classification. The design is divided into four sub-modules:

1. **Data Collection**: We gathered more than $10,000$ Android applications (benign and malware) from various sources for our experimental analysis.
2. **Feature Extraction**: Features are the backbone of any machine learning solution. We extracted Android permissions from the applications to be used as features for our models.
3. **Feature Engineering**: It is the process of understanding features using domain knowledge and statistical tools to improve the effectiveness and performance of a classification model. We used correlation analysis followed by feature reduction methods like variance threshold, principal component analysis and auto-encoders to reduce the size of the Android permission set used for building the malware detection models to avoid the curse of dimensionality.
4. **Classification Models**: Various machine learning and deep learning algorithms can be used to build the detection models. We used traditional classifiers, ensemble methods and deep neural network algorithms to build an efficient Android malware detection system. All the above steps are discussed in-depth later in the paper.

3.2 Performance Metrics

A classification model is evaluated on the following four values (*True Positive* (TP), *False Positive* (FP), *True Negative* (TN), and *False Negative* (FN). From these predicted values, various metrics can be derived to measure and understand the performance of the classification model.

1. Accuracy: It is the ratio of the correct predictions to the total number of predictions.

$$Accuracy = \frac{TP + TN}{TP + FP + TN + FN} \tag{1}$$

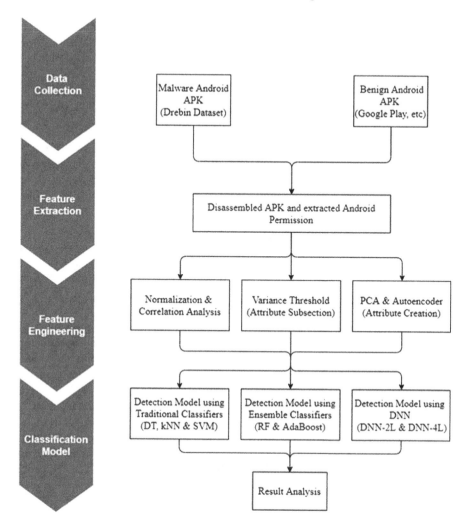

Fig. 1. Procedure for the construction of an efficient Android malware detection system

2. Recall (TPR): The Recall is the ratio of correctly predicted positive values to the total actual positive values.

$$Recall = \frac{TP}{TP + FN} \qquad (2)$$

3. Specificity (TNR): TNR is the ratio of the number of correctly classified benign apps to the total number of benign apps.

$$TNR = \frac{TN}{TN + FP} \qquad (3)$$

4. Receiver Operating Characteristic (ROC): It illustrates the separability of classes in a model, which is the ability of a model to classify malicious application as malware and benign application as benign. The ideal model has AUC value at 1.

4   Experimental Setting and Analysis

This section discusses the dataset (malware and benign), the process of feature extraction, feature engineering methods performed on the dataset and different classification algorithms used to build the efficacious Android malware detection system.

4.1   Malware and Benign Datasets

Input data quality holds the vital key for building any effective classification model. Daniel Arp and others compiled the Drebin dataset containing $5,560$ Android malware samples downloaded from the Google Play store and various other sources [1]. It also contains all the malicious applications from the Android Malware Genome Project [29]. Drebin includes apps from multiple malware families like *FakeInstaller*, *DroidKungFu*, *GoldDream*, and *GingerMaster*. After reviewing the different model proposed by various authors, we have also used the benchmark Drebin dataset as the representative of malicious Android applications for all our experiments [1,10,28].

Google Play Store[5] and other third-party apps stores are the primary distributors of Android applications (.apk) to users. For obtaining the benign samples, we downloaded ~$8,000$ Android apps from the Google Play store. To validate whether the downloaded apps are malicious or not, we used the services of Virus-Total[6] (a subsidiary of Alphabet Inc., which aggregates result of many AV products and online search engines). The reports generated by VirusTotal were used to segregate the benign samples for our experiments. An Android application is labelled as benign only if all the AVs from VirusTotal declare it as non-malicious. The remaining samples were non benign and hence discarded. Thus the final dataset for our analyses contained $5,560$ malware and $5,721$ benign samples.

4.2   Feature Extraction

Features can be extracted by static/dynamic analysis of Android applications to build a classification model. Essentially the feature vector is a fundamental pillar of any malware detection system. In this project, Android applications were disassembled using a reverse engineering software called Apktool[7]. A disassembled app contains AndroidManifest.xml, smali files, library files, assets, etc.

---

[5] https://play.google.com/store.

[6] https://www.virustotal.com/gui/home/upload.

[7] https://ibotpeaches.github.io/Apktool/.

The list of Android permissions to be used by an application are declared in the AndroidManifest.xml file. We handcrafted the extensive list of all the permissions using original Android documentation [8]. The list contains 197 permissions and their respective API level. We have considered all the permissions from API level 1 to API level Q(29) (launched in 2019). The list also contains depreciated permissions like $PERSISTENT\_ACTIVITY$ in API level 15, GET_TASKS in level 21, etc. which cannot be used in the newer version of Android. Finally, all the apps from malware and the benign dataset were decompiled using Apktool. Few Android applications were corrupted and thus were discarded. Lastly, the parser scanned through AndroidManifest.xml of each application to generate the feature vector containing the list of permissions used by that application. Thus the final feature vector representing the dataset is $11,274 \times 197$, where a row represents a particular Android app (malware or benign), and a column represents Android permission.

4.3   Feature Engineering

After rigorous feature extraction from Android applications, the next step was to perform feature engineering and to develop the classification models. Initial analysis of the feature vector revealed some useful insights into the usage of the Android permissions. In total, 59 permissions have never been used by any applications (malware/benign) in the dataset. Individually the number is 82 and 67 for malware and benign applications respectively. Analyzing further, some applications were using deprecated permissions (like $RESTART\_PACKAGES$ in API level 15, GET_TASKS in level 21, etc.) which cannot be used in the newer versions of Android. Also, the distribution of permission usage is not uniform across all applications. Some permissions are heavily used by malicious applications while others by benign applications. Figure 2 shows the detailed visualization of permissions and their normalized frequency in the dataset. Android permissions like $ACCESS\_NETWORK\_STATE$, $INTERNET$ and

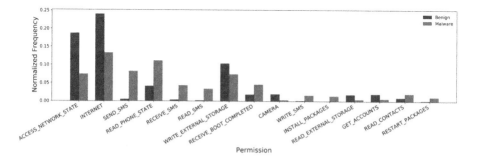

Fig. 2. Normalized frequency of the permissions in malicious and benign applications

---

[8] https://developer.android.com/reference/android/Manifest.permission.

WRITE_EXTERNAL_STORAGE are used by both benign and malware samples but extensively by benign applications. Also, permissions like *SEND_SMS*, *RECEIVE_SMS*, *READ_SMS*, *WRITE_SMS* and *INSTALL_PACKAGES* are heavily used by malicious applications but rarely by benign applications.

Correlation grid describes the degree of linear relationship between two variables. Figure 3 shows the correlation between the top fifteen features (Android permissions) derived from the random forest in malicious applications. *READ_SMS* & *WRITE_SMS* and *SEND_SMS* & *RECEIVE_SMS* has the highest correlations of 0.68 followed by *ACCESS_NETWORK_STATE* & *ACCESS_WIFI_STATE*, *READ_SMS* & *RECEIVE_SMS*, *ACCESS_NETWORK_STATE* & *RECEIVE_BOOT_COMPLETED* of 0.53, 0.47 and 0.45 respectively. *READ_PHONE_STATE* is often used by malware to gather phone number, current cellular network information and personal information like call list, SMS etc. *SEND_SMS* is also used by malware to subscribe to the victim to unwanted paid services. All these permissions are used in tandem with each other to perform the desired malicious task.

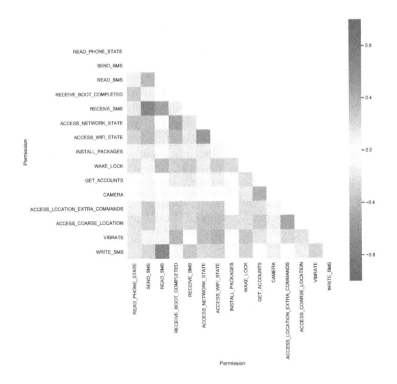

Fig. 3. Correlation matrix of permissions used in the malicious applications

4.4   Feature Reduction

As the number of unique system-defined Android permissions are 197, thus the feature vector also consists of 197 attributes. A classification model that builds on a large number of attributes will be computationally expensive, have higher train/test time, be less interpretable and is more likely to suffer from the curse of dimensionality. Thus, we performed feature reduction using both feature subset selection method (variance threshold) and attribute creation techniques (principal component analysis and autoencoder).

Variance Threshold (VT): VT is a feature reduction technique in which the variance of each feature in a dataset is calculated and features having less variance (below a threshold value) are dropped from the final vector. Figure 4 shows the plot between the features and corresponding variance values in the dataset. The plot clearly shows many permissions have very low variance, and thus have less predictive power during classification. Fifty-nine permissions have zero variance, and hence they do not contribute to the classification. Ten permissions have variance less than 0.0001 and remaining features have variance between 0.0001 and 0.24. Permissions *READ_PHONE_STATE*, *WRITE_EXTERNAL_STORAGE*, and *ACCESS_WIFI_STATE* have the highest variance of 0.24, 0.23, and 0.23 respectively. In Fig. 4, an elbow is visible at 0.10 (set as threshold value), and thus the final VT feature vector consists of only 16 permissions. Table 1 list all the 16 Android permissions arranged in descending order based on the variance.

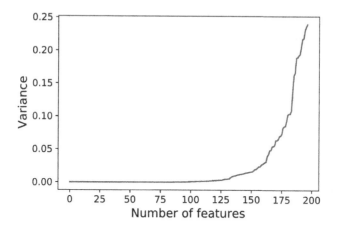

Fig. 4. Variance in Android permissions

Principal Component Analysis (PCA): PCA is another feature reduction technique where the dimensionality of a dataset is reduced by transforming the data to new orthogonal coordinate axes such that loss of information and variance is minimum. Further, highly correlated dimensions are dropped at the cost of a small decrease in the accuracy to reduce the curse of dimensionality. Figure 5 shows the model accuracy with the number of principal components by random forest classifier. Initially, as the principal components are added there is a sudden

Table 1. Significant permission ranking

Android permission	Ranking
READ_PHONE_STATE	1
WRITE_EXTERNAL_STORAGE	2
ACCESS_WIFI_STATE	3
RECEIVE_BOOT_COMPLETED	4
WAKE_LOCK	5
SEND_SMS	6
ACCESS_COARSE_LOCATION	7
ACCESS_NETWORK_STATE	8
ACCESS_FINE_LOCATION	9
VIBRATE	10
RECEIVE_SMS	11
READ_SMS	12
READ_CONTACTS	13
GET_ACCOUNTS	14
WRITE_SMS	15
CHANGE_WIFI_STATE	16

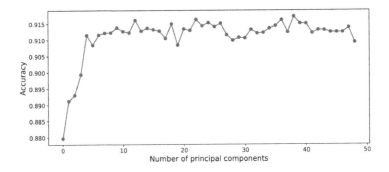

Fig. 5. Principal component analysis for Android permissions

increase in the model accuracy, which stabilizes around 16 principal components. Hence top 16 principal components are chosen to represent the data with PCA feature reduction technique. Since PCA is an attribute creation method, thus a particular principal component can represent one or more Android permissions.

Auto Encoder (AE): AE uses deep learning to reduce the dimensionality of a dataset. AE takes the set of features as the input and produces a reduced set as the output. AE consists of an encoder (input layer to code layer) which maps the input data to reduced latent space, and a decoder (code layer to the last layer) which tries to reconstruct the input data back. The number of neurons in the hidden layer(s) in AE is decreased gradually during encoding and increased again during decoding. AE is first trained on a complete network after which decoder is discarded, and the only encoder is used for feature reduction. We have designed a shallow and deep AE to achieve two distinct data transformations on the dataset.

- **AE with 1 Layer (AE-1L)** is a shallow autoencoder with only one hidden layer/code layer with 64 neurons. The design of AE-1L is 197-64-197.
- **AE with 3 Layer (AE-3L)** is a deep autoencoder with three encoding layers having 64, 32 and 16 neurons consecutively. The overall design of AE-3L is 197-64-16-64-197.

By design, all the layers (encoder and decoder) in both the AEs are fully connected with Rectified Linear Unit (ReLU) activation function except the code layer, which uses the sigmoid function because of the binary data. A dropout of 0.4 is set at all the layers for better generalization and to avoid overfitting. Adam optimizer is used to train both the AE with mean square error (MSE) as the loss function. The training and validation split of 80 : 20 is maintained, and both the AE are trained for 80 epochs with a batch size of 64. After training, Keras is used in the backend to derive an output from the code layer. Figure 6 and Fig. 7 shows the mean square error and AUC for the training and validation data over different epochs for AE-1L. During initial cycles, both MSE and AUC are jittery but become stable after training the AE-1L for 80 epochs. It also signifies that both the AEs are trained well and are not over-fitting or under-fitting the dataset.

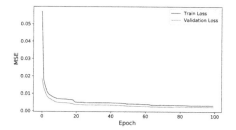 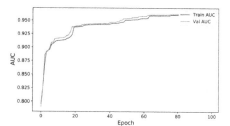

Fig. 6. Training and validation loss at different epochs for AE-1L

Fig. 7. Training and validation AUC at different epochs for AE-1L

Finally, Table 2 shows the different feature reduction techniques and the number of output features produced by each method. Original data contains all the 197 features without any feature reduction. VT performs attribute sub-selection, and top 16 Android permissions as features were selected based on variance for the final vector. Attribute creation method like PCA, AE-1L and AE-3L have created the new feature set of size 16, 64 and 16 respectively.

Table 2. Feature reduction technique and corresponding reduced vector size

Feature reduction	Number of features
OD[1]	197
VT[2]	16
PCA[3]	16
AE-1L[4]	64 (code layer)
AE-3L[5]	16 (code layer)

[1] Original Data [2] Variance Threshold [3] Principal
Component Analysis
[4] AE with 1 Layer [5] AE with 3 Layers

5   Malware Detection Models

We used three different categories of classifiers for building a permission-based Android malware detection system. The first group contain traditional classifiers like Decision Tree (DT), Support Vector Machine (SVM), and k-Nearest Neighbour (kNN). The second group include ensemble methods like Random Forest (RF) and Adaptive Boosting (AdaBoost). The third group consists of Deep Neural Network (DNN) of different depths.

5.1   Detection Model Using Traditional Classifiers

DT is a tree-based supervised learning algorithm which maximizes the information gain at every decision node. Gini impurity was used as the support criteria to choose the best split at each stage. There was no limit on the maximum depth of the tree, but the minimum number of samples at each leaf node was set to five to avoid overfitting. kNN classifies data based on its nearest k-neighbours in feature vector space. We considered five nearest neighbours to classify the data point with each neighbourhood weighted equally. SVM uses hyperplane and support vector to classify data into different classes. It is also called the maximum margin classifier since it tries to maximize the margin between the data and the hyperplane. We used LinearSVC kernel for classification, and decision function shape was one vs rest. The penalty parameter was set to *l1* since the feature vector space was sparse.

5.2   Detection Model Using Ensemble Classifiers

RF is also a supervised machine learning algorithm, which is an ensemble of a large number of DTs with different parameters. The class which is predicted by the majority of trees is the final output. Due to a large number of independent trees, the error of an individual tree does not affect the overall outcome. RF also perform feature sub-selection to avoid overfitting. The number of DTs in our model was 100 with Gini impurity as the split criteria. Bootstrapping and Out-of-bag was set to true for better generalization. There was no limit on the maximum depth of the tree, but the minimum number of samples to the leaf node was set to five. AdaBoost uses a series of weak classifiers for the final classification. The base estimator (weak classifiers) was DT with a maximum depth of one. *SAMME.R* was used to boost the results of the base estimators. The number of estimators was set to 50, and the learning rate was 1.

5.3   Detection Model Using DNN

DNN is a supervised learning technique which uses deep learning to build classification models. We have built three different DNN models with one hidden layer (shallow network), three hidden layers and five hidden layers (deep network) with the following design:

- **DNN with 2 Layers (DNN-2L)** has one input layer and a hidden layer containing 197 and 64 neurons, respectively. The output layer acts as the decision point and has only one neuron. The design of DNN-2L is 197-64-1.
- **DNN with 4 Layers (DNN-4L)** has one input layer of 197 neurons, followed by three hidden layers containing 128, 32, and 8 neurons, respectively. The design of DNN-4L is 197-128-32-8-1.
- **DNN with 7 Layers (DNN-7L)** is a deep network with six hidden layers containing 128, 64, 32, 16, 8, and 4 neurons, respectively. The design of DNN-7L is 197-128-64-32-16-8-4-1.

All the DNNs are fully connected network with ReLU as activation function at all the layers except the output layer, which has a sigmoid function. A split ratio of 80 : 20 for training and validation set is used to train the model. Again, the dropout rate of 0.4 is used to avoid overfitting of DNN models. For training, Adam optimizer with a learning rate of 0.1 and binary cross-entropy loss function is used. The DNNs are trained over 150 epochs with a batch size of 64. Figure 8 and Fig. 9 shows binary cross-entropy loss and AUC values for training and validation set of DNN-4L with VT data. The figures clearly show that the DNN-4L become stable after training for 150 epochs and does not over-fit or under-fit the dataset.

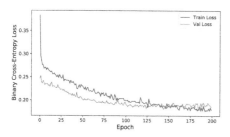
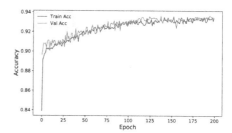

Fig. 8. Training and validation loss at different epochs for DNN-4L

Fig. 9. Training and validation AUC at different epochs for DNN-4L

5.4 Results and Discussion

Table 4 shows the performance of selected classification models with different feature reduction techniques. Random forest models produced most balanced classifications results (highest AUC) with original data (98.1), VT data (97.0), AE-1L data (97.7), PCA data (97.6) and AE-3L data (97.2). On the other hand, classification models based in kNN tended to overfit the malware class.

In terms of Accuracy (Acc) RF with the original data achieved the highest score of 94.0, followed by RF with VT data at 93.3. In neural network models, both DNN-4L (VT data) and DNN-2L (AE-1L) achieved a high accuracy score of 93.1. kNN (original data) and kNN (VT data) reported the lowest accuracy of 78.7 and 78.4 respectively since they were overfitting the malware class. As far as TPR is a concern, kNN (original data) and kNN (VT data) achieved the highest rates of 97.8 and 96.4, respectively. It also demonstrates that malicious applications use similar permission sets. The lowest TNR has also been provided by kNN with original and VT data at 59.7 and 60.4 respectively, which implies that benign apps use a diverse set of permissions. Highest TNR was recorded for DNN-7L (AE-1L data) and DNN-7L (original data) at 95.8 and 95.4 respectively, which is skewed towards the benign class.

In general, lower training time was reported for kNN, DT and RF with less number of features like VT data (16 features), PCA data (16 features), and AE-3L data (16 features). Also, there is a considerable reduction in train and test time when the model is trained on smaller feature vectors (VT, PCA and AE-3L) without much penalty on model accuracy. In the case of RF, train time was reduced to half for smaller vectors (VT data) with less than 1% penalty on the model accuracy. It signifies that only 16 features from VT, PCA and AE-3L are enough to represent that data and can be effectively used to build the classification model with less training and test time. Since kNN models store the feature vector with minimal preprocessing, thus they have considerably less training time. On the other hand, all DNNs have extremely large training time for building classification models. Although training time is a one-time activity in case of malware detection, the model needs to be updated quite frequently based on current telemetry. Similarly, reducing the feature vector has a positive impact on test time as well, where DT and RF outperformed other classifiers. Test time is particularly relevant because AV engines might have to run throughout 24×7 for detecting malicious activities.

Table 3 shows the detection rate of our proposed model with ten popular AVs. Our model w/RF achieved a higher detection rate of 93.3% with only 16 Android permissions which is much higher than most AV engines. On the other hand, Drebin used 5, 45, 000 features to achieve 93.90% detection rate with SVM, but their model suffered from the curse of dimensionality. Li et al. achieved detection rate of 91.36% with 22 features with a computationally expensive three-stage pruning approach [10].

Table 3. Malware Detection Rates (Our model vs Antivirus)

Our Model w/RF	Our Model w/DNN-4L	AV1	AV2	AV3	AV4	AV5	AV6	AV7	AV8	AV9	AV10
93.3	93.1	88.22	83.62	83.60	83.28	81.57	56.02	19.28	7.93	7.91	4.22

Table 4. Performance of multiple classifiers with different feature reduction techniques

Feature reduction	Classifier	Accuracy	TPR	AUC	Train Time (sec)	Test Time (sec)
OD[1]	DT[6]	92.6	91.9	94.5	0.052	0.003
VT[2]	DT	92.3	90.9	94.7	0.012	**0.001**
PCA[3]	DT	91.2	90.7	92.6	0.059	0.002
AE-1L[4]	DT	91.4	91.1	92.7	0.258	0.003
AE-3L[5]	DT	90.5	89.8	91.6	0.476	0.002
OD	kNN[7]	78.7	**97.8**	84.2	0.133	4.044
VT	kNN	78.4	96.4	84.5	0.080	0.421
PCA	kNN	91.4	91.3	95.7	**0.005**	0.119
AE-1L	kNN	90.8	93.0	95.4	0.100	1.950
AE-3L	kNN	88.4	90.3	94.7	0.084	0.327
OD	SVM[8]	91.0	89.4	96.3	5.634	0.929
VT	SVM	89.1	87.3	95.2	1.186	0.116
PCA	SVM	87.3	87.6	94.1	0.624	0.088
AE-1L	SVM	89.5	86.9	95.4	6.372	1.061
AE-3L	SVM	86.6	86.2	93.0	7.200	1.185
OD	RF[9]	**94.0**	93.0	**98.1**	0.674	0.036
VT	RF	93.3	92.0	97.7	0.328	0.028
PCA	RF	93.1	91.7	97.6	0.870	0.026
AE-1L	RF	93.2	91.7	97.7	1.281	0.029
AE-3L	RF	91.9	91.1	97.2	2.087	0.028
OD	AdaBoost[10]	90.6	90.6	96.4	1.488	0.063
VT	AdaBoost	89.1	88.7	95.3	0.352	0.031
PCA	AdaBoost	89.9	89.1	96.1	0.828	0.029
AE-1L	AdaBoost	91.1	89.8	96.6	2.881	0.048
AE-3L	AdaBoost	89.0	87.6	95.4	5.029	0.048
OD	DNN-2L[11]	93.0	93.5	93.0	162.624	0.195
VT	DNN-2L	92.6	91.7	92.6	175.512	0.225
PCA	DNN-2L	86.9	86.1	86.9	160.566	0.259
AE-1L	DNN-2L	93.1	91.4	93.2	162.066	0.200
AE-3L	DNN-2L	87.6	87.0	87.6	165.436	0.215
OD	DNN-4L[12]	93.0	93.0	94.2	191.264	0.310
VT	DNN-4L	93.1	92.0	93.2	207.849	0.400
PCA	DNN-4L	90.2	87.3	90.2	207.461	0.434
AE-1L	DNN-4L	93.1	91.0	93.1	193.373	0.333
AE-3L	DNN-4L	88.9	86.0	88.9	200.711	0.355
OD	DNN-7L[13]	93.0	92.8	94.0	254.377	0.521
VT	DNN-7L	92.6	90.5	92.6	269.323	0.664
PCA	DNN-7L	89.5	89.2	89.5	264.253	0.717
AE-1L	DNN-7L	92.5	89.3	92.6	247.947	0.557
AE-3L	DNN-7L	88.3	83.6	88.4	255.443	0.598

[1] Original Data [2] Variance Threshold [3] Principal Component Analysis [4] AE with 1 Layer [5] AE with 3 Layers [6] Decision Tree [7] k-Nearest Neighbour [8] Support Vector Machine [9] Random Forest [10] Adaptive Boosting [11] DNN with 2 Layers [12] DNN with 4 Layers [13] DNN with 7 Layers

6   Conclusion and Future Work

Over the last decade, smartphones and Android OS have been growing at a tremendous pace. Such devices store a lot of personal user information which is an obvious target of cybercriminals. Research shows detection engines based on signature and heuristic methods will be unable to cope with next-generation malware.

Our extensive analysis indicates that feature engineering produces efficacious Android malware detection without significant reduction in model accuracy. We found that instead of considering all the permissions for building classification model, only 16 permissions acquired from feature reduction (variance threshold/auto-encoder/principal component analysis) saves considerable model train and test time without significant penalty on accuracy.

Overall the baseline random forest model built with original data was able to balance both TPR and TNR to achieve highest AUC score of 98.1. Also, Tree-based classification models like random forest and decision tree are more accurate, time-efficient and have high interpretability, which makes them suitable for real-time deployment. Also, deep neural network based models achieved a comparable accuracy but with a massive penalty of training and testing time. Furthermore, malicious applications tend to use a similar permission set which can be explained by high TPR of k-nearest neighbour based models.

We are also designing an online tool for Android malware detection that can perform real-time analysis of Android applications. In addition to the above, we are also analyzing other deep learning-based feature reduction techniques like variational autoencoder coupled with classification models built with a recurrent neural network, long short-term memory, echo state network, deep belief networks, etc. for more effective and efficient detection of Android malicious apps which may be published elsewhere.

References

1. Arp, D., Spreitzenbarth, M., Hubner, M., Gascon, H., Rieck, K., Siemens, C.: Drebin: effective and explainable detection of android malware in your pocket. NDSS Symp. **14**, 23–26 (2014)
2. Daniel, W., Liu, X., Nusaputra, C., Hu, B., Wang, Y., Xing, M.: Strategies in improving android security. In: Pacific Asia Conference on Information Systems (PACIS) (2014). https://aisel.aisnet.org/pacis2014/275
3. Enck, W., Gilbert, P., Han, S., Tendulkar, V., Chun, B.G., Cox, L.P., Jung, J., McDaniel, P., Sheth, A.N.: Taintdroid: an information-flow tracking system for realtime privacy monitoring on smartphones. ACM Trans. Comput. Syst. (TOCS) **32**(2), 1–29 (2014)
4. Faruki, P., Bharmal, A., Laxmi, V., Ganmoor, V., Gaur, M.S., Conti, M., Rajarajan, M.: Android security: a survey of issues, malware penetration, and defenses. IEEE Commun. Surv. Tutorials **17**(2), 998–1022 (2014)
5. G DATA: Cyber attacks on Android devices on the rise (2018). https://www.gdatasoftware.com/blog/2018/11/31255-cyber-attacks-on-android-devices-on-the-rise. Accessed May 2020

6. Harris, M.A., Brookshire, R., Patten, K., Regan, B.: Mobile application installation influences: have mobile device users become desensitized to excessive permission requests. In: Americas Conference on Information Systems (AMCIS), pp. 13–15 (2015).https://aisel.aisnet.org/amcis2015/ISSecurity/GeneralPresentations/4/

7. Hicks, C., Dietrich, G.: An exploratory analysis in android malware trends. Americas Conference on Information Systems (AMCIS) (2016). https://aisel.aisnet.org/amcis2016/ISSec/Presentations/35/

8. Hou, S., Saas, A., Ye, Y., Chen, L.: DroidDelver: an android malware detection system using deep belief network based on API call blocks. In: Song, S., Tong, Y. (eds.) WAIM 2016. LNCS, vol. 9998, pp. 54–66. Springer, Cham (2016). https://doi.org/10.1007/978-3-319-47121-1_5

9. Kemp, S.: GLOBAL DIGITAL REPORT (2018). https://digitalreport.wearesocial.com/. Accessed May 2020

10. Li, J., Sun, L., Yan, Q., Li, Z., Srisa-an, W., Ye, H.: Significant permission identification for machine-learning-based android malware detection. IEEE Trans. Ind. Inf. **14**(7), 3216–3225 (2018)

11. Li, W., Wang, Z., Cai, J., Cheng, S.: An android malware detection approach using weight-adjusted deep learning. In: International Conference on Computing, Networking and Communications (ICNC), pp. 437–441. IEEE (2018)

12. Lindorfer, M., Neugschwandtner, M., Weichselbaum, L., Fratantonio, Y., Van Der Veen, V., Platzer, C.: Andrubis-1,000,000 apps later: a view on current Android malware behaviors. In: IEEE BADGERS, pp. 3–17. IEEE (2014)

13. McAfee: McAfee Labs Threats Report: December 2018, January 2019. https://www.mcafee.com/enterprise/en-us/assets/reports/rp-quarterly-threats-dec-2018.pdf. Accessed May 2020

14. Nguyen, T., McDonald, J.T., Glisson, W.B.: Exploitation and detection of a malicious mobile application. In: Hawaii International Conference on System Sciences (HICSS) (2017). https://aisel.aisnet.org/hicss-50/st/mobile_app_development/4

15. Patri, O., Wojnowicz, M., Wolff, M.: Discovering malware with time series shapelets. In: Hawaii International Conference on System Sciences (HICSS) (2017). https://aisel.aisnet.org/hicss-50/st/digital_forensics/4

16. Rhue, L.: Beauty's in the AI of the beholder: how AI anchors subjective and objective predictions. In: International Conference on Information Systems (ICIS) (2019). https://aisel.aisnet.org/icis2019/future_of_work/future_work/15/

17. O'Dea, S.: Global smartphone shipments forecast from 2010 to 2019 (2016). http://www.statista.com/statistics/263441/global-smartphone-shipments-forecast/. Accessed May 2020

18. Sahay, S.K., Sharma, A., Rathore, H.: Evolution of malware and its detection techniques. In: Tuba, M., Akashe, S., Joshi, A. (eds.) Information and Communication Technology for Sustainable Development. AISC, vol. 933, pp. 139–150. Springer, Singapore (2020). https://doi.org/10.1007/978-981-13-7166-0_14

19. Sarma, B.P., Li, N., Gates, C., Potharaju, R., Nita-Rotaru, C., Molloy, I.: Android permissions: a perspective combining risks and benefits. In: ACM symposium on Access Control Models and Technologies (SACMAT), pp. 13–22 (2012)

20. Sewak, M., Sahay, S.K., Rathore, H.: Comparison of deep learning and the classical machine learning algorithm for the malware detection. In: 19th IEEE/ACIS SNPD, pp. 293–296. IEEE (2018)

21. Sewak, M., Sahay, S.K., Rathore, H.: Deepintent: implicitintent based android ids with e2e deep learning architecture. In: 2020 IEEE 31st Annual International Symposium on Personal, Indoor and Mobile Radio Communications, pp. 1–6. IEEE (2020)

22. Sharma, A., Sahay, S.K.: An investigation of the classifiers to detect android malicious apps. In: Information and Communication Technology, pp. 207–217. Springer (2018)

23. Symantec: Internet Security Threat Report (2019). https://www.symantec.com/content/dam/symantec/docs/reports/istr-24-2019-en.pdf. Accessed May 2020

24. Tam, K., Feizollah, A., Anuar, N.B., Salleh, R., Cavallaro, L.: The evolution of android malware and android analysis techniques. ACM Comput. Surv. (CSUR) **49**(4), 1–41 (2017)

25. Tao, G., Zheng, Z., Guo, Z., Lyu, M.R.: Malpat: mining patterns of malicious and benign android apps via permission-related APIS. IEEE Trans. Reliab. **67**(1), 355–369 (2017)

26. Wang, Z., Cai, J., Cheng, S., Li, W.: DroidDeepLearner: identifying android malware using deep learning. In: IEEE 37th Sarnoff Symposium, pp. 160–165. IEEE (2016)

27. Wu, D.J., Mao, C.H., Wei, T.E., Lee, H.M., Wu, K.P.: Droidmat: android malware detection through manifest and API calls tracing. In: Asia Joint Conference on Information Security, pp. 62–69. IEEE (2012)

28. Ye, Y., Li, T., Adjeroh, D., Iyengar, S.S.: A survey on malware detection using data mining techniques. ACM Comput. Surv. **50**(3), 1–40 (2017)

29. Zhou, Y., Jiang, X.: Dissecting android malware: characterization and evolution. In: IEEE Symposium on Security and Privacy (IEEE S&P), pp. 95–109 (2012)

Energy Efficiency Optimization for RF Energy Harvesting Relay System

Guangjun Liang[1,2] , Jianfang Xin[3(✉)] , Qun Wang[1,2] , Lingling Xia[1,2] , and Meng Li[1,2]

[1] Department of Computer Information and Network Security,
Jiangsu Police Institute, Nanjing, China
{liangguangjun,wqun}@jspi.cn
[2] Jiangsu Provincial Public Security Department Key Laboratory of Digital
Forensics, Nanjing, China
[3] Electrical Engineering School, Anhui Polytechnic University, Wuhu, China
xinjfang@163.com

Abstract. This paper conducts research on the RF energy harvesting relay network, and proposes an improved energy harvesting relay protocol, which allows the energy harvesting source node to retransmit data to improve the system diversity gain, and constructs energy harvesting slot allocation, subcarrier pairing, and power Optimized model of distributed system energy efficiency. A resource allocation algorithm based on optimal energy efficiency is further proposed. The Dinkelbach method is used to transform the nonlinear programming problem into a linear programming problem. Then, the Hungarian algorithm and the sub-gradient method are used to obtain the iterative algorithm based on energy efficiency optimization. Simulation shows that the algorithm reduces the complexity of the algorithm and has good global convergence.

Keywords: RF energy harvesting · Energy efficiency · Power allocation · Subcarrier pairing

1 Introduction

Radio frequency energy harvesting (RF-EH) technology can extend the life of wireless networks, improve energy efficiency, and reduce the total greenhouse gas emissions of green wireless communications [1,2].

Reference [3] applied RF energy harvesting technology to the cognitive radio (CR) network scenario earlier, considering a random geometric model of the

This research has been supported by the National Natural Science Foundation of China (No. 61802155), the High-level Introduction of Talent Scientific Research Start-up Fund of Jiangsu Police Institute (JSPI19GKZL407) and the General Research Project of Anhui Higher Education Promotion Plan (Grant TSKJ2015B18, KZ00215021, KZ00215022), Innovation project for postgraduates of Jiangsu province (KYCX19-0887), Youth Foundation of Anhui Polytechnic University (2014YQ40).

H. Gao et al. (Eds.): BROADNETS 2020, LNICST 355, pp. 53–66, 2021.
https://doi.org/10.1007/978-3-030-68737-3_4

homogeneous Poisson point process (HPPP) where the primary user and the secondary user are independent, the secondary user can obtain the environmental RF energy from the transmission, analyze the transmission probability and throughput of the secondary user, and get the best transmission power and user distribution density. Literature [5] conducts research on cognitive D2D communication based on energy harvesting in heterogeneous cellular networks. Cognitive D2D users can obtain energy from environmental interference, and analyzes two types of uplink or downlink for cellular communication Spectrum access strategy, namely random spectrum access (RSA) strategy and priority spectrum access (PSA) strategy. Literature [4] studies the transmission scheduling strategy in RF energy harvesting communication. In order to describe the actual environmental energy harvesting process more accurately, a nonlinear recursive model including the feedback loop of data transmission to the energy harvesting process is proposed, and a design based on The optimal transmission scheduling strategy of the recursive algorithm.

Literature [6,7] assumes that the secondary user node of the cognitive energy harvesting network satisfies the causal limitation of harvested energy. Literature [6] assumes that a system throughput optimization model of primary user interference limitation is constructed and proposes a system based on system Power allocation algorithm. Reference [7] considers the differences in energy acquisition capabilities, channel perception energy and channel quality of secondary users, and proposes a joint resource allocation algorithm for secondary user transmission channel selection, transmission power allocation, and transmission time assignment.

The collaborative communication technology represented by relays can significantly improve the average throughput of the system and expand the network coverage, and has received extensive attention from academia and industry. The literature [8–14] focuses on the application of energy harvesting technology in the field of collaborative communication the study.

Literature [8] studies a bidirectional relay scenario with energy harvesting nodes, proposes a dynamic selection relay strategy to improve throughput, and maximizes offline throughput through an iterative generalized water injection algorithm, and further gives a dynamic programming method Get the best online relay selection strategy. References [9,10] study the performance optimization scheme of the three-node energy harvesting bidirectional relay network (TWRN). Reference [9] assumes that energy transfer is allowed between nodes for energy collaboration. Under the constraints of energy harvesting (EH) and peak power, an optimal resource allocation scheme based on offline scheduling is proposed, and a dynamic programming-based Of the online scheduling scheme to approximate the offline optimal solution. Reference [10] assumes that the relay collects energy from the received information signal and co-channel interference signal, and then uses the collected energy to forward the correctly decoded signal to the receiver, and the receiver switches between decoding information and collecting energy Time switching scheme (TS), and power receiving scheme (PS), part of the received power is used for energy collection, and the remaining power is used for information processing information, given the decoding and forwarding energy collection relay system traversal capacity and Analytical expression of interruption capacity. Reference [11] studies the maximum throughput of the end-to-end system of the energy harvesting two-hop relay communication network. Assuming that the energy arrival and channel state are known, the optimal offline time scheduling and power are obtained through the Karush-Kuhn-Tucker condition. Distribution, further proposed two sub-optimal low complexity online transmission strategies. Reference [12] studies the optimal design of bidirectional decoding and forwarding (DF) energy harvesting relay networks, and examines power split relay (PSR) and time switching relay (TSR) strategies, respectively, and applies the fairness max-min criterion and maximum According to the max-sum criterion of resource utilization, the optimal power allocation coefficient and the optimal time switching coefficient of the network based on PSR and TSR are obtained, and the maximum transmission rate is analyzed. Literature [13] studied the substrate-based energy harvesting cognitive relay scenario, assuming that the energy harvesting device has hardware damage, proposed a hardware damage-based substrate-based energy harvesting bidirectional cognitive relay network model, and deduced the secondary network in Sweden Closed solution of the probability of outage in a fading block fading channel. Reference [14] considers a two-way relay cooperative cognitive radio network for cooperative transmission of energy and information. The secondary user adopts two-way cooperative relay transmission. The relay adopts cooperative transmission of energy and information to derive the outage probability of the system and the traversal of secondary users. Closed solution of capacity.

This article considers an RF-EH multi-relay scenario, which includes a base station BS, a source node, and relay nodes. The HTC relay mechanism is used in the network. The BS broadcasts energy to the source node and the relay node on the downlink channel, and receives signals from the source node and the relay node on its upstream channel. After the source node collects radio frequency energy from the BS, it uses the collected Energy transmission data. Taking the maximum energy efficiency of the system as the optimization goal, the transmission power of the entire network is restricted as the constraint condition, and then the energy efficiency optimal model of joint subcarrier pairing, power allocation and time slot assignment is concluded. The proposed optimization model is a mixed integer nonlinear programming problem, which can be simplified by the equivalent channel gain method and solved by the dual method. First, the Dinkelbach method is used to transform the nonlinear programming problem into a linear programming problem. Then, the Cauchy inequality and the Hungarian algorithm are used to solve the power allocation and subcarrier allocation problems of the current iteration. Finally, the sub-gradient method is used to obtain the iterative algorithm based on energy efficiency optimization.

The main contributions of this paper are summarized as follows:

- An improved HTC relay mechanism is proposed to allow the source node to retransmit the unsuccessful signal in the last time slot on another subcarrier.

Such a scheme can significantly improve the energy efficiency performance of the system.

- The proposed optimization model is a mixed integer nonlinear programming problem. The method of deriving the equivalent channel gain simplifies the objective function and reduces the computational complexity of the objective function.
- For an iterative process of energy efficiency optimization, a joint resource allocation algorithm is proposed. Joint allocation is based on the principle of energy efficiency optimization, power allocation, subcarrier pairing and time slot assignment.

The rest of this article is organized as follows. The second chapter is the system model and problem description, elaborating on the improved HTC protocol proposed in this paper, which comes down to the optimization problem. The third chapter is the energy efficiency optimization outer loop algorithm. Sect. 3 describes the energy efficiency optimization inner loop algorithm. Sect. 4 is the simulation results and analysis. Sect. 5 presents the conclusion of this study.

2   System Model and Problem Description

2.1   System Model

As shown in Fig. 1, this chapter studies the RF-EH multi-relay network scenario, including a base station BS, a source node S and K relay nodes, each relay works in AF half-duplex mode, the entire transmission bandwidth is divided equally into N sub-carriers. BS has a constant energy supply to ensure reliable communication. The source node S and all relays are equipped with rechargeable batteries without a stable energy supply device, and must rely on energy harvesting to complete data transmission.

Unlike the HTC relay mechanism in [16], it is assumed that the source node S and all K relay nodes can collect energy and use it to transmit data. The transmission process T of each data block is divided into two stages, an energy transmission stage $\tau_E T$ and a data transmission stage $\tau_I T$, and thus $\tau_E + \tau_I = 1$.

In the energy transmission phase $\tau_E T$, the BS broadcasts energy to the source node S and all K relay nodes in the downlink channel. After the source node S and the K relay nodes collect enough energy for the signal transmission of the next two time slots, the energy transmission phase ends.

In this paper, the subscript B indicates BS, the subscript S indicates the source node, and the subscript $R_k, k = 1, 2, ..., K$ indicates each relay node. h^{BS} and h_k^{BR} represent the channel gain from BS to source node S and BS to relay node R_k on subcarrier i, respectively, and the channel gain follows the complex Gaussian distribution, defined as $h^{BS} \sim CN\left(0, \sigma_{BS}^2\right)$ and $h_k^{BR} \sim CN\left(0, \sigma_{BR,k}^2\right)$, where σ_{BS}^2 and $\sigma_{BR,k}^2$ represent the Gaussian white at the receiving end noise. P_B represents the transmission power of BS. In order to ensure that the relay and the source collect enough energy to work properly,

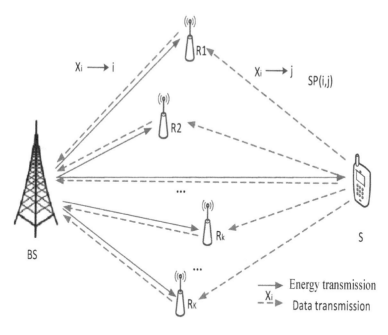

Fig. 1. RF-EH multi-relay network scenario.

the P_B needs to be large enough so that the energy collected from the noise can be ignored. In the energy transmission phase, the energy collected by the source node S and the relay node R_k and the total energy collected are expressed as

$$E^S = \zeta_S \tau_E Th^{BS} P_B \tag{1}$$

$$E_k^R = \zeta_k^R \tau_E Th_k^{BR} P_B, \quad k \in \{1, 2, ..., K\} \tag{2}$$

$$E^{EH} = \tau_E T \left(\zeta_S h^{BS} + \sum_{k=1}^{K} \zeta_k^R h_k^{BR} \right) P_B \tag{3}$$

where ζ_S and ζ_k^R are the energy collection efficiency of the source node S and the relay node R_k, which meets $0 < \zeta_S < 1$, $0 < \zeta_k^R < 1$. Based on the AF relay protocol, a subcarrier pairing strategy is applied. Each relay receives the signal from the source node S on the subcarrier i, and then amplifies and forwards the signal on the subcarrier j in the next time slot. Define the $N \times N$ decision matrix $\Phi_{N \times N} = \{\phi_{i,j}\}$, where $\phi_{i,j}$ is the subcarrier pairing factor. $\phi_{i,j} = 1$ means that subcarrier i is paired with subcarrier j, denoted as $SP_{i,j}$, and conversely, $\phi_{i,j} = 0$ means that subcarrier i is not paired with subcarrier j. At the same time, it is stipulated that each subcarrier must be paired with only one subcarrier, so that $\phi_{i,j}$ meets the following

$$\phi_{i,j} \in \{0,1\}, \forall i, j \tag{4}$$

$$\sum_{i=1}^{N} \phi_{i,j} = 1, \sum_{j=1}^{N} \phi_{i,j} = 1, \forall i, j \tag{5}$$

It is worth noting that the solution proposed in this chapter is suitable for indoor and outdoor application scenarios. For example, for indoor scenarios, intelligent terminals need to collect and process information about the indoor environment. The source node and relay node may have flexible locations and unstable power supplies. Power supply smart terminal, and BS stands for smart terminal with relatively fixed position and stable power supply. For outdoor scenes, this system model can also be a wireless sensor network with cooperative relay function, where the BS can be regarded as a gateway node of the wireless sensor network with a relatively fixed position, and the relay node and the source node can be regarded as wireless Sensor network nodes, with the help of EH technology, increase the energy endurance of sensor nodes, thereby increasing the stability and reliability of the network and reducing network maintenance costs.

2.2   Improve HTC Relay Protocol

As shown in Fig. 2, the transmission process T of each data block of the improved HTC relay protocol is divided into an energy transmission stage $\tau_E T$ and a data transmission stage $\tau_I T$. In the data transmission phase, $\tau_I T$ is used for uplink cooperative data communication and includes two time slots: information transmission time slot and information cooperation time slot. To simplify the expression, we assume that the two time slots in the data transmission phase are of equal length and are both $\tau_I T/2$ in length.

In the first time slot of $\tau_I T$ in the data transmission phase, the source node S broadcasts the signal to the relay node and the base station BS simultaneously. $g_{i,1}^{SB}$ and $g_{i,k}^{SR}$ represent the channel gains on the subcarrier i from the source node S to BS and from the source node S to the relay node R_k respectively. The channel gains follow the complex Gaussian distribution and are defined as $g_{i,1}^{SB} \sim CN\left(0, \sigma_{SB,1}^2\right)$ and $g_{i,k}^{SR} \sim CN\left(0, \sigma_{SR,k}^2\right)$, respectively, where $\sigma_{SB,1}^2$ and $\sigma_{SR,k}^2$ represent the receiving end Gaussian white noise.

On the subcarrier i, the signals received by the k-th relay and BS are represented as $y_{i,k}^R$ and y_i^B, respectively.

$$y_{i,k}^R = g_{i,k}^{SR} \sqrt{P_i^{S1}} x_i + n_{i,k}^{SR} \quad \forall i, k \tag{6}$$

$$y_i^B = g_{i,1}^{SB} \sqrt{P_i^{S1}} x_i + n_{i,1}^{SB} \quad \forall i \tag{7}$$

where P_i^{S1}, x_i, $n_{i,1}^{SB}$ and $n_{i,k}^{SR}$ represent the power allocated to the source node S in the first time slot, the transmission signal from the source node S to the BS, the source node S and the k-th relay on the subcarrier i of the first time slot Gaussian white noise.

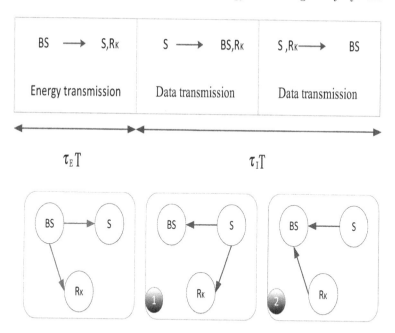

Fig. 2. Proposed improved HTC relay protocol.

In the second time slot of $\tau_I T$ during data transmission, all relays forward the signal received in the first time slot to the BS. Different from the HTC relay mechanism in [15], the signal of the previous time slot is retransmitted by S on another subcarrier which can further improve system performance. For the $SP_{i,j}$, the joint signal received from the source node S and all relays received at the BS can be expressed as

$$y_{(i,j)}^{B} = g_{j,2}^{SB}\sqrt{P_{i,j}^{S2}}x_i + \sum_{k=1}^{K} g_{j,k}^{RB}\alpha_{i,k}^{R}y_{i,k}^{R} + n_{j,2}^{SB} \tag{8}$$

where $P_{i,j}^{S2}$, $\alpha_{i,k}^{R}$ and $n_{j,2}^{SB}$ represent the power allocated by the second time slot source node S on the subcarrier pair $SP_{i,j}$, the amplification factor of the k-th relay and the Gaussian white noise of the source node S on the j-th subcarrier, $\alpha_{i,k}^{R}$ can expressed as

$$\alpha_{i,k}^{R} = \sqrt{P_{i,j,k}^{R}\Big/\left(\left|g_{i,k}^{SR}\right|^{2}P_i^{S1} + \sigma_{R,k}^{2}\right)} \tag{9}$$

where $P_{i,j,k}^{R}$ represents the power allocated to the k-th relay by the second time slot on the j-th subcarrier.

Using the improved HTC relay mechanism, the signal-to-interference and noise ratio of the first and second time slots on the subcarrier pair $SP_{i,j}$ are expressed as SNR_i^{TS1} and $SNR_{(i,j)}^{TS2}$, respectively, which can be expressed as follows

$$SNR_i^{TS1} = \left|g_{i,1}^{SB}\right|^2 P_i^{S1} \Big/ \sigma_{SB,1}^2 \qquad (10)$$

$$SNR_{(i,j)}^{TS2} = \frac{\left(\sum_{k=1}^{K} \frac{\left|g_{j,k}^{SR} g_{j,k}^{RB}\right|\sqrt{P_i^{S1} P_{i,j,k}^R}}{\sqrt{P_i^{S1}\left|g_{j,k}^{SR}\right|^2 + \sigma_{SR,k}^2}} + \left|g_{j,2}^{SB}\right|\sqrt{P_{i,j}^{S2}}\right)^2}{\sigma_{SB,2}^2 + \sum_{k=1}^{K} \left(\frac{\left|g_{j,k}^{RB}\right|\sqrt{P_{i,j,k}^R}}{\sqrt{P_i^{S1}\left|g_{j,k}^{SR}\right|^2 + \sigma_{SR,k}^2}}\right)^2 \sigma_{SR,k}^2} \qquad (11)$$

2.3   Problem Description

Using the maximum ratio combining method to combine the received signals from two time slots, the end-to-end transmission rate of the subcarrier pair $SP_{i,j}$ can be expressed as

$$R_{(i,j)} = \frac{\tau_I}{2} \log(1 + SNR_i^{TS1} + SNR_{(i,j)}^{TS2}) \qquad (12)$$

Therefore, the total reachable rate of the system can be expressed as

$$R_{total}(\mathbf{\Phi}, \mathbf{P}) = \sum_{i=1}^{N} \sum_{j=1}^{N} \phi_{i,j} R_{(i,j)} \qquad (13)$$

where $\mathbf{\Phi} = \{\phi_{i,j}\}$, $\mathbf{P} = \{P_{i,j}\}$.

In order to better characterize the energy consumption of the system, the energy consumption of the system is divided into two parts: transmission power consumption and inherent power consumption of the circuit, the former mainly refers to the energy overhead caused by the transmission data of users and relays, expressed as

$$P_{trans}(\mathbf{\Phi}, \mathbf{P}) = \sum_{i=1}^{N} \sum_{j=1}^{N} \left(P_i^{S1} + P_{i,j}^{S2}\right) + \sum_{i=1}^{N} \sum_{j=1}^{N} P_{i,j,k}^R = \sum_{i=1}^{N} \sum_{j=1}^{N} \phi_{i,j} P_{(i,j)} \qquad (14)$$

The latter's inherent power consumption of the circuit is positioned as P_C, which mainly includes system overhead such as digital-to-analog converters and power amplifiers. This chapter considers it as a constant and specifies that $\frac{1}{\varsigma}$ represents power conversion efficiency. For example, when $\varsigma = 2$, the efficiency of the system power amplifier is 50%. Summing the energy consumption of the two parts, the total energy expenditure of the system is obtained as follows

$$P_{total}(\mathbf{\Phi}, \mathbf{P}) = P_C + \varsigma P_{trans}(\mathbf{\Phi}, \mathbf{P}) \qquad (15)$$

This article considers joint subcarrier pairing and power allocation on different subcarriers and terminals, and the following constraints must be met

$$\sum_{i=1}^{N}\sum_{j=1}^{N}\left(P_i^{S1}+P_{i,j}^{S2}\right)\leq P^S=\frac{1-\tau_I}{\tau_I}2\zeta_s h^{BS}P_B \tag{16}$$

$$\sum_{i=1}^{N}\sum_{j=1}^{N}\sum_{k=1}^{K}P_{i,j,k}^R\leq\sum_{k=1}^{K}P_k^R=\frac{1-\tau_I}{\tau_I}2\zeta_k^R P_B\sum_{k=1}^{K}h_k^{BR} \tag{17}$$

where Among them, P^S and P_k^R represent the sum of the transmission power of the source node S and the k-th relay in the two time slots, respectively. According to (4)–(5), the total transmit power consumed by the sub-carriers for $SP_{i,j}$ in the first and second time slots is expressed as $P_{i,j}$, thus giving the limitation of the total transmission power P_T

$$\sum_{i=1}^{N}\sum_{j=1}^{N}\phi_{i,j}P_{i,j}=P^S+\sum_{k=1}^{K}P_k^R\leq P_T \tag{18}$$

In summary, the energy efficiency optimization problem of the energy harvesting multi-relay system is expressed as follows

$$P1: \max_{\tau_I,P_i^{S1},P_{i,j}^{S2},P_{i,j,k}^R,\phi_{i,j}} \frac{R_{total}(\mathbf{\Phi},\mathbf{P})}{P_{total}(\mathbf{\Phi},\mathbf{P})}$$

$$s.t.\phi_{i,j}\in\{0,1\},\forall i,j \tag{19A}$$

$$\sum_{i=1}^{N}\phi_{i,j}=1,\sum_{j=1}^{N}\phi_{i,j}=1,\forall i,j \tag{19B}$$

$$\sum_{i=1}^{N}\sum_{j=1}^{N}\left(P_i^{S1}+P_{i,j}^{S2}\right)\leq P^S=\frac{1-\tau_I}{\tau_I}2\zeta_s h^{BS}P_B \tag{19C}$$

$$\sum_{i=1}^{N}\sum_{j=1}^{N}\sum_{k=1}^{K}P_{i,j,k}^R\leq\sum_{k=1}^{K}P_k^R=\frac{1-\tau_I}{\tau_I}2P_B\sum_{k=1}^{K}\zeta_k^R h_k^{BR} \tag{19D}$$

$$\sum_{i=1}^{N}\sum_{j=1}^{N}\phi_{i,j}P_{i,j}=P^S+\sum_{k=1}^{K}P_k^R\leq P_T \tag{19E}$$

(19)

The objective function of P1 is to maximize $\sum_{i=1}^{N}\sum_{j=1}^{N}\phi_{i,j}R_{(i,j)}$, where $R_{(i,j)}$ and $\phi_{i,j}$ respectively represent the end-to-end transmission rate and the subcarrier pairing factor on the subcarrier pair $SP_{i,j}$. Constraints (19A)–(19B) indicate that each subcarrier must be paired with only one subcarrier. Constraints (19C)–(19E) represent constraints on the source node S, relay, and total transmit power, respectively. Generally speaking, P1 is a mixed integer nonlinear programming problem with high computational complexity, which is usually solved by the dual method.

In the following content, we will transform the optimization problem P1 into other forms and use the Dinkelbach method to solve the optimal energy efficiency.

3 Energy Efficiency Optimization Algorithm

3.1 Continuous Relaxation of Optimization Problem

The optimization problem P1 gives an optimization model that maximizes the average energy efficiency of the system. It is easy to find that the optimization problem P1 is a Mixed-Integer Nonlinear Programming (MINLP) problem. Such problems can usually be solved by branch and bound methods [16] Solution, but the computational complexity is extremely large, it is difficult to be applied in the actual system. In order to reduce the computational complexity, this section proposes a low complexity optimization method that can find the optimal solution in polynomial time.

First, ignore the physical meaning of formula (4), in order to convert the optimization problem P1 into a quasi-convex function form, we will relax the binary integer constraint to the real number constraint and rewrite Eq. (4) as

$$\phi_{i,j} \in [0,1], \forall i,j \tag{20}$$

So we can get the relaxation problem of the original problem P1

$$
P2: \quad \max_{\tau_I, P_i^{S1}, P_{i,j}^{S2}, P_{i,j,k}^R, \phi_{i,j}} \frac{R_{total}(\mathbf{\Phi},\mathbf{P})}{P_{total}(\mathbf{\Phi},\mathbf{P})}
$$

$$
s.t. \phi_{i,j} \in [0,1], \forall i,j
$$

$$
\sum_{i=1}^{N} \phi_{i,j} = 1, \sum_{j=1}^{N} \phi_{i,j} = 1, \forall i,j
$$

$$
\sum_{i=1}^{N} \sum_{j=1}^{N} \left(P_i^{S2} + P_{i,j}^{S3} \right) \leq P^S = \frac{1-\tau_I}{\tau_I} 2\zeta_S h^{BS} P_B \tag{21}
$$

$$
\sum_{i=1}^{N} \sum_{j=1}^{N} \sum_{k=1}^{K} P_{i,j,k}^R \leq \sum_{k=1}^{K} P_k^R = \frac{1-\tau_I}{\tau_I} 2P_B \sum_{k=1}^{K} \zeta_k^R h_k^{BR}
$$

$$
\sum_{i=1}^{N} \sum_{j=1}^{N} \phi_{i,j} P_{i,j} = P^S + \sum_{k=1}^{K} P_k^R \leq P_T
$$

Note that the traditional convex optimization software package can be used to solve the relaxation problem P2 to obtain the solution to the original problem P1, but the solution efficiency is very low, because it is not guaranteed that the $\mathbf{\Phi}^*(\alpha,\beta)$ returned by the iteration is binary. Since there is no available method to convert the real $\mathbf{\Phi}^*(\alpha,\beta)$ into a binary solution, the Hungarian algorithm based on the equivalent channel gain $A_{i,j}$ is usually used to perform subcarrier pairing $\phi_{i,j}$. The use of the improved HTC protocol in this paper will lead to more complicated derivation based on equivalent channel gain, which will be explained in detail in the next section.

3.2 Energy Efficiency Optimization Iterative Algorithm

Analyze the optimization problem P2, define the optimal value of energy efficiency as η^*, and its feasible region is as $\mathbf{T}$, adopt Dinkelbach method [24]

$$\eta^* = \max_{\mathbf{\Phi},\mathbf{P}} \frac{R_{total}(\mathbf{\Phi},\mathbf{P})}{P_{total}(\mathbf{\Phi},\mathbf{P})} = \frac{R_{total}(\mathbf{\Phi}^*,\mathbf{P}^*)}{P_{total}(\mathbf{\Phi}^*,\mathbf{P}^*)}, \forall\{\mathbf{\Phi},\mathbf{P}\} \in \mathbf{T} \tag{22}$$

$$F(\eta) = \max_{\mathbf{\Phi},\mathbf{P}} [R_{total}(\mathbf{\Phi},\mathbf{P}) - \eta P_{total}(\mathbf{\Phi},\mathbf{P})] \tag{23}$$

The Dinkelbach fractional planning method can obtain the optimal energy efficiency value η^* through the iterative method under the premise of given power allocation $\mathbf{P}$ and subcarrier assignment $\mathbf{\Phi}$ to users. The detailed algorithm flow is shown in Table 1.

Table 1. Energy efficiency optimization iterative algorithm.

Algorithm 1 Energy efficiency optimization iterative algorithm.

1. **Initialize.**

2. Set the iteration termination times N_{outer}^{max}, iteration termination accuracy ϖ_{outer}, and the initial iteration value $\eta_0 = 0$ and $n = 0$.

3. **Loop body**

4. Update iteration index $n = n + 1$.

5. Solving the Optimization Problem $F(\eta_{n-1}) = \max_{\mathbf{\Phi},\mathbf{P}} [R_{total}(\mathbf{\Phi},\mathbf{P}) - \eta_{n-1}P_{total}(\mathbf{\Phi},\mathbf{P})]$

gain $\{\mathbf{\Phi}^*,\mathbf{P}^*\}$

6. Calculate the energy efficiency under the current iterative index using $\{\mathbf{\Phi}^*,\mathbf{P}^*\}$, $\eta_n = R_{total}(\mathbf{\Phi}^*,\mathbf{P}^*)/P_{total}(\mathbf{\Phi}^*,\mathbf{P}^*)$.

7. **End Condition:** $|\eta_n - \eta_{n-1}| < \varpi_{outer}$ or $n > N_{outer}^{max}$.

8. Output optimal solution $\{\eta^*, \mathbf{\Phi}^*, \mathbf{P}^*\}$.

---

4   Simulation and Analysis Results

In this section, we compare the performance of the proposed energy efficiency-based joint resource allocation algorithm with other resource allocation schemes. The channel gain of each subcarrier is modeled as a complex Gaussian distribution with a mean value of 0 and a variance of $c \cdot d_{i,j}^{-v}$, satisfying the $h_{i,j} \sim CN\left(0, c \cdot d_{i,j}^{-v}\right)$. The hypothetical scenario is a circular region with a relay node centered at $500\,\mathrm{m}$ radius. As shown in Fig. 1, the base station BS is distributed in the left semicircle, the source node is S distributed in the right semicircle, the K relays are randomly distributed in the circle, and the number of subcarriers of the OFDM system is $N=16$. AWGNs variance $\sigma_r^2 = \sigma_k^2 = N_0 = -131\,\mathrm{dBm}$, circuit power consumption set to $P_C = 30\,\mathrm{dBm}$.

Compare the proposed EE optimization algorithm with the literature [6,17,18] algorithm's spectral efficiency performance, as shown in Fig. 3. The purpose of the resource allocation algorithm proposed in [6,17,18] is to maximize the SE of the system, so as the P_B increases, the performance curve increases monotonously. It can be seen from the figure that the EE optimization algorithm is proposed in this paper. When $P_B \leq 18$ dBm, the spectrum efficiency continues to increase, and when $P_B > 18$ dBm the curve tends to be stable, this is because the proposed EE maximization resource optimization algorithm does not sacrifice energy consumption for spectrum Increased efficiency. In addition, at $P_B \leq 18$ dBm, the proposed algorithm has higher SE performance than the algorithms in [17,18], and [6], and can achieve performance gains of approximately 3.0 dB, 2.0 dB, and 1.6 dB, respectively.

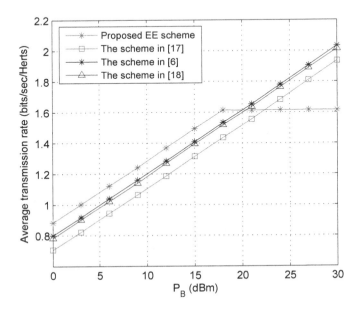

Fig. 3. Comparison of spectrum efficiency performance of different resource allocation algorithms.

Figure 4 shows the energy efficiency performance comparison between the proposed EE optimization algorithm and the literature [6,17,18] algorithm. Due to the optimization goal of literature [6] and literature [17], the spectrum efficiency is maximized, so when $P_B \leq 18$ dBm, the energy efficiency curve increases monotonously, and when $P_B > 18$ dBm decreases monotonously. However, the algorithm proposed in this chapter and the algorithm proposed in [18] both pursue the maximization of EE, and increase monotonously when $P_B \leq 18$ dBm, and remain stable until $P_B > 18$ dBm. In particular, when $P_B > 18$ dBm, the algorithm proposed in this chapter keeps the average EE unchanged and reaches the optimal value, which is about 5.6 bit/J/Hz. This is because once the maximum EE value of the system is reached, the source node and the relay node will not consume extra energy for useless data transmission. As can also be seen in Figs. 3 and 4, due to the use of joint channel-user assignment and a new relay strategy, when $P_B \leq 18$ dBm, the EE scheme proposed in this chapter can achieve better EE and SE performance, literature [18] Although the algorithm also considers joint channel user assignment, it does not consider the improvement of the relay strategy, so its EE performance is lower than the algorithm proposed in this chapter.

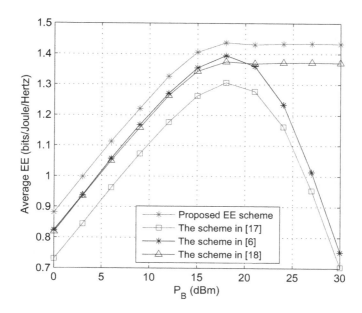

Fig. 4. Comparison of energy efficiency performance of different resource allocation algorithms.

5   Conclusions

Aiming at the RF energy harvesting relay network scenario, this paper proposes a resource allocation algorithm based on optimal energy efficiency, and constructs a system energy efficiency optimization model including energy harvesting time slot allocation, subcarrier pairing, and power allocation. Dinkelbach method, Cauchy inequality and Hungarian algorithm are used to solve the problem of time slot assignment, power allocation and subcarrier allocation based on energy efficiency. Simulation shows that the algorithm reduces the complexity of the algorithm and has good global convergence.

References

1. Lu, X., Wang, P., Niyato, D., et al.: Wireless networks with RF energy harvesting: a contemporary survey. IEEE Commun. Surv. Tutor. **17**(2), 757–789 (2014)
2. Hao, Z.: Development of Low Power RF Energy Acquisition System. Nanjing University of Posts and Telecommunications (2015)

3. Lee, S., Zhang, R., Huang, K.: Opportunistic wireless energy harvesting in cognitive radio networks. IEEE Trans. Wirel. Commun. **12**(9), 4788–4799 (2013)
4. Sakr, A.H., Hossain, E.: Cognitive and energy harvesting-based D2D communication in cellular networks: stochastic geometry modeling and analysis. IEEE Trans. Commun. **63**(5), 1867–1880 (2015)
5. Luo, Y., Pu, L., Zhao, Y., Wang, W., Yang, Q.: A nonlinear recursive model based optimal transmission scheduling in RF energy harvesting wireless communications. IEEE Trans. Wirel. Commun. (2020). https://doi.org/10.1109/TWC.2020.2973967
6. Xie, Z.-W., Zhu, Q.: Power allocation algorithm for cognitive radio energy harvesting networks based on energy cooperation. J. Commun. **38**(9), 176–184 (2017)
7. Long, Y., Zhang, X., Fang, X., He, R.: Resource allocation in cognitive radio network with energy harvesting. J. Commun. **39**(9), 67–75 (2018)
8. Tutuncuoglu, K., Varan, B., Yener, A.: Throughput maximization for two-way relay channels with energy harvesting nodes: the impact of relaying strategies[J]. IEEE Trans. Commu. **63**(6), 2081–2093 (2015)
9. Chen, Z., Dong, Y., Fan, P., et al.: Optimal throughput for two-way relaying: energy harvesting and energy co-operation. IEEE J. Sel. Areas Commun. **34**(5), 1448–1462 (2016)
10. Gu, Y., Aissa, S.: RF-based energy harvesting in decode-and-forward relaying systems: ergodic and outage capacities. IEEE Trans. Wirel. Commun. **14**(11), 6425–6434 (2015)
11. Qian, L.P., Feng, G., Leung, V.C.M.: Optimal transmission policies for relay communication networks with ambient energy harvesting relays. IEEE J. Sel. Areas Commun. **34**(12), 3754–3768 (2016)
12. Ju, M.C., Yang, H.C.: Optimum design of energy harvesting relay for two-way decode-and-forward relay networks under max? Min and max-sum criterions. IEEE Trans. Commun. **67**(10), 6682–6697 (2019)
13. Yi, L., Ronghua, S., Jian, D., et al.: Outage performance analysis of two-way underlay cognitive relay network with energy harvesting. J. Nanjing Univ. Sci. Technol. **43**(03), 292–299 (2019)
14. Xu, J., Zeng, F., Li, K., Li, Y.: Performance analysis of two-way relay cooperation underlay cognitive radio networks based on WIPT. J. Commun. **40**(2), 129–136 (2019)
15. Chen, Y., Shi, R., Feng, W., et al.: AF relaying with energy harvesting source and relay. IEEE Trans. Veh. Technol. **66**(1), 874–879 (2016)
16. Boyd, S., Mattingley, J.: Branch and bound methods. Stanford University, Stanford (2003)
17. Chen, Y., Fang, X.M., Zhao, Y.: Energy-efficient adaptive power allocation in orthogonal frequency division multiplexing-based amplify-and-forward relay link. IET Commun. **7**(15), 1676–1687 (2013)
18. Wang, Y., Zhang, J., Zhang, P.: Low-complexity energy-efficient power and subcarrier allocation in cooperative networks. IEEE Commun. Lett. **17**(10), 1944–1977 (2013)

Communication Quality

Analysis of QoS Schemes and Shaping Strategies for Large Scale IP Networks Based on Network Calculus

Lihao Chen$^{(\boxtimes)}$, Jiayi Zhang, Tao Gao, and Tongtong Wang

Huawei Technologies Co., Ltd., Beijing, China
`lihao.chen@huawei.com`

Abstract. IP network experts and engineers have been working on solutions for decades to promote the network QoS. Latency guarantee, as one of the key aspects of the QoS, is attracting increasing attentions with requirements from time-critical applications and the vision of building a fully connected, intelligent world. Meanwhile, Network Calculus is a theory that focuses on performance bound analysis for communication networks, and has been used in avionic networks. However, because of the extremely large scale and high complexity of IP networks, few works gave theoretically modeling and systematically analyzing for the QoS (i.e., latency bound) of IP networks. In this paper, three QoS schemes for IP networks are summarized and the performance on the perspective of efficiency is analyzed. The effect of ingress shaping is also investigated, and results show that a proper ingress shaping could benefit the overall network latency performance, and could be adapted to all three QoS schemes. An IP network use case is given with different QoS schemes applied and the performance is evaluated by using Network Calculus.

Keywords: Quality of Service (QoS) · IP network · Latency bound · Shaping · Network Calculus (NC)

1 Introduction

Quality of Service (QoS) requirements have always existed in the history of network development. One of the earliest solutions is Asynchronous Transfer Mode (ATM), then IntServ (Integrated Services) [1]. However, DiffServ (Differentiated Services) dominates IP networks of today, which specifies a simple and scalable differentiation for managing traffic on an essentially best-effort (BE) network. Although priorities are defined, DiffServ provides no quantifiable QoS guarantee (e.g., the latency bound) even for the highest priority traffic, unless specific traffic constraints are applied [2]. 5G, Time-sensitive Networking (TSN) and other emerging technologies are bringing new QoS ideas, such as the Credit-based Shaping (CBS) and Time-aware Shaping (TAS) in TSN [3], and the network slicing for carrier networks in 5G, aiming to provide bounded latency for time-critical services.

© ICST Institute for Computer Sciences, Social Informatics and Telecommunications Engineering 2021
Published by Springer Nature Switzerland AG 2021. All Rights Reserved
H. Gao et al. (Eds.): BROADNETS 2020, LNICST 355, pp. 69–89, 2021.
https://doi.org/10.1007/978-3-030-68737-3_5

In statistical multiplexing networks, like IP networks, latency upper-bound guarantee is required by a part of traffics. For this purpose, 3 major types of QoS schemes are designed, which we name them *None-time-based QoS, Time-based QoS, and Logical Separated Network (LSN)*. These QoS schemes are evaluated mainly on the perspective of efficiency, and a more efficient QoS scheme can provide a latency upper-bound guarantee for more flows under a given bandwidth allocation.

Regardless of QoS schemes, when applied in a specific use case, it is necessary to determine the latency upper-bound for certain flows. Network Calculus is a theory that focuses on analysing the network performance bounds, and has successfully been used in avionic networks. In this paper, the latency upper-bound of the 3 schemes as well as the impact of shaping are analyzed mainly based on Deterministic Network Calculus (DNC), based on which shaping schemes are investigated.

Real IP network use cases are also important. In this work, we study traffics that are abstracted from three typical applications: The smart grid differential protection, VR interactive applications, and VR video applications. Different latency bounds are required for these different traffics, and numerical analysis and comparisons are made.

Literature that apply network calculus in real networks can be seen for decades. Early works in [4] showed network calculus' usage in ATM, IntServ, DiffServ and many other scenarios. [5] investigated providing QoS in an ideal model using per-flow queues and Weighted Fair Queuing (WFQ) schedulers, and analyzed the result with three flows. Considering transport layer, [6] analyzed the TCP performance in the sense of NC. Recently, as TSN and DetNet came into sight, [7,8] integrated NC to analysis delay and backlog upper bounds. However, few works could be found that linked the academic NC theory to engineering solutions on the QoS guarantee in IP service provider networks.

The main contribution of this paper is to provide handful results and comparisons on latency upper-bound with a huge amount of traffic flows in IP networks. We quantitatively demonstrate that the None-time-based QoS scheme outperforms the other two schemes on the perspective of efficiency, no matter with or without the ingress shaping.

The paper is organized as the following. Section 2 introduces 3 major types of QoS schemes. Section 3 summarizes methods to get performance bounds, i.e., simulations, and theoretical analysis methods like the Network Calculus. Section 4 discusses quantitative analysis of the performance of QoS schemes, as well as the influence of shaping. Section 5 gives a use case and its analysis results. Section 6 presents conclusions and future works.

2   Three Major Paths Towards a Better Quality of Service

The QoS discussed in this paper, if not specifically stated, refers to the QoS of the latency upper-bound of traffics. To determine this bound, the most important thing is to characterize the queuing delay, which may vary significantly with different traffic and scheduler. Except for the queuing delay, other delays (e.g., the process delay of routers, the transmission delay of links) are relatively fixed or with achievable bound, which are not take into consideration in this paper.

Considering the implementation of hardware, in this paper, the queuing and forwarding behavior is discussed at the level of a single data message, i.e., a packet. Various channel multiplexing techniques are out of the scope.

2.1 None-Time-Based QoS

IntServ (Integrated Services), proposed by IETF [1], and the Credit-based Shaping (CBS) and Asynchronous Traffic Shaping (ATS), proposed by IEEE 802.1 [3], are classified into the None-time-based QoS scheme. They have similar ways of working:

– Resource reservations are needed so that competitions for forwarding services are limited,
– Packets can be classified by networking devices (routers, switches, etc.) so as to give corresponding services.

By modeling the reserved flow and the service considering the worst-case competition, latency upper-bounds of queuing and forwarding for these packets can be calculated.

The CBS combined with the Stream Reservation Protocol (SRP) has been used in Audio-Video Bridging (AVB) networks [9]. The Avionics Full-Duplex Switched Ethernet (AFDX) is also a None-time-based QoS technique which has been used in A380, B787, and A350 aircrafts [10].

Routers in current IP network are mainly using priority and round-robin based methods as queuing and forwarding mechanisms. Without resource reservations (i.e., the behaviour of users are unknown and unlimited), what a router can do is to try its best to forward packets priority by priority, or queue by queue. However, with proper planning and configuration on schedulers, latency guarantees can be achieved for certain users or flows with current devices.

2.2 Time-Based QoS

The Time-aware Shaping (TAS), proposed by IEEE 802.1 [3], controls the packet forwarding by enabling the configuration of queue gates, and the state of gates (i.e., open or close) switches based on the time. These gates are called time-based gates, which are the main characteristic to identify a group of Time-based QoS schemes. An ideal deployment of the Time-based QoS scheme is to perfectly design the gate open time for any "express" traffics along their paths. However this is extremely difficult for large scale IP networks due to many implementation considerations, such as the difficulty of gate schedule designs and time synchronizations, the wasted bandwidth (to protect the gate changing actions), and the lack of hardware supports. IEEE 802.1 gives the Cyclic Queuing and Forwarding (CQF) [3] as an alternate approach, without relying on perfectly synchronization, and more CQF-like approaches are summarized here [11].

The Time-based QoS is often used together with the Non-time-based QoS. In TTEthernet, Time-Triggered traffics are protected by time-based gates, while Rate-Constrained traffics and Best Effort traffics use the remaining time slots [12]. In Profinet IRT, Isochronous Real-Time traffics are protected by time-based gates, while Real-Time traffics and TCP/IP traffics use the remaining time slots [13].

2.3 Logical Separated Network (LSN)

The basic idea of LSN, sometimes called the network slicing, is to divide a physical network into multiple logical sub-networks. More specifically, one physical link can be divided into multiple non-interfering logical sub-links. As traffics transmitted on different sub-networks do not interfere with each other, the QoS can be guaranteed more easily.

There are more than one techniques to realized the LSN, such as the channelized sub-interfaces, the Flexible Ethernet (FlexE) [14]. This article does not discuss the difference of these techniques, but assuming the ideal logical isolation can be achieved.

2.4 How to Compare the QoS Schemes

Table 1. Feasibilities of using the 3 QoS schemes in IP network

QoS scheme	Feasibility	Description
None-time-based QoS	Moderate	Need to configure the existing routers and switches based on network planning (resource reservation)
Time-based QoS	Hard	Need special-made hardware. Need accurate planning of the whole network
Logical Separated Network	Moderate	Need new hardware or need to buy extra bandwidth (more costs)

Feasibilities of the 3 QoS schemes are evaluated in Table 1, however, this paper will focus more on efficiency comparisons.

One of the most famous features for IP networks is statistical multiplexing, i.e., if a transmission port or a link has a bandwidth of 10 Gbps, it serves every packets in a work-conserving method and the sum of the service rate is 10 Gbps. The statistical multiplexing feature provides an excellent efficiency of bandwidth usage. As a result, no matter which QoS scheme is used to provide the latency upper-bound guarantee, the *efficiency* of the QoS scheme must be carefully evaluated.

– **Efficiency** refers to provide lower latency upper-bound guarantees for a same set of traffics under a given bandwidth allocation. Equivalently, a more efficient QoS scheme can convey more time-critical traffics under a given bandwidth allocation, thus achieving higher bandwidth utilization.

Intuitively, the None-time-based QoS scheme has better efficiency, benefit from the nature of statistical multiplexing. Meanwhile, the Time-based QoS scheme's statistical multiplexing characteristic is deteriorated because some specific time slots will belong to some specific flows. And for the LSN scheme, the total bandwidth is separated into several LSNs and one LSN can not multiplexing another LSN's bandwidth, which also weaken the efficiency.

A quantitative analysis is given in Sect. 4 to prove that None-time-based QoS scheme has better efficiency than the other two, without or with shaping.

3   Analytical Tools

In real network use cases, no matter which QoS scheme is used to build up a solution for QoS guarantee, it is necessary to quantitatively analyze whether the provided QoS fulfills the need of delay requirement, especially for time-critical traffics.

3.1   Simulation

Simulation is a commonly used method for network performance verification, by using simulation software, emulations, testbeds or the Telemetry. The idea of simulation is to gradually determine the approximate range of QoS performance through repeated iterations.

The shortcoming of simulation is that, within finite number of repetitions, it is not always possible to reach the actual worst-case result. In other words, the theoretical latency upper-bound can hardly be attained by simulation, which makes simulation insufficient for applications that requires high reliability and performance guarantee. In addition, the larger the use case is, the more time and computational resources the simulation will consume, which restricts the applicability of simulation in online adjustments of network resource allocation.

3.2   Theoretical Analysis

Theoretical analysis is another commonly used method. The idea is to abstract the traffic and the network into mathematical models, and to derive the theoretical performance in a quick and elegant manner. Theoretical analysis is notable in predicting rarely happened cases, which is especially suitable for latency upper-bound analysis.

Network Calculus (NC) is one of the theoretical analysis methods for performance bounds in communication networks. By modeling the maximum arrival traffic and the least provided service during any duration, NC can be used to calculate latency upper-bounds for the None-time-based QoS scheme, as well as QoS solutions that use the Time-based QoS scheme combined with the None-time-based QoS scheme. NC also applies for the LSN scheme, as the None-time-based scheme can be used within a sub-network.

In this work, we take the continuous-time model for traffics and services of networks. Consider a two-port network element with accumulative input traffic $R(t)$ and output traffic $R^*(t)$. To character the input, *arrival curve* $\alpha(t)$ is defined as the upper-bound of accumulative arrival traffic during any time intervals, $\alpha(t) \geq R(s+t) - R(s), \forall s, t \geq 0$, and $\alpha(t) = 0, t \leq 0$. The network element provides storing and forwarding services to the traffic, which is modeled as *service curve* $\beta(t)$, so that the lower-bound of accumulative output traffic R^* satisfies $(R \otimes \beta)(t) \leq R^*(t), \forall t \geq 0$, where $\otimes$ is the convolution defined in min-plus algebra[1]. Then, the latency upper-bound at this network element is given by

$$D = \sup_{s}\{\inf_{t}\{t \geq 0 \mid \alpha(s) \leq \beta(s+t)\}\} \tag{1}$$

The latency upper-bound D is the maximum horizontal deviation between the arrival curve and the service curve, as an example shown in Fig. 1.

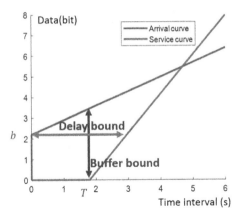

Fig. 1. Computing the bounds from arrival curve and service curve

Consider a traffic flow traverses multiple network nodes, each providing a service curve $\beta_i(t), i = 1, \cdots, N$. In order to calculate the end-to-end latency upper-bound, one simple way is to separately calculate per-hop latency upper-bounds and add them up. Another way is to model these nodes as a concatenated service curve $\beta_c(t) = (\beta_1 \otimes \cdots \otimes \beta_N)(t)$. Advanced methods could also be used in calculating delay bounds [22–25].

Shaping is generally used in networks, in order to control the traffic to satisfy certain regulations so as to avoid overflow congestion. In NC, a shaper is characterized with the shaping curve $\sigma(t)$, which regulates the upper-bound of

---

[1] Operator $\otimes$ is defined as $(f \otimes g)(t) = \inf_s\{f(s) + g(t-s)\}$.

output traffics of the shaper. When a shaper $\sigma(t)$ is implemented at the edge of the network, the core network would have shaped traffics with arrival curves as $\sigma(t)$. Although shapers seem to introduce additional delay to flows, it is proven in [4] that greedy shapers do not increase end-to-end latency upper-bounds, if $\sigma \geq \alpha^2$.

With the mathematical modeling of traffics, and schedulers and shapers, quantitative analysis of network's queuing latency upper-bounds can be obtained by NC.

4   Analysis of QoS Performance and Shaping Strategies

4.1   The Basic Modeling of QoS

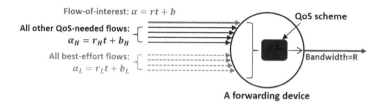

Fig. 2. One-hop model

The one-hop model used in this section to analyze QoS schemes is shown as Fig. 2. Flows entering the node can be firstly classified into

1. QoS-needed Flows that require latency guarantee, and
2. Best-effort Flows that do not need latency guarantee.

Consider flows satisfying token bucket arrival curves, the initial behaviour of flows are described by the form of arrival curves as below

$$\alpha(t) = rt + b \tag{2}$$
$$\alpha_H(t) = r_H t + b_H \tag{3}$$
$$\alpha_L(t) = r_L t + b_L \tag{4}$$

where α is the arrival curve of the flow that needs latency guarantee and will be observed and analyzed (namely, *Flow-of-Interest, FoI*), α_H is the aggregated

---

[2] This property gives more freedom in the design of reshaping in networks, since the output of a service node does not conform to the traffic regulation at source α, that the output arrival curve is updated to $\alpha^* = \alpha \oslash \beta$, which is larger than α. While one can reshape the flow's arrival curve back to α without deteriorate the delay upper-bound, one should note that a shaper violating $\sigma \geq \alpha$ may cause additional worst-case latency.

arrival curve of QoS-needed flows, r_H is the sum of the (average) rate of all QoS-needed flows and b_H is the sum of the burst, α_L is the aggregated arrival curve of other best-effort flows.

The capability of the network forwarding device is described by the form of service curve as below

$$\beta(t) = \max(0, R(t - T)) \tag{5}$$

where R is the bandwidth or sending rate of the output port, and T is maximum waiting time determined by the queuing and forwarding mechanism specified by the applied QoS scheme.

In IP networks, the total amount of QoS-needed flows is huge, therefore, for a Flow-of-Interest, it always holds:

$$r \ll r_H, b \ll b_H, L_L \ll b_H \tag{6}$$

where L_L is the length of the longest packet of any best-effort flows.

4.2   Latency Upper-Bound Analysis for QoS Schemes

The queuing latency upper-bound on one hop is calculated by using NC, and comparisons are provided among several QoS schemes. For fairness, the same model and assumptions in Sect. 4.1 are used among the comparisons.

A - FIFO. As the baseline for comparisons, all flows go into a single FIFO queue. The worst-case delay (i.e., latency upper-bound) is calculated as

$$D_{FIFO} = \frac{b + b_H + b_L}{R} \approx \frac{b_H + b_L}{R} \tag{7}$$

A easy way to explain the derivation process of (7) is to look at Fig. 1. The burst b in Fig. 1 is $b + b_H + b_L$ in (7), as all flows are going into the same FIFO queue so that the aggregated arrival curve can be used as the maximum burst of the queue. The T in Fig. 1 is zero because there is no other competing queues. The slope of the service curve in Fig. 1 is the port's bandwidth, which is R in (7).

What can be observed is, the worst-case delay of the Flow-of-Interest is approximately proportional to the total burst of all other flows, and is independent of the total rate of all other flows, as long as the total rate does not excess the bandwidth that the port provides.

B1 - None-Time-Based QoS - SP. Strict priority (SP) is use to obtain the QoS guarantee. The Flow-of-Interest and all other QoS-needed flows go into a high priority FIFO queue, and all best-effort flows go into low priority FIFO queues. The latency upper-bound is given as

$$D_{SP} = \frac{b + b_H + L_L}{R} \approx \frac{b_H}{R} \tag{8}$$

The $\frac{L_L}{R}$ in (8) is the T in Fig. 1, as the influence from all best-effort flows is no more than a packet length, indicating that the influence from the total burst of all best-effort flows is isolated by strict priority queues. The worst-case delay of the Flow-of-Interest is now approximately proportional to the total burst of all other QoS-needed flows.

B2 - None-Time-Based QoS - SP+DRR. In this scheme, two strict priorities are defined, each of which is shared by Deficit Round-Robin (DRR). The Flow-of-Interest, along with some part of QoS-needed flows go into a high priority DRR queue i, the other QoS-needed flows go into other high priority DRR queues, and all best-effort flows go into low priority queues. The delay upper-bound is given as

$$D_{SP+DRR} = \frac{b_i}{R\frac{Q_i}{\Sigma_j Q_j}} + T_{DRR} \approx \frac{b_i}{R\frac{Q_i}{\Sigma_j Q_j}} \tag{9}$$

where b_i is the total burst of flows (including the Flow-of-Interest and some part of QoS-needed flows) in the high priority DRR queue i, Q_i is the quanta of this DRR queue i, $\Sigma_j Q_j$ is the sum of quanta of all high priority DRR queues, and T_{DRR} is the T in (5). T_{DRR} is caused by the combination of the SP and DRR scheduler [16] and can be derived from [15]

$$T_{DRR} = \frac{L_L + \sum_{j \neq i} L_j}{R} + \frac{\sum_{j \neq i} Q_j(Q_i + L_i)}{Q_i R} \tag{10}$$

where j belongs to any high priority DRR queues, L_j is the maximum packet length in that queue. Generally, the number of high priority DRR queues used in one output port is a single digit (typically 8) and the quantum Q is set to be as the same order of magnitude as the maximum packet length L, and $b_i \gg L$ (same reason as for (6)). Therefore, T_{DRR} is much less than the first item in (9).

What can be observed is, as all QoS-needed flows are separated into a number of high priority DRR queues, the total burst reduces from b to b_i, and the ability to "digest" the burst also reduces from R to $R\frac{Q_i}{\Sigma_j Q_j}$. So whether the Flow-of-Interest can get a better or worse worst-case delay, comparing SP+DRR with SP, will depend on the design of DRR queues (i.e., b_i and quanta Q_i configurations). So SP+DRR is generally more flexible, but with the cost of T_{DRR}.

C - Logical Separated Network (LSN). The Flow-of-Interest and all other QoS-needed flows go into an exclusive sub-network where there is one FIFO queue. The delay upper-bound is

$$D_{LSN} = \frac{b + b_H}{R_H} \approx \frac{b_H}{R_H} \tag{11}$$

where R_H is the bandwidth of this sub-network/network-slice. Now the worst-case delay of the Flow-of-Interest is proportional to the total burst of all other

QoS-needed flows that share the same sub-network, and influence of all best-effort flows are isolated, with the cost that $R_H < R$. However this cost will not be a problem if money is not a problem for the buyer of the sub-network.

D1 - Time-Based QoS - CQF. Suppose a three buffer switching CQF mechanism [11] is used, the Flow-of-Interest and all other QoS-needed flows go into one dedicated buffer, and all other best-effort flows go into the other two buffers

$$D_{CQF} = (2+2)T_c > \frac{4(b+b_H)}{R} \approx \frac{4b_H}{R} \quad (12)$$

where T_c is the buffer switching time, i.e., each one of the three output buffers has a time of T_c to forward its packets. According to [11], the maximum per-hop queuing delay is $2T_c$, if a packet can enter any of the three buffers. However, as the packets of QoS-needed flows go to one dedicated buffer, they could have to wait another $2T_c$ in maximum. And the length of T_c must be able to "digest" the total burst of QoS-needed flows, and some extra costs (e.g., the guard band before the buffer switching time) are needed to make sure the CQF function works correctly, thus

$$T_c > \frac{b+b_H}{R} \quad (13)$$

Ideally, the extra costs are not so much, the worst-case delay of the Flow-of-Interest can be approximately proportional to the total burst of all other QoS-needed flows.

D2 - Time-Based QoS - CQF+SP. In every nodes, high and low priorities are defined, sharing a three buffer switching CQF mechanism. The Flow-of-Interest and all other QoS-needed flows go into any buffers with the high priority, and all other best-effort flows go into any buffers with the low priority. In this scheme, latency upper-bound is

$$D_{CQF+SP} = 2T_c = \frac{2(b+b_H+L_L)}{R} \approx \frac{2b_H}{R} \quad (14)$$

This time, the packets of the Flow-of-Interest as well as all other QoS-needed flows can enter any of the three buffers with high priority. The cost is each buffer has to have at least 2 priority queues. And (13) becomes $T_c > \frac{b+b_H+L_L}{R} \approx \frac{b_H}{R}$. The worst-case delay of the Flow-of-Interest is approximately proportional to the total burst of all other QoS-needed flows.

4.3   Efficiency Comparison Between QoS Schemes

Assuming that, the bandwidth $R = 1\,\text{Gbps}$, and for the Flow-of-Interest, $b = 10\,\text{Kbit}, r = 1\,\text{Mbps}$, for all other QoS-needed flows, $b_H = 990\,\text{Kbit}, r_H = 99\,\text{Mbps}$, and for all best-effort flows, $b_L = 5000\,\text{Kbit}, L_L = 12\,\text{Kbit}$. When using SP conbined with DRR (B2), all the QoS-needed flows including the Flow-of-Interest is divided evenly by the amount of bursts into 4 parts, each part enters a high priority DRR queue, and 4 high priority DRR queues have the same quanta. When using LSN scheme (C), all the QoS-needed flows use a third of the total bandwidth, or use a half of the total bandwidth as LSN+, shown in Fig. 3. When using the CQF scheme (D1), all the QoS-needed flows use only one of the three buffers.

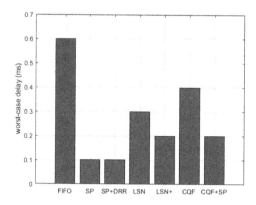

Fig. 3. Worst-case delay for FoI under different QoS schemes

Under these assumptions, results of worst-case latency of Flow-of-Interest under all QoS schemes are shown in Fig. 3. Apparently, comparing with the simplest FIFO queue, all QoS schemes significantly lower the worst-case delay. This result also indicates that the None-time-based QoS scheme (i.e., SP or SP+DRR) is better than the other two from the perspective of efficiency, as all QoS schemes in the example are using the same total bandwidth for all flows. In other words, if the goal is to provide a specific worst-case delay, the None-time-based QoS scheme can bear more QoS-needed flows than the other two schemes using the same total bandwidth, or, if the goal is to provide a specific worst-case delay to some specific flows, the None-time-based QoS scheme can achieve this goal by using less bandwidth than the other two.

Please note that the worst-case delay calculated above is the delay for one hop. However for end-to-end delay upper-bounds, the above comparison results can remain unchanged. For the CQF scheme (D1, D2), it can be calculated by summing up per-hop worst-case delays, according to the per-hop buffer switching time of CQF. And for all other schemes (A, B1, B2, C), the end-to-end worst-case delay can also be calculated by summing up per-hop worst-case delays, which should consider the burst increment hop-by-hop.

Literature show that more algorithms in NC can be used for end-to-end worst-case latency calculation for None-time-based QoS schemes, such as SFA, PMOO, ULP [22–24]. These algorithms can provide much tighter delay bounds than just summing up per-hop delay bounds, which implicates the efficiencies of the None-time-based QoS scheme and the LSN scheme are even better comparing to the result of Fig. 3. However, the exact effects on calculating end-to-end delay bounds of these algorithms also vary significantly depending on the network topology and traffics. So, we do not take these algorithms into consideration when comparing.

4.4 Trade-Offs Besides Efficiency

Although the None-time-based QoS scheme has a better efficiency, the author wants to emphasize that no one QoS scheme is absolutely superior to others. For example, a Time-based QoS method can provide a very low jitter, and for applications like industrial automation where messages are sent at each control loop cycle, a specifically designed Time-based QoS method can suit well. For critical applications and cost insensitive users, LSN can be a straight-forward and easy-proved method to provide bounded latency. All in all, the performance of these QoS schemes can vary for different use cases, and the design of QoS solution should consider the feature of the use case and try to use a QoS scheme or a combination of QoS schemes that fit the use case well.

4.5 Shaping for the Overall Network QoS Enhancement

The word "shaping" discussed in this paper, if not specifically stated, refers to the ingress shaping (or the source shaping). Shaping can be applied to all three QoS schemes, and the fundamental idea of shaping is to limit the burst of a flow before the flow enters the network or at the first forwarding node of the network. Shaping can cause additional delay. Whether the benefit is worth the additional 1shaping delay and how to set the shaping strategy will be discussed in this section.

The end-to-end model is shown as Fig. 4. Later, ingress shaping is introduced and its influence on end-to-end worst-case delay will be analyzed based on this model.

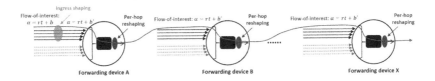

Fig. 4. End-to-end model

Shaping for None-Time-Based QoS. The initial behaviour of the Flow-of-Interest is described by the form of arrival curve as $\alpha(t) = b + rt$. If this burst b is shaped into $\frac{b}{N}$ at the ingress of the network, $N > 1$, then the maximum shaping delay imposed on this flow can be described as

$$D_{shaping} = \frac{b - \frac{b}{N}}{r} \tag{15}$$

The reason is shown in Fig. 5. Shaping will not change r, the long term average rate of a flow. Only the burst b is reduced. And N is named as the *shaping multiple* (SM).

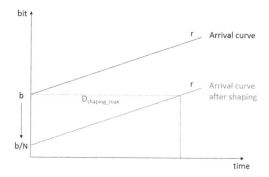

Fig. 5. The effect of ingress shaping on the arrival curve

Consider the scenario B1 in chapter IV - A. If the bursts of the Flow-of-Interest and all other QoS-needed flows are reduced by N times (name this kind of shaping mechanism as FIS - Fair Ingress Shaping), according to (8) and (15), the worst-case delay for the Flow-of-Interest becomes

$$D_{SP+shaping} = \frac{\frac{b+b_H}{N} + L_L}{R} + \frac{b - \frac{b}{N}}{r} \approx \frac{b_H}{NR} + \frac{b}{r} \qquad (16)$$

Because of (6), $\approx$ in (16) stands when $N \gg 1$ and $\frac{b_H}{N} \gg L_L$. Note that R refers to the bandwidth of the output port and r refers to the rate of Flow-of-Interest. Define the burst share as $\frac{b}{b_H+b}$ and the bandwidth share as $\frac{r}{R}$. What can be derived from (8) and (16) is,

Theorem 1. *Using FIS (Fair Ingress Shaping) mechanism, the WCD-IM (worst-case delay improvement multiple) of a flow will not exceed the shaping multiple N.*

Theorem 2. *Using FIS mechanism, the WCD-IM of a flow will approach N if the burst share of the flow gets lower while the bandwidth share is fixed.*

The WCD-IM can be calculated as

$$\frac{D_{SP}}{D_{SP+shaping}} = \frac{N \times (b + b_H)}{b + b_H + (N-1)b \times \frac{R}{r}} = \frac{Np}{p + (N-1)q} \qquad (17)$$

where $p = \frac{b_H+b}{b}$ is the inverse of burst share of Flow-of-Interest and $q = \frac{R}{r}$ is the inverse of bandwidth share. Apparently, WCD-IM calculated by (17) is less than N, which proves Theorem 1.

If the bandwidth share is fixed, and the burst share is getting lower until $p \gg q$, then

$$WCD - IM = \frac{Np}{p + (N-1)q} \approx \frac{Np}{p} \to N^-$$ (18)

which proves Theorem 2. The larger the value of WCD-IM is, the better benefit that the Flow-of-Interest can get through FIS.

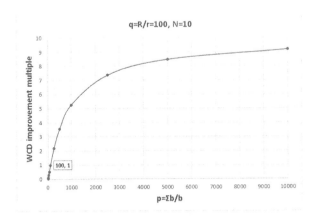

Fig. 6. A trend of WCD-IM

As shown in Fig. 6, the bandwidth share and the shaping multiple (SM) are fixed, and with the increase of p (i.e., decrease of burst share), the WCD-IM increases towards the SM $N = 10$. The point $(100, 1)$ is called the "Equivalence Point", meaning that FIS has no effect on one hop worst-case delay for a flow that has an identical burst share and bandwidth share. This kind of flow is called a neutral flow. If the WCD-IM for a flow is less than 1, that means the benefit which FIS brings to that flow will not be able to compensate the extra shaping delay, at least within one hop. This is because the flow has a large burst, and we call it a bursty flow. On the other hand, a smooth flow (above Equivalence Point $(100, 1)$) can enjoy the benefit from FIS.

All discussed above are about making comparisons between the cost of shaping and the benefit of shaping on one hop. What makes ingress shaping much more attractive is, the cost has to be paid only once, i.e., at the ingress point that shaping is executed, however, the benefit can be accumulated and magnified hop by hop. So the end-to-end worst-case delay (with per-hop reshaping that does not increase end-to-end latency upper-bounds) is

$$
\begin{aligned}
D_{e2e+SP+shaping} &= N_{hop} \times D_{SP} + D_{shaping} \\
&= \frac{N_{hop} \times (b + b_H)}{NR} + \frac{(N-1)b}{Nr}
\end{aligned}
$$ (19)

Theorem 3. *Using FIS mechanism together with per-hop reshaping, while the burst share and the bandwidth share of the flow and the shaping multiple are fixed, the more the number of hop on the flow's path is, the larger the end-to-end WCD-IM for that flow will be. The end-to-end WCD-IM will not exceed the shaping multiple N.*

Compare (8), (16) and (19), it is easy to prove Theorem 3. And a more intuitive comparison is shown in Fig. 7. The Equivalence Point $(100, 1)$ on 1 hop moves to $(10, 1)$ on 10 hops, meaning that a lot more bursty flows will get the benefit from shaping, unless its burst share is more than 10 times its bandwidth share.

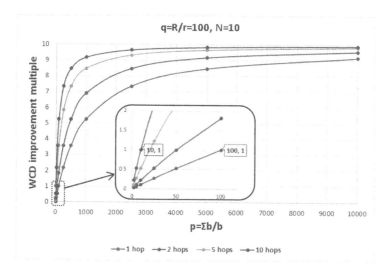

Fig. 7. A trend of end-to-end WCD-IM for different hops

If the None-time-based QoS scheme with shaping is used to design a network QoS solution, the solution does not have to use FIS. A general feasible method is shape as much as possible for all flows until there is no latency margin to bear the extra shaping delay for those bursty flows.

Shaping for Time-Based QoS. In IP networks, the total number of flows is almost countless and the fact that most flows entering the network is independent of time. Therefore, it is almost impossible to design a time-based scheduling for every QoS-needed flows. CQF or a CQF-like scheme would be a possible approach, and the buffer switching time T_c has to be wisely chosen with the constrain of (13), as all the bursts of all QoS-needed flows can arrive at the same time and need to enter the same buffer within T_c.

Consider the scenario D2 in chapter IV - A. Shaping can be implemented at the ingress, with the SM of N. Therefore, the total burst of Qos-needed flows reduces to $\frac{b+b_H}{N}$, and the constrain of T_c becomes $T_c > \frac{b+b_H}{NR}$.

With shaping, T_c can be reduced significantly. The cost is the extra delay induced by shaping. According to (14), the end-to-end worst-case delay can be calculated as

$$
\begin{aligned}
D_{e2e+CQF+SP+shaping} &= N_{hop} \times D_{CQF+SP} + D_{shaping} \\
&= N_{hop} \times 2T_c + D_{shaping} \\
&\approx \frac{2N_{hop}(b+b_H)}{NR} + \frac{(N-1)b}{Nr}
\end{aligned}
\tag{20}
$$

This result is computed as $T = \frac{b+b_H}{NR}$. Actually, T must be larger because of overheads, i.e., costs to implement the CQF scheme [11]. And the higher the SM N is, the shorter T will be, and the impact of overheads will become more significant.

Shaping for Logical Separated Network. If there are multiple flows using one LSN, None-time-based QoS, Time-based QoS or their combinations are all applicable within that LSN. Then the analysis of the effect of shaping will be the same as in the previous two sections.

Supposing M to be the share of bandwidth for the LSN serving all QoS-needed flows. E.g., $M = 1/3$ means the QoS-needed flows use a third of the total bandwidth as a LSN, in other words, $R_H = MR$. And there is a FIFO queue in this LSN. Then,

$$
\begin{aligned}
D_{e2e+LSN+shaping} &= N_{hop} \times D_{LSN} + D_{shaping} \\
&= \frac{N_{hop} \times (b+b_H)}{NMR} + \frac{(N-1)b}{Nr}
\end{aligned}
\tag{21}
$$

Comparison of Three QoS Schemes with Shaping. Comparing (19), (20) and (21), one can easily tell that shaping with None-time-based QoS scheme provides the lowest latency bound (noticing that $0 < M < 1$ in (21)). This again indicates that the None-time-based QoS scheme is better than the other two from the perspective of efficiency when all three schemes use the same shaping strategy.

5 Use Case and Analysis

An IP network use case is provided, and end-to-end latency upper-bounds (worst-case delays) are analyzed with different QoS schemes.

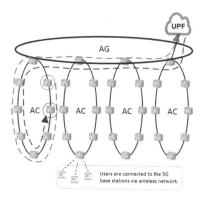

Fig. 8. The use case network topology

5.1   An IP Network Use Case

A typical IP carrier topology is shown in Fig. 8. Each Access (AC) ring connects eight 5G base stations, and Access rings are connected to the Aggregation (AG) ring. The bandwidths of AC rings are 10 Gbps and AG ring is 20 Gbps.

All QoS-needed flows in this use case are shown in Table 2. The type "Electric" refers to traffics used for current differential protections. The Virtual Reality (VR) traffics have two types, VR-interact traffics and VR-video traffics, however their upstream traffics have the same behaviour. The latency requirements are the 2-way end-to-end latency, including only the IP wired part, i.e., from the base station to the UPF (User Plane Function [17]) and then all the way back to the base station. More specifically, for current differential protections, the destination base station of a flow is next to its source base station, as shown in Fig. 8. For VR flows, the sources and the destinations are the same.

Table 2. Traffic description

Traffic type	Description	Latency requirement
Electric	A burst with 14 packets in every 15 ms, each packet is 380 Bytes	2 ms
VR upstream	1.6 Kbit burst and 50 Mbps rate per-user flow	/[a]
VR-interact downstream	750 Kbit burst and 50 Mbps rate per-user flow	8 ms [18]
VR-video downstream	1500 Kbit burst and 50 Mbps rate per-user flow	can > 8 ms [18]

[a] A VR upstream traffic corresponds to either a VR-interact downstream or a VR-video downstream traffic

For each base station, suppose there is one "Electric" user, three "VR-interact" users, and three "VR-video" users.

5.2 Results and Analysis

Six specific QoS-schemes are designed, and worst-case delays for electric and VR traffics are calculated. Three methods are used to calculate, one is Pay Multiplexing Only Once (PMOO) [19], one is the software RTaW-Pegase [20], and the other is the CQF worst-case latency analysis proposed by (14). PMOO is a promising candidate to reduce NC's pessimism of worst case delay calculation by considering multiplexing only once of cross traffics compared to SFA (while in some specific cases PMOO performs worse than SFA [26]). In this use case, VR (-interact and -video) downstream flows share a long common path with electric flows, where PMOO is appropriate to be adopted.

For simplicity, we just analyze downstream flows in which case the bursts of VR traffics have a significant effect on the worst case delay of electric traffics. As shown in Fig. 9, the electric and VR traffics share a complete common path from UPF to access ring. Consequently, a single node with service curve β^* can be obtained by convoluting service curves of each node in the aggregated ring with (22), where R_1 and T_1 are the rate and latency of each node. Next, for each node in the access ring, the cross-traffic is subtracted to calculate the left-over service curve, where as long common path as possible is considered to decrease the effect of multiplexing. Hence, the end-to-end left-over service curve $\beta^{l.o.}$ can be obtained in (23), where R_2 and T_2 are the rate and latency of each node in access ring, and b is the burst of the VR traffic. Furthermore, parameter δ^* is presented in (24).

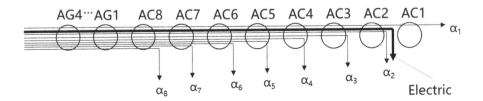

Fig. 9. A sketch of downstream traffic for the analysis with PMOO

$$\beta^* = \beta_{ag1} \otimes \beta_{ag2} \otimes \beta_{ag3} \otimes \beta_{ag4} = R_1(t - 4T_1)^+ \tag{22}$$

$$\beta^{l.o.} = (((\beta^* \otimes \beta_8 - \alpha_8) \cdots \otimes \beta_2) - \alpha_2 - \alpha_1)^+$$
$$= (R_2 - 8r)(t - 4T_1 - 7T_2 - b\delta^*)^+ \tag{23}$$

$$\delta^* = \frac{1}{R_2 - r} + \frac{\frac{1}{R_2-r} * r + b}{R_2 - r} + \cdots \tag{24}$$

Results are shown in Table 3. There are multiple flows for each traffic type, and the worst-case delays shown in the table (except for CQF) is the largest of the worst-case delays for all flows of that traffic type, calculated by both PMOO and RTaW-Pegase. Column 2 FIFO means all electric and VR traffics are going into one FIFO queue. Column 3 SP means electric traffics have a higher priority than all VR traffics, i.e., VR packets can not be forwarded unless there are no electric packets waiting in the queue at the moment. Column 4 SP+ means electric traffics have the highest priority, VR-interact traffics have a higher priority than VR-video traffics. Column 5 LSN means to allocate a 1G LSN on AC ring to electric traffics and to allocate the other 9G to all VR traffics. Column 6 LSN+ means to allocate a 1G LSN on AC ring to electric traffics, a 3G LSN to VR-interact traffics, and the other 6G to VR-video traffics. Column 7 CQF means all electric and VR traffics are entering cyclic switched buffers with high priority, and the per-hop worst-case delay is calculated based on (14). There can be other best-effort traffic in the network, and these traffics are assigned with the lowest priority, so their influences to electric and VR traffics are no more than a maximum packet length, which are neglected.

Table 3. Worst-case delay of different QoS-scheme

Traffic	FIFO	SP	SP+	LSN	LSN+	CQF
Electric	2.97	0.12	0.11	0.45	0.45	174
VR-interact	5.76	7.00	2.68	6.30	3.20	174
VR-video	5.76	6.95	16.64	6.29	12.50	174

Results show that, the None-time-base QoS scheme and the LSN scheme can improve the worst-case delay of electric traffics comparing to FIFO. However the impact on VR flows are different. Generally, because of the efficiency advantage, None-time-based schemes (SP, SP+) are a bit better than LSN schemes. On the other hand, the specific Time-based QoS mechanism, CQF, gives a very bad result. The reason is that the bursty and non-cyclical features of VR downstream traffics are very incompatible with the Time-based QoS method. Therefore, the buffer switching time T_C has to be very large in case that the bursts of all traffics arrive simultaneously. Another reason is that this use case fits PMOO perfectly. As all flows join the AC ring from the base station one by one, and after aggregation, go all the way together until the flow reaches its destination base station, they do multiplexing only once. The worst-case delay results from PMOO almost equal to the one-hop worst-case delay if all flows aggregate at this hop. Therefore, the pessimism of NC analysis is greatly reduced, resulting in tight results for SP, SP+, LSN, and LSN+.

6   Conclusion and Future Work

Non-time-based QoS, Time-based QoS, and Logical Separated Network are summarized as the three major QoS schemes that could provide bounded latency in IP networks. Their cons and pros are compared, and network calculus quantitatively proves that Non-time-based QoS is superior to the other two schemes in terms of efficiency of bandwidth utilization. The effect of ingress shaping is studied. Results show that applying ingress shaping to any specific flow could improve the overall network performance on the perspective of worst-case latency, and the benefit of reducing the worst-case latency to that flow could outweigh the extra delay caused by imposing ingress shaping. An IP network use case is used to compare the performance of these QoS schemes.

Because of the large scale and high complexity of IP networks, using network calculus to accurately calculate latency bounds under these QoS schemes is still a great challenge. There are two major to-do tasks for future works. One is to wisely choose network calculus algorithms, and improvements to the algorithm may be needed, to make trade-off between calculation accuracy and complexity. The other is to consider stochastic network calculus (SNC) [21], to take advantage of the statistical property of large-scale network and overcome the pessimism of DNC.

References

1. Braden, R.: Integrated Services in the Internet Architecture: an Overview, RFC 1633 (1994)
2. G. Armitage, B. Carpenter, A. Casati, et al.: A Delay Bound alternative revision of RFC 2598, RFC 3248 (2002)
3. IEEE 802.1. IEEE 802.1Q-2018 - IEEE Standard for Local and Metropolitan Area Networks-Bridges and Bridged Networks, IEEE WG 802.1, July 2018. http://www.ieee802.org/1/
4. Le Boudec, J.-Y., Thiran, P. (eds.): Network Calculus. LNCS, vol. 2050. Springer, Heidelberg (2001). https://doi.org/10.1007/3-540-45318-0
5. Fgee, E., Phillips, W.J., Robertson, W., Elhounie, A., Smeda, A.: A scalable mathematical QoS model for IP networks. In: 2008 3rd International Conference on Information and Communication Technologies: From Theory to Applications, Damascus, pp. 1–5 (2008)
6. Kim, H., Hou, J.C.: Network calculus based simulation for TCP congestion control: theorems, implementation and evaluation. In: IEEE INFOCOM 2004, Hong Kong, vol. 4, pp. 2844–2855 (2004)
7. Jiang, Y.: A basic result on the superposition of arrival processes in deterministic networks. In: IEEE Global Communications Conference (GLOBECOM), Abu Dhabi, United Arab Emirates, pp. 1–6 (2018)
8. Mohammadpour, E., Stai, E., Le Boudec, J.: Improved credit bounds for the credit-based shaper in time-sensitive networking. IEEE Netw. Lett. 1(3), 136–139 (2019)
9. Kreifeldt, R.: AVB for Professional A/V Use, AVnu Alliance White Paper (2009)
10. Wikipedia. Avionics Full-Duplex Switched Ethernet
11. Finn, N.: Multiple Cyclic Queuing and Forwarding, IEEE 802.1 public files (2019)

12. TTTech, Time-Triggered Ethernet - A Powerful Network Solution for Multiple Purpose
13. PROFINET University, Isochronous Real-Time (IRT) Communication. https://profinetuniversity.com/profinet-basics/isochronous-real-time-irt-communication/
14. OIF. Flex Ethernet 2.0 Implementation Agreement (2018)
15. Boyer, M.: Deficit round robin with network calculus. In: 6th International ICST Conference on Performance Evaluation Methodologies and Tools (2012)
16. Boyer, M.: Combining static priority and weighted round-robin like packet scheduling in AFDX for incremental certification and mixed-criticality support. In: 5th European Conference for Aeronautics and Space Sciences (2013)
17. 3GPP TS 23.501. Technical Specification Group Services and System Aspects, System Architecture for the 5G SYstem (2019)
18. Huawei, Cloud VR Network Solution White Paper (2018)
19. Schmitt, J.: Improving performance bounds in feed-forward networks by paying multiplexing only once. In: 14th GI/ITG Conference - Measurement, Modelling and Evaluation of Computer and Communication Systems (2008)
20. RealTime-at-Work. http://www.realtimeatwork.com/software/rtaw-pegase/
21. Fidler, M., Rizk, A.: A guide to the stochastic network calculus. IEEE Commun. Surv. Tutor. $\mathbf{17}$(1), 92–105 (2014)
22. Bondorf, S.: Quality and cost of deterministic network calculus - design and evaluation of an accurate and fast analysis. In: Measurement and Analysis of Computing Systems, no. 16 (2017)
23. Bouillard, A., Jouhet, L., Thierry, E.: Tight performance bounds in the worst-case analysis of feed-forward networks. In: Proceedings IEEE INFOCOM, San Diego, CA, pp. 1–9 (2010)
24. Schmitt, J.B., Zdarsky, F.A., Fidler, M.: Delay bounds under arbitrary multiplexing: when network calculus leaves you in the lurch. In: IEEE INFOCOM 2008 - The 27th Conference on Computer Communications, Phoenix, AZ, pp. 1669–1677 (2008)
25. Geyer, F., Bondorf, S.: DeepTMA: predicting effective contention models for network calculus using graph neural networks. In: IEEE INFOCOM 2019 - IEEE Conference on Computer Communications, Paris, France, pp. 1009–1017 (2019)
26. Schmitt, J., Zdarsky, F., Fidler, M.: Delay bounds under arbitrary multiplexing: when network calculus leaves you in the lurch. In: IEEE INFOCOM 2008-The 27th Conference on Computer Communications (2008)

Research on Information Transmission Characteristics of Two-Layer Communication Network

Zhenghui Li[1,2,3](✉), Yuzhi Xiao[1,2,3], Haixiu Luo[1,2,3], and Chunyang Tang[1,2,3]

[1] Computer Department, Qinghai Normal University, Xining 810016, Qinghai, China
qh_xiaoyuzhi@139.com
[2] Tibetan Information Processing and Machine Translation Key Laboratory of Qinghai Province, Xining 810008, Qinghai, China
[3] Key Laboratory of Tibetan Information Processing, Ministry of Education, Xining 810008, Qinghai, China

Abstract. With the development of the Internet, the marketing model of the communications industry has transformed from call-based to social application-based. Analyzing information transmission of social application helps to develop marketing strategy for different customers' needs. The paper proposes and constructs a two-layer communication user spreading model based on the SIR information dissemination model. Then we analyze the traditional model of virus spread on the network's application, and get the simulation results of immunization strategy and the communication process of social application information on WeChat, microblog and QQ. Combining with the actual data, simulation results show that the spread of the three types of social applications reaches a peak in a short time with the increase of the spreading rate. The spreading scale of WeChat application is larger than the other two types of applications on the same spread rate. Based on the acquaintance (target) immune strategy, the three types of applications have faster transmission inhibition than the random immune strategy. The research results of this paper provide an effective theoretical base for setting up individuality service combination of mobile communication enterprise.

Keywords: Immune strategy · Information dissemination · Social application · Two-layer communication network

1 Introduction

Nowadays, the way people get information turns from traditional media to social application platform, and social network has become the main place for publishing public opinion, forwarding information, product marketing and so on. With the increase of the number of Internet users and the diversification of social platforms, users have frequent

Supported by the National Science Foundation of China (No. 61763041), the Science Found of Qinghai Province (No. 2020-GX-112).

H. Gao et al. (Eds.): BROADNETS 2020, LNICST 355, pp. 90–108, 2021.
https://doi.org/10.1007/978-3-030-68737-3_6

exchanges and interactions, resulting in more rapid and extensive information dissemination. Different social networks have different characteristics of information transmission process due to their different structures, functions and emphases. At the beginning of 2020, the COVID-19 outbreak attracted the attention of the world, and the open and transparent release of epidemic information has become an important measure when China fought against the epidemic. The high efficiency, timeliness and universality of information dissemination have won precious time for people to enhance their awareness of self-isolation and stop the spread of the epidemic. In the research on information transmission during the epidemic, Li Jianjun et al. [1] proved that high information transmission efficiency can effectively reduce population mobility and slow down the spread of disease. He Zijie et al. [2] proposed that timely release of foreign-related epidemic information would help foreigners to participate in the prevention and control actions, while the lag or absence of information would easily lead to rumors and even panic. Therefore, in the process of information transmission, positive information should be spread quickly, while some rumors or statements that are not conducive to social stability should be suppressed in a timely manner. Preventing and controlling rumor spreading is of great significance to safeguarding citizens' rights and interests, public interests, national security and social stability.

In order to study the dynamic characteristics of information transmission on social networks, researchers proposed many mathematical models similar to the spread of infectious diseases. Xu et al. [3] introduced information value and user behavior into the information transmission model of social networks, improved and modified the traditional SEIR model, and proposed a new S-SEIR model. Rozenfeld et al. [4] embedded scale-free networks in European space, and found that such networks could promote information transmission and effectively inhibit rumor transmission. Zhu et al. [5] studied the influence of human heterogeneity on information transmission from the perspective of sociology. Zhang Zhaowen et al. [6] explored from the perspective of node heterogeneity that the information transmission process is more consistent with the information transmission in the real world.

At present, many scholars believe that most complex networks are coupled and interact with each other. So, "The network of networks" [6], "Multiplex Networks" [7] and "Multiplex Networks and Interdependent Network" [8] have become the vanguard of research in the field of complex networks. Research on information transmission in multi-layer networks has attracted extensive attention from many researchers [9–12]. The research foundation of information transmission process is the construction of network model. The two-layer social network model originates from the real social communication network. The network layers influence each other, depend on each other, and the nodes have heterogeneity. Du Rong [13] took urban activities in douban film review websites as research objects, analyzed the characteristics of information transmission in the network, and concluded that online information interaction effectively promoted the development of offline activities. Taking the online virtual community platform as the research object, Zhou Junjie [14] constructed the online and offline two-layer network model, proposed the mixed communication mode, and expanded the interaction scope and influence of Shared knowledge and information. By studying symmetric and asymmetric information transmission mechanisms. Yu Kai [15] constructed an information transmission model on online and offline BCN. Wang [16] constructed an asymmetric two-layer network of "information-disease" and found that faster information.

According to the 42nd Statistical Report on the Development of Internet in China [17]. As of June 30, 2018, the number of Internet users in China has reached 802 million, and the Internet penetration rate has also increased. The utilization rate of comprehensive social applications is relatively high, with WeChat APP ranking the first at 84.3%, QQ at 65.8% and microblog users at 38.7%. The utilization rate of all kinds of social software continues to rise, which enhances the maximum influence of information interaction and information dissemination. Meanwhile, it is also very necessary to suppress the dissemination of negative information such as online public opinion and rumors [18–23].

Aiming at the above problems, this paper constructs a two-layer communication user network model and analyzes the topology characteristics of the network. Based on the classic SIR communication mechanism and combined with the actual data of a university, the communication trajectories of users' information interaction through social software under different transmission rates are analyzed. At the same time, random immunization strategy, acquaintance immunization strategy and target immunization strategy were used to analyze the suppression process of information transmission under different immunization strategies of different social software, and the time window for the maximum influence of social software was obtained, which provided a theoretical basis for the design of traffic packages in the communication industry.

2   Introduction of Basic Concepts

2.1   SIR Spreading Model

The analysis of information spreading model started from the disease spreading model. At present, the classic spreading models are SI, SIS and SIR models [24–27]. Building a reasonable information spreading model can generally accurately describe the process of information spreading in the network, and can predict the flow direction of information. Based on SIR spreading model, this paper analyzes the process of information dissemination. In this model, the S state means that the individual has not received the propagation information, but may receive the information after contacting with the propagating state individual. I state means that the individual has received the information and is able to transmit the information to the susceptible individual, R state means that the information cannot be transmitted to the other state.

In the SIR information spreading model, all nodes are in the unknown state S in the initial stage, and the nodes have not contacted the information; when some unknown individuals receive the information, they will have a certain probability Then, some individuals who lose interest in the information will be transformed into information immune state R with a certain probability, and the immune individuals will not continue to spread after receiving the information. The dynamic propagation mechanism and differential equation of SIR model are shown in formulas 1 and 2.

$$s(i) + I(j) \xrightarrow{\beta} I(i) + I(j) \tag{1}$$

$$I(i) \xrightarrow{\gamma} R(i)$$

$$\begin{cases} \frac{ds(t)}{dt} = -\beta i(t)s(t) \\ \frac{di(t)}{dt} = \beta i(t)s(t) - \gamma i(t) \\ \frac{dr(t)}{dt} = \gamma i(t) \end{cases} \qquad (2)$$

Figure 1 shows the change of individual density in each state of SIR propagation model with time. The initial node of the network is 100, where the initial unknown state $S(0) = 0.92$, the information dissemination state $I(0) = 0.07$ I (0) = 0.07, the immune state $R(0) = 0.01$, the propagation rate $\beta = 0.8$, and the recovery rate $\gamma = 0.2$. When the transmission time is $t = 6$, the nodes of the three states are similar, but after that, the number of immunized people increases rapidly until the later stage of the transmission cycle, the number of immune persons reaches stable, and the transmission and susceptible individuals tend to 0, which is in line with the law of the transmission cycle of a conquered disease in real life.

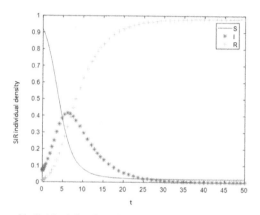

Fig. 1. Change of individual density with time in each state of SIR spreading model

2.2 Introduction of Immunization Strategy

For the information spreading on complex networks, it is a very significant and challenging problem to choose appropriate immune strategies to suppress the spread of negative information. The traditional immune strategies mainly include random immunization, target immunization and active immunization [28].

Random immunization strategy completely random selection of nodes in the network for immunization. Target immunization is carried out selectively. All nodes in the network are not equal and have different positions in the network. If these nodes with relatively important positions are found for immunization, better effects may be achieved. Acquaintance immunization: randomly select a certain proportion of nodes from the network for immunization, and then randomly select neighbor nodes from the selected nodes for immunization. Therefore, acquaintance immunization strategy can achieve good immune effect without knowing the information of global nodes. At present, the commonly used immune algorithms are target immunity and acquaintance immunity and the improvement of these two immune algorithms. In order to reduce the harm caused by rumors and public opinions on the complex network, immunization strategy arises at the right moment. Whether the current immunization strategy meets the requirements of the actual network and whether it can be used in the actual network is still a problem to be solved.

3 Two-Layer Network Modeling

In the real world, many complex networks are not running in isolation, but connected and influenced each other. The heterogeneity of nodes can divide the network into different levels. In online social network, different types of people are distributed at different levels, and they are related to each other. Aiming at the multi-path and multi-level problems of information dissemination in real life, this paper constructs a double-layer network model, and explores and analyzes the process of information dissemination based on the characteristics of the two-layer network model.

In this paper, the BA-BA two-layer network model is constructed. The BA-BA scale-free network generation algorithm is used in the model layer, and the random connection algorithm is used to connect the edges between interlayers. The network does not contain duplicate edges.

Step 1 Initialization: The scale of the two single layer networks is N, at the beginning, the single layer network has m_0 node and m_1 edges.

Step 2 Growth and preferential connection of scale-free network: In each time step, a new node is introduced and connected to m existing old nodes. Here $m \leq m_0$, at the same time, the probability $\prod_i$ of a new node connecting with an existing old node satisfies the following relationship with the degree of the node k_i: $(k_i + 1) / \sum (k_j + 1)$, when the total network node reaches N, the algorithm ends.

Step 3 Interlayer connection: Given that the interlayer connection probability is P, traverse the nodes i in the Layer A layer and the nodes j in the Layer B, and generate a probability P_2 randomly. If $P > P_2$, then in the adjacency matrix $a(i, j) = 1$, otherwise $a(i, j) = 0$, node traversal in the Layer A is completed, and the algorithm is finished.

As shown in Fig. 2, the topological structure diagram of the network is given. The node scale of the single layer network is set as $N = 30$, $m_0 = 5$, $m = 3$, and the link probability between layers is $P = 0.2$.

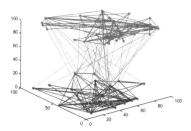

Fig. 2. Two-layer network model

4 Information Spreading Model of Two-Layer Communication Network

The information transmission between two-layer communication users can effectively observe the information transmission path between different types of nodes, and through the analysis of the information transmission of the whole network, we can get how the information is transmitted across layers and achieve the overall range of transmission between different levels. Therefore, this paper constructs a two-layer communication network based on the mobile communication data of college students, and analyzes the information transmission process between college students based on wechat, QQ, microblog and other application platforms combined with the information interaction data in popular social software. Based on the mobile communication data of college students, this paper constructs a two-layer communication network between sophomores and juniors, and analyzes the information dissemination process of popular social software such as WeChat, microblog, QQ based on SIR communication mechanism.

4.1 Data Preprocessing

The data of communication users comes from the actual questionnaire, and the data of information transmission between users comes from the data analysis library of mobile system. Based on the real data of mobile communication behavior, the information dissemination process is analyzed. In order to ensure the validity of the data, the communication data between students of a university from 2016 to 2019 are processed, and their social behaviors are analyzed. The usage of WeChat, QQ and microblog obtained from the data are shown in Tables 1 and 2.

Table 1. Total user data table

Years	2016	2017	2018	2019
Users	873	470	354	101

From Table 2, we can see that in 2017 and 2018, the APP ranked high in frequency: APP, QQ and microblog; low frequency APP used basketball forum, tiktok, short video

Table 2. Statistical table of average daily usage times

Users		Average open times		
		≤50	50–100	≥100
Second year class	WeChat	87	127	140
	QQ	274	71	9
	Microblog	133	56	2
	Douyin	153	2	0
	Hupu	8	0	0
	Alpay	149	0	0
	Mooc	28	0	0
Third Years class	WeChat	105	177	188
	QQ	337	83	20
	Microblog	172	43	5
	Douyin	15	10	0
	Hupu	17	2	0
	Alpay	173	1	0
	Mooc	53	0	0

APP, voice, APP Alipay, and learning software APP Mogao. It is not difficult to see that students tend to use social apps such as wechat. At the same time, it can be seen that the average daily number of users using wechat in 2017 was 72 times, and that in 2018 was 76 times. The WeChat utilization rate of Internet users in the past two years was very close. WeChat has its own social communication function, which can quickly spread and spread information. Therefore, it can be used as a source of information dissemination between users who have access to the network in 2017 and users who have access to the network in 2018. In the experiment, users who use WeChat more than 100 times a day are defined as communicators, and users who use less than 20 times a day are defined as immune users. The propagation rate is set according to the experience value. The experiment analyzes the spread of WeChat, QQ and microblog.

4.2 Model Construction and Characteristic Analysis of Two-Layer Communication Network

4.2.1 Construction of Two-Layer Network Model

In 2017, the number of communication users accessing the network was 354, and that in 2018 was 474. According to the actual data, a two-layer communication user network is constructed.

Step 1 Initialization: The scale of the two single-layer networks are 354 and 474, layer a is the network access users in 2017, and layer B is the access communication users in 2018.

Step 2 Intra layer connection: The number of calls between two mobile phone communication users is greater than or equal to 1, and the two user nodes are connected with edges, excluding duplicate edges.

Step 3 Inter layer connection: If the number of calls between two mobile communication users is greater than or equal to 1, an edge is added between the two user nodes, otherwise, no edge is added.

According to the above algorithm, a two-layer network model of communication between sophomores and juniors in a university is constructed. The network diagram is shown in Fig. 3.

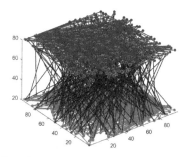

Fig. 3. Topology of two-layer communication network

4.2.2 Analysis of Topology Characteristics of Two-Layer Communication Network

According to the network model, the degree distribution, average clustering coefficient and average path length are analyzed.

1) Degree distribution

The degree k_i of a node v_i refers to the total number of other nodes adjacent to the node, which is recorded as the average degree of all nodes in the network, and is recorded as $\langle k \rangle$. For a given adjacency matrix $A = (a_{ij})_{N \times N}$ of network G, the calculation formulas of node degree and average degree are as follows:

$$k_i = \sum_{j=1}^{N} a_{ij} \tag{1}$$

$$\langle k \rangle = \frac{1}{N} \sum_{i=1}^{N} k_i = \frac{1}{N} \sum_{i,j=1}^{1} a_{ij} \tag{2}$$

In the two-layer communication network, the degree value of the node represents the number of users who have called with other users. This parameter is one of the indexes reflecting the importance of nodes. The node degree distribution of the two-layer network is calculated as shown in Fig. 4. The analysis shows that the overall node degree distribution of the network tends to power-law distribution, most users have small degree value, only a few users have larger degree value and stronger activity.

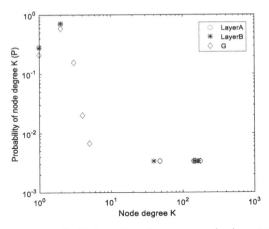

Fig. 4. Degree distribution of two-layer communication network

2) Average clustering coefficient

The clustering coefficient is used to quantitatively describe the probability that any two of your friends are friends with each other in complex networks. It reflects the aggregation of the whole network. The larger the clustering coefficient, the better the clustering of the network. The formula is defined as follows:

$$C_j = \frac{2M_j}{N_j(N_j - 1)} \tag{3}$$

Where, M_j is the actual number of connected edges between adjacent nodes N_j, and $N_j(N_j - 1)/2$ is the estimated maximum number of connected edges between adjacent nodes N_j. By averaging the aggregation coefficients of all nodes in the network, the aggregation coefficient of the whole network can be obtained

$$C = \frac{1}{N} \sum_{i=1}^{N} C_i \tag{4}$$

The average aggregation coefficient of the two-layer network is 0.187, and the network connection is sparse (Fig. 5).

3) Average path length

The average path length is defined as the average distance between any two nodes, also known as the average distance or characteristic path length, which is usually used

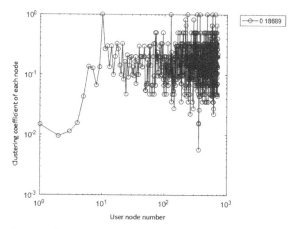

Fig. 5. Average clustering coefficient of two-layer communication network

to measure the speed of information transmission between nodes. The expression is as follows:

$$L = \frac{2}{N(N-1)} \sum_{i \geq j} d_{ij} \tag{5}$$

Where d_{ij} is the number of connected edges on the shortest path from node i to node j. Through numerical calculation, the average shortest path of the network is 2.4569 (Fig. 6).

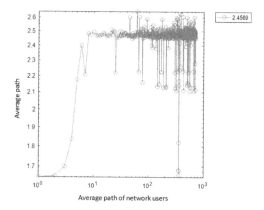

Fig. 6. Average path length of two-layer communication network

By analyzing the topological properties of degree distribution, average clustering coefficient and average path length of the two-layer communication user network, it is found that the user interaction distribution of the two-layer network is extremely uneven. Most of the users have less interaction, only a small number of users have dense connections, frequent and extensive communication, and the overall aggregation coefficient of the network is small, which is due to the number of inter layer connections of the two-layer network model. Therefore, the overall network connection is sparse. This also contributes to the shorter average path length of the network, which also helps users to connect to each other over a shorter path.

5 Information Dissemination of Two-Layer Communication Network Based on SIR

This section studies and analyzes the information transmission in the Sir Propagation mechanism of the two-tier user communication network. By adjusting the propagation rate and recovery rate, we can observe the network transmission at different times and the state transition of individuals at different times. At the same time, through the analysis of the corresponding immune strategy results, we can know how to control the spread of information, so that the research results can be better applied to real life, and provide corresponding reference for communication operators to make better decisions.

5.1 Analysis of Propagation Threshold Conditions

1. The influence of different transmission rates on individual density of simultaneous interpreting
    Table 3 shows the frequency statistics of users' daily use of WeChat app. It can be concluded from the table that the average daily frequency of using WeChat app was 72 times among the communication users who had access to the network in 2017, and 76 times in 2018. In the SIR communication mechanism, users who use WeChat more than 100 times a day at the initial time are regarded as transmission individuals, those who use WeChat less than 20 times a day are regarded as immune individuals, and other users are set as susceptible individuals. Thus, the initial conditions are obtained as follows: $s(0) = 0.814$, $i(0) = 0.16$, $r(0) = 0.026$, the propagation rate β is 0.3, 0.5, 0.8, and the recovery rate is $\gamma = 0.2$. The test results are shown in Fig. 7(a). In order to further explore whether the propagation process is related to the clustering coefficient and average path length of the network, set $\beta = C/L$. The ratio of the average clustering coefficient to the average path length is 0.08, and the recovery rate is $\gamma = 0.2$. Through 100 simulations, the experimental results as shown in Fig. 7(b) are obtained.

Table 3. Statistics of WeChat users

| Years | Average daily openning times | | | | |
	Less than 20 times	More than 80 times	More than 100 times	More than 150 times	More than 200 times
2017	8	115	61	14	4
2018	11	139	63	8	2

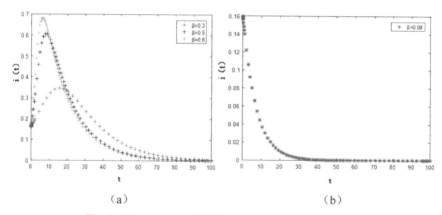

Fig. 7. Change trend of WeChat app propagation behavior

Based on the analysis of the experimental results, two different situations are obtained: (1) from Fig. 7(a), when $t = 9$, the proportion of disseminators reached the peak at $\beta = 0.8$. When $t = 11$, the proportion of disseminators reached the peak at $\beta = 0.5$. When $t = 15$, the proportion of disseminators reached the peak at $\beta = 0.3$. The results show that with the increase of the transmission rate, the time when the proportion of communicators reaches the peak decreases in turn. At $t \approx 90$, the proportion of communicators reaches the steady state under three kinds of transmission rates.

2) The ratio of the average clustering coefficient and the average path length of the network can get a smaller propagation rate. The number of communicators has reached the peak at the initial time, but when the network reaches the peak, the proportion of communicators is 0.16, which indicates that the overall propagation is slow and the spread range is small due to the sparse connection. To sum up, with the increase of propagation rate, the propagation speed is accelerated and the propagation range is expanded, and the influence of network communication is also enhanced.

5.1.1 Analysis of Three Types of APP Communication Behavior

In addition to WeChat, QQ and microblog usage frequency can also be used to analyze users' communication behavior. According to the empirical data, the daily average usage data of QQ and microblog are obtained, as shown in Table 4.

Similarly, users who use more than 100 times a day are regarded as communicators; those who use less than 10 times a day are regarded as immune individuals, and other users are regarded as vulnerable individuals. The initial conditions are as follows: in QQ social software, the proportion of susceptible individuals, transmission individuals and immune individuals is $s(0) = 0.58$, $i(0) = 0.26$, $r(0) = 0.16$; In microblog social software, the proportion of susceptible individuals, communicators and immune individuals is $s(0) = 0.74$, $i(0) = 0.15$, $r(0) = 0.11$; Let the transmission rate β be 0.3, 0.5 and 0.8 respectively, and the recovery rate $\gamma = 0.2$. The results of 100 simulation experiments are shown in Fig. 8.

Table 4. Statistics of daily average usage times (microblog, QQ)

Years	Average daily openning times		
	Less than 10 times	More than 50 times	More than 100 times
2017 (QQ)	56	80	9
2017 (microblog)	63	103	20
2018 (QQ)	33	58	2
2018 (microblog)	47	48	5

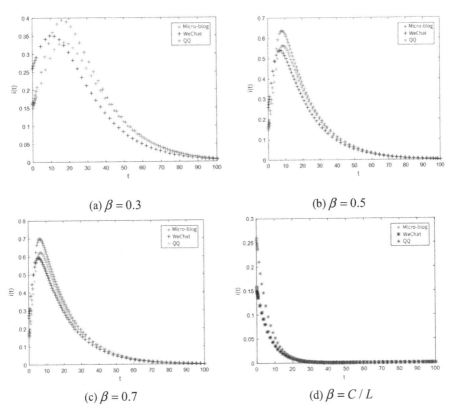

(a) $\beta = 0.3$

(b) $\beta = 0.5$

(c) $\beta = 0.7$

(d) $\beta = C / L$

Fig. 8. Trend of density spread of individuals with different propagation rates in three types of APP simultaneous interpreting

According to the analysis of the experimental results, two different situations are obtained: (1) according to the analysis of Fig. 8(a) (b) (c), the communication rate of $\beta = 0.3$, $\beta = 0.5$ and $\beta = 0.5$, microblog app communication individuals first reached the peak, QQ and WeChat users almost reached the peak at the same time, when the peak, WeChat users accounted for the largest proportion of individuals, followed by WeChat, the smallest was QQ. Among them, the higher the transmission rate, the faster the peak time of the three apps. (2) It can be seen from Fig. 8(d) that when the transmission rate is $\beta = C/L$, at the initial stage of transmission, the size of individual network communication is the peak value. Due to the low transmission rate, the transmission efficiency in the network is also very limited.

Comprehensive analysis shows that with the increase of the transmission rate, the propagation speed of the three types of app is accelerated, among which WeChat app has the highest transmission efficiency. When the network transmission rate is very small, the number of people affected in the network transmission process is the least, that is, the communication effect is weak.

5.2 Research on Immune Strategy in Two-Layer Communication Network

By analyzing the structural properties of double-layer network and the dynamic process of information dissemination, the corresponding immune strategies are formulated to suppress the spread of rumors and rumors. The communication behavior is analyzed by implementing immune strategies in WeChat, QQ and microblog.

5.2.1 Immune Strategy Analysis Based on WeChat Communication

Based on SIR propagation mechanism, immune results were analyzed on the two-layer network, and the immune results were analyzed in WeChat app using random immunization, target immunization and acquaintance immunization strategies. The initial setting parameters of the experiment are as follows: $s(0) = 0.814$, $i(0) = 0.16$, $r(0) = 0.026$; The recovery rate is set to $\gamma = 0.2$, and the propagation rate is set to $\beta = 0.5$. In the two-layer network, the nodes with F = 5% and F = 15% are immunized respectively, and the propagation experiment is simulated for 100 times. The experimental results are shown in Fig. 9.

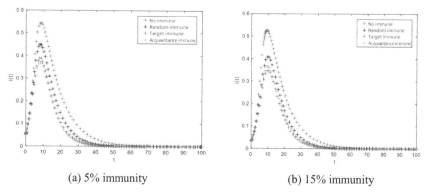

(a) 5% immunity   (b) 15% immunity

Fig. 9. Change trend of network infection index QC of double layer communication users with time step (WeChat)

Through the analysis of the experimental results, two cases are obtained: (1) in Fig. 9(a), it can be seen that when 5% of the nodes are immunized, when $t = 10$, the density of communicators under the non-immune strategy and the three immune strategies reaches the peak almost at the same time; the number of communicators without immune strategy is the largest, and the density is close to 0.55. The second is random immunization, and the transmission trend and peak value of target immunization and acquaintance immunization are almost the same. (2) It can be seen from Fig. 9(b) that when the time step t = 12, the immune strategies reach the peak. Under the non-immune strategy, the number of communicators is the largest, followed by the non-immune strategy, and the change trend of target immunization and acquaintance immunity is roughly the same.

5.2.2 Analysis of Immune Strategy Based on QQ Propagation

In the QQ application data center, the initial setting parameters of the experiment is $s(0) = 0.58$, $i(0) = 0.26$, $r(0) = 0.16$; $\gamma = 0.2$, $\beta = 0.5$. In the two-layer network, the nodes with F = 5% and F = 15% are immunized respectively, and the propagation experiment is simulated for 100 times. The experimental results are shown in Fig. 10.

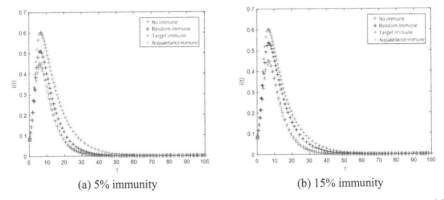

(a) 5% immunity   (b) 15% immunity

Fig. 10. Change trend of network infection index QC of double layer communication users with time step (QQ)

By analyzing the experimental results, two cases are obtained: (1) In Fig. 10(a), we can see that when 5% of the nodes are immunized, the density of communicators under the no immune strategy and the three immune strategies almost reach the peak at the same time in time step $t = 10$; the number of communicators without immune strategy is the largest, and the density is close to 0.6. The second is random immunization, and the transmission trend and peak value of target immunization and acquaintance immunization are almost the same. (2) It can be seen from Fig. 9(b) that when the time step t = 12, the immune strategies reach the peak. Under the non-immune strategy, the number of communicators is the largest, followed by the non-immune strategy, and the change trend of target immunization and acquaintance immunity is roughly the same.

5.2.3 Immune Strategy Analysis Based on Microblog

In the microblog application data center, the initial setting parameters are as follows: $s(0) = 0.74$, $i(0) = 0.15$, $r(0) = 0.11$, $\gamma = 0.2$, $\beta = 0.5$. In the two-layer network, the nodes with F = 5% and F = 15% are immune respectively, and the simulation of propagation experiment is carried out for 100 times. The experimental results are shown in Fig. 11.

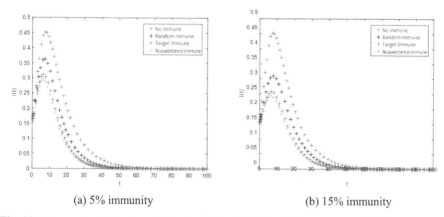

(a) 5% immunity   (b) 15% immunity

Fig. 11. Change trend of network infection index QC of double layer communication users with time step (Microblog)

Through the analysis of the experimental results, two cases are obtained: (1) In Fig. 11(a), it can be seen that when 5% of the nodes are immunized, the density of the communicators under the no immune strategy and the three immune strategies almost reaches the peak at $t = 10$; The number of communicators under the non-immune strategy is the largest, and the density is close to 0.45. The second is random immunization, and the transmission trend and peak value of target immunization and acquaintance immunization are almost the same. (2) It can be seen from Fig. 9(b) that when the time step $t = 12$, the immune strategies reach the peak at the same time when 15% nodes are immunized. Under the non-immune strategy, the number of communicators is the largest, followed by the non-immune strategy, with the same target immunization and maturity. The change trend of human immunity was similar.

In this two-layer communication user network, the non-immune strategy is compared with other immune strategies, and it is known that the random immune strategy, the target immune strategy and the acquaintance immune strategy have good network inhibition effect. Under different transmission rates, the impact of the ratio of the three APP carriers to the network propagation and the characteristics of the simultaneous interpreting of the two tier networks are very consistent with the characteristics of the research.

Through a series of simulation experiments on the empirical network, it is concluded that the information dissemination of social app with high utilization rate has similar propagation rules, but in the process of communication, the scale of individuals in each state, network topology index and immune strategy will affect the propagation trajectory. The larger the scale of the network, the larger the clustering coefficient and the smaller the average path, the more widely the use of app and the spread of information. In this paper, the immune strategy involved is applied to the fixed-point traffic package publicity strategy in real life. As the empirical network in the long-term development, there will be stagnant state, this is because people are immune to the old information, resulting in burnout. Therefore, we should always keep innovation and update the operation system to achieve long-term, stable and sustainable development. In Sir Propagation mechanism, with the increase of time in the network, most node states will be transformed into immune state. The immune state includes either saturated or low utilization rate. Therefore, immune strategy is introduced to carry out fixed-point traffic package publicity strategy for users with low utilization rate. In the process of transmission, the peak size of individual disseminator is particularly important, communication operators can observe the scale of individual communication, and observe the use of an app and its joint effect to achieve a communication effect. For example, starting from WeChat, QQ and microblog apps, they can bundle and set their traffic packages to better meet people's demand for traffic packages. However, in real life, there will be a small number of APP usage rate is low. In order to meet the growing demand of communication network traffic packages, we can bundle the app with high utilization rate with the app with low utilization rate to serve the people with demand, so that the communication operators can better maximize the communication and make its benefits grow steadily.

6 Conclusion

In this paper, a double-layer B-B network model is constructed, and the Sir Propagation mechanism is introduced to analyze the relevant characteristics of propagation in the double-layer network. At the same time, a two-layer homogeneous communication network is constructed by using the communication data of college students. The communication process of WeChat, microblog, QQ and other apps in the communication network is analyzed. The results show that the communication of the empirical communication network conforms to the characteristics of information dissemination in the two-layer network. At the same time, according to the analysis of the three types of APP propagation path, the corresponding marketing strategy is formulated, which provides a theoretical basis for the communication operators to set and promote the app traffic package better.

Compared with the information dissemination in real life, there is still a lot of work to be improved. There is still a lot of room for development of the current communication mechanism in the application of the two-layer network. For example, the construction of two-layer network model, the diversity of the connection between layers, the heterogeneity of network level, and the more complex network model. Secondly, it is the improvement of immunization and marketing strategy, which can make the effect more obvious by hierarchical immunization or marketing recommendation through the attribute structure of the network itself, and also provide reference for the control of communication phenomenon in real life in the future.

References

1. Li, J.J., He, S.: Population movement. Information dissemination efficiency and disease control: evidence from coronavirus disease 2019. J. Central Univ. Finance Econ. **4**, 116–128 (2020)
2. He, Z.J., Tang, J.M., Wan, Q.Q., et al.: The release and dissemination of information on the epidemic among foreign nationals in China. External Commun. **04**, 31–33 (2020)
3. Xu, R., Li, H., Xing, C.: Research on information dissemination model for social networking serever. Int. J. Comput. Sci. Appl. **2**(1), 1–6 (2013)
4. Rozenfeld, A.F., Cohen, R., Ben, A.D., et al.: Scale-free networks on lattices. Phys. Rev. Lett. **89**(21), 1662–1666 (2002)
5. Zhu, Z.Q., Liu, C.J., Wu, J.L., et al.: The influence of human heterogeneity to information spreading. J. Stat. Phys. **152**, 1569–1577 (2014)
6. Verbrugge, L.M.: Multiplexity in adult friendships. Soc. Forces **57**(4), 1286–1309 (1979)
7. Wasserman, S., Faust, K.: Social Network Analysis: Methods and Applications. Cambridge University Press, Cambridge (1994)
8. De, D.M., Nicosia, V., Arenas, A., et al.: Structural reducibility of multilayer networks. Nat. Commun. **6**, 6864 (2015)
9. Boccaletti, S., Bianconi, G., Criado, R., et al.: The sturcture and dynamics of multilayer networks. Phys. Rep. **544**(1), 1–122 (2014)
10. Nicosia, V., Bianconi, G., Latora, V., et al.: Growing multiplex networks. Phys. Rev. Lett. **111**(5), 058701 (2013)
11. Min, B., YiS, D., Lee, K.M., et al.: Network roustness of multiplex networks with inter layer correlations. Phys. Rev. E **89**(4), 042811 (2014)
12. Lee, K.M., Kim, J.Y., Cho, W.K., et al.: Correlated multiplexity and connectivity of multiplex random network. New J. Phys. **14**(3), 033027 (2012)
13. Du, R., Yu, Z.W., Liu, Z.L., Guo, B., et al.: Social Influence of online and offline based on events. J. Comput. Sci. **37**(1), 238–245 (2014)
14. Zhou, J.J., Zuo, M.Y.: Research on the relationship among the online/offline interaction group differentiation and knowledge sharing: an empirical analysis based on virtual community. Chin. J. Manage. Sci. **20**(6), 185–192 (2012)
15. Yu, K.: Research on information spreading model layer couple network. Dalian University of Technology (2015)
16. Wang, W., Tang, M., Yang, H., et al.: Asymmetrically interacting spreading dynamics on complex layered networks. Sci. Rep. **4**, 5097 (2014)
17. China internet network information center: The 42nd Statistical Report on Internet Development in China. CNNIC, Beijin (2018)
18. Wang, X.F., Li, X.F., Chen, G.R.: Complex Network Theory and its Application. Tsinghua University Press, Beijing (2006)
19. Zhang, Z.W.: Research on information flow Behavior of Heterogeneous nodes in complex networks. Shijiazhuang Railway University (2016)
20. Biswas, M.H.A., Paiva, L.T., Pinho, M.D.: ASEIR model for control of infectious diseases with constraints. Math. Biosci. Eng. **11**(4), 761–784 (2014)
21. Tao, Z., Zhong, F.U., Binghong, W.: Epidemic dynamics on complex networks. Prog. Nat. Sci. **16**(005), 452–457 (2006)
22. Granell, C., Gómez, S., Arenas, A.: Competing spreading processes on multiplex networks: awareness and epidemics. Phys. Rev. E **90**(1), 012808 (2014)
23. Gomez, S.A., Diaz, G.J., Gomez, G., et al.: Diffusion dynamics on multiplex networks. Phys. Rev. Lett. **110**(2), 028701.1–028701.5 (2013)

24. Lee, K.M., Kim, J.Y., Cho, W.K., et al.: Correlated multiplexity and connectivity of multiplex random networks. New J. Phys. **14**(3), 033027 (2012)
25. Gómez-Gardenes, J., Reinares, I., Arenas, A., et al.: Evolution of cooperation in multiplex networks. Sci. Rep. **2**, 620 (2012)
26. Li, X.N., Zhang, Q.M.: Stability analysis of an SIRS epidemic with information intervention. J. South China Normal Univ. (Nat. Sci. Edn.) **51**(05), 98–103 (2019)
27. Qin, W.T.: Research on information propagation model of online/ offline network based on couple network. Shijiazhuang Railway University (2018)

Detection of Malicious Android Applications: Classical Machine Learning vs. Deep Neural Network Integrated with Clustering

Hemant Rathore[✉], Sanjay K. Sahay, Shivin Thukral, and Mohit Sewak

Department of CS and IS, Goa Campus, BITS Pilani, Goa, India
{hemantr,ssahay,f201500350,p20150023}@goa.bits-pilani.ac.in

Abstract. Today anti-malware community is facing challenges due to ever-increasing sophistication and volume of malware attacks developed by adversaries. Traditional malware detection mechanisms are not able to cope-up against next-generation malware attacks. Therefore in this paper, we propose effective and efficient Android malware detection models based on machine learning and deep learning integrated with clustering. We performed a comprehensive study of different feature reduction, classification and clustering algorithms over various performance metrics to construct the Android malware detection models. Our experimental results show that malware detection models developed using Random Forest eclipsed deep neural network and other classifiers on the majority of performance metrics. The baseline Random Forest model without any feature reduction achieved the highest AUC of 99.4%. Also, the segregating of vector space using clustering integrated with Random Forest further boosted the AUC to 99.6% in one cluster and direct detection of Android malware in another cluster, thus reducing the curse of dimensionality. Additionally, we found that feature reduction in detection models does improve the model efficiency (training and testing time) many folds without much penalty on effectiveness of detection model.

Keywords: Android malware · Cyber security · Deep neural network · Machine learning · Malware detection · Static analysis

1 Introduction

Mobile phone and internet are increasingly becoming an integral part of our daily life. A recent report suggests that there are around 5.13 billion mobile phone users, which is more than 65% of the world's population [10]. The mobile phone market is currently dominated by the Android Operating System (OS), which runs on more than 70% of the devices [3]. Surprisingly there are 8.485 billion mobile connections which are even more than the world's current population [22]. Also, around 50% of internet traffic flows through mobile phones

© ICST Institute for Computer Sciences, Social Informatics and Telecommunications Engineering 2021
Published by Springer Nature Switzerland AG 2021. All Rights Reserved
H. Gao et al. (Eds.): BROADNETS 2020, LNICST 355, pp. 109–128, 2021.
https://doi.org/10.1007/978-3-030-68737-3_7

[10]. Mobile phones hold a large amount of personal user data like documents, pictures, contacts, messages etc. and are an easy target of malware designers to steal the above information.

Malware (**Mal**icious Soft**ware**) is a universal name given to any program performing any malicious activity. The first known malware (*Creeper*, 1971) was designed for TENEX OS to display taunting messages [28]. In the initial years, attackers would design malware to show their knowledge or for fun. These attacks would pose low-security threat risk to the system, but today it is a profit-driven industry. Individuals, groups, states, etc. perform malware attacks motivated by gains associated with it. The first Android OS malware (*ANDROI-DOS_DROIDSMS.A*[1], 2010) was developed to perform SMS fraud [28]. According to G DATA CyberDefense, 214,327 new Android malware were detected in 2012 [4]. Since then, there has been an exponential growth in the velocity of incoming Android malware. Another recent report by G DATA CyberDefense shows 4 million new malware was detected in 2018 [4]. Last year Symantec blocked 10,573 malicious Android applications every day which were trying to steal user's information [21].

Anti-malware detection engines developed by Avast, Kaspersky, McAfee, Symantec etc. are the primary defence to protect the genuine user from malware attacks [28]. Traditionally, these engines were based on signature based malware detection mechanism. A signature is a short unique byte sequence used to identify a particular malware [28]. However, the signature generation is often human-driven and time-consuming process. Also, malware can easily evade signature based detection by modifying a small amount of malicious code without affecting the overall semantic [14]. Automated malware development toolkits viz. *Zeus*[2] can generate thousands of variants of malware in a single day using obfuscation techniques [28]. Creating different signatures for the detection of all the malware variants is an infeasible task. Also, signature based detection does not provide security against a zero-day attack[3]. Thus, Heuristic-based detection was developed where domain experts write generic rule/pattern to discriminate malicious and benign applications [7]. Ideally, rules/pattern should be comprehensive so that they do not increase false positives and false negatives which is often unacceptable for any real-world deployment and achieving it is a tough task. Thus scientists and researchers are developing new intelligent Android malware detection system based on machine learning and deep learning techniques which are less human-driven, and more effective, efficient, and scalable.

Malware analysis and detection using machine learning and deep learning is a two-step process: feature engineering followed by classification/clustering. The performance of any malware detection system is highly dependent on the feature set, and the category of the machine learning/deep learning algorithm used to build the model. Researchers have used feature set like permission [1,20], intent

---

[1] https://www.trendmicro.com/vinfo/us/threat-encyclopedia/malware/ANDROID OS_DROIDSMS.A.

[2] https://usa.kaspersky.com/resource-center/threats/zeus-virus.

[3] https://www.avast.com/c-zero-day.

[2,24], API calls [9,25], opcode [17] in the past for detecting malicious Android applications. After feature vector creation, classification/clustering algorithm is used to build the malware detection model. The selection of the feature set is critical since they might contribute to many limitations of the malware detection systems. For example, a detection model based on Android permission can detect malicious activity performed through permission module only. Often researchers combine multiple feature sets and create huge vector space to build the detection model. The disadvantages of these models are that they suffer from the curse of dimensionality, need of a sophisticated classifier to construct the detection model, a large model size for any real-time deployment, huge train time and test time. Also, explainability of these models is very poor. Therefore in this paper, we propose to use Android opcodes as a feature for malware detection. Opcodes are at the lowest abstraction of Android OS architecture[4] and can detect malware attack designed at higher OS abstraction as well. We performed an extensive feature vector analysis with different feature reduction techniques like attribute sub-selection and new attribute creation methods. Also, we used three categories of classification algorithms viz. classical machine learning, ensemble learning and deep neural network to build malware detection models and analyzed them using different performance metrics. Lastly, to further improve performance, we used clustering to divide the feature vector into smaller spaces (clusters) and then built classification models on each one of them to reduce the curse of dimensionality. Therefore in this paper, we performed extensive work for effective and efficient Android malware detection models and made the following contributions:

- Our baseline Android malware detection model developed using random forest achieved the highest AUC (99.4). The reduced feature model based on random forest with only 12% opcodes obtained an AUC of 99.1 and reduction in the training and testing time by 47% and 8% respectively.
- Segregating of vector space using clustering followed by classification further boosted the performance of malware detection models with a higher AUC of 99.6 (using random forest) in one cluster and direct detection of Android malware in another cluster. Experimental results show that the construction of a single complex malware detection model on the complete dataset may overfit/underfit the data. Thus segregation of vector space (clusters) integrated with classification can reduce the above effect by reducing the curse of dimensionality.
- Android malware detection models based on autoencoder and deep neural network perform poorly as compared to machine learning models. They achieved comparable effectiveness in detection but with substantially higher train and test time.

The rest of the paper is organized as follows. Related work based on malware analysis and detection is discussed in Sect. 2. The proposed experimental setup and various performance metrics used in the paper are introduced in Sect. 3.

---

[4] https://developer.android.com/guide/platform.

Experimental results including feature reduction, classification models and segregation of the feature vector (using clustering) integrated with classification are explained in Sect. 4. Finally, Sect. 5 concludes the paper and discuss future work.

2   Related Work

Malware analysis and detection is an endless competition between malware designers and the anti-malware community. Traditional malware detection systems are based on the signature, heuristic, and cloud-based engines which are not able to cope-up with new-age sophisticated malware attacks. Thus anti-malware community is trying to construct next-generation Android malware detection systems based on machine learning and deep learning [6,18,28]. These systems are developed using the two-step process (1) Feature Engineering (2) Classification. Thus we have also divided the literature survey into two lines of research **(1) Feature Engineering** consists of feature extraction and feature selection. Hou et al. [9] developed DroidDelver (2016) for Android malware detection based on API calls as features on comodo dataset. Wang et al. [23] proposed DroidDeepLearner, which used features like permission and API call extracted from Android applications. DroidMat [24] extracted features including permission, application component, intent, and API call for building the detection model. Drebin [1] extracted permission, intent, app component, API call and network address from the Android applications for the construction of malware detection. Most of the above work combines multiple features set for the development of Android malware detection models. For example, Drebin used roughly 545,000 different features extracted from Android applications to build the malware detection model and thus suffers heavily from the curse of dimensionality. Literature shows that various feature selection methods viz. Document Frequency [8,28], Information Gain [13,28], Hierarchical Feature Selection [28], Max-Relevance Algorithm [8,28], etc. have been used for construction of malware detection system but the cost of feature reduction is rarely discussed. On the other hand, Lindorfer et al. in Andrubis [12] gathered more than 1 million Android applications dated between 2010 to 2014. They found exponential growth in the number of Android applications (both malicious and benign) in the same time frame. They also found that the average number of permission requested by benign applications is less than malicious ones. Sarma [15] also found that certain permissions like *READ_SMS*, *WRITE_CONTACTS* etc. are used extensively by malicious applications as compare to benign application. Yang et al. [27] tracked the flow of intent to differentiate malicious and benign behaviour. Sharma et al. [19] performed grouping of Android applications using permissions and then performed classification using opcodes in each group. Zhou et al. [29] found 86% repacked benign applications to be containing some malicious payload and 93& of malicious application exhibited bot-like capabilities. They also show that the anti-virus engine performed poorly and are unable to detection next-generation Android malware. **(2) Building classification model:** After the development of feature vector, various machine learning and deep learning algorithms can be used for the construction of the Android malware detection system. Arp et al. [1] in Drebin used 545,000 different features and support vector machine as the classification algorithm for the construction of the Android malware detection model, which achieved 93.80% detection accuracy. DroidMat [24] used permission, intent and API call as features combined with k-means, naive bayes, k-nearest neighbour algorithms to propose a detection model which achieved the f-measure of 91.8%. Sharma et al. [19] on Drebin dataset first performed permission-based grouping and then used opcode for construction of detection model. They used a variety of tree-based classification algorithm like J48, functional trees, NBTree, logistic model tree, random forest and attained 79.27% accuracy with functional trees. Sewak et al. [16] on Malicia dataset used opcode as the feature and explored models based on random forest and deep neural network to achieve 99.78% detection accuracy with the random forest model. DroidDeepLearner [23] developed a deep belief network for malware detection and achieved 92.67% accuracy in malware classification. Li et al. [11] on Drebin dataset used kirin rules and attained 94.29% recall in Android malware detection. DroidDelver [9] used decision tree, naive bayes, support vector machine and deep learning to build detection models and attained 94.04% of detection accuracy with decision tree-based model.

3 Experimental Setup and Performance Metrics

In this section, we will discuss the dataset (malicious and benign apps), feature vector generation and various evaluation metrics used to design Android malware detection models.

3.1 Malicious and Benign Apps

We downloaded real Android malware applications from the *Drebin* project [1]. Arp et al. downloaded 131,611 Android applications from Google Play Store[5] and various other sources for the construction of the Drebin dataset. All these downloaded applications were inspected by a list of 10 popular antivirus scanners and then labelled as malware or benign. Additionally, the dataset al.so includes all the 1,260 malicious applications from the Android Malware Genome Project [29]. The final published Drebin dataset consists of 5,560 malicious Android applications from more than 50 different malware families.

For this project, we collected 9,823 Android apps from the Google Play Store between August 2018 to December 2018. We used the services of Virus-Total[6] to label applications as malware or benign. VirusTotal is a subsidiary of Chronicle/Google which provides APIs to scan Android applications by a list of antiviruses (viz. AVG, McAfee, Symantec, etc.). We scanned all the downloaded Android applications with VirusTotal and labelled them as benign or malicious.

---

[5] https://play.google.com/store?hl=en.
[6] https://www.virustotal.com/.

A sample was labelled benign if all the antiviruses from virustotal.com platform declared it as benign. We deleted applications which are reported malicious by VirusTotal. Finally, we marked a set of 5,592 Android applications as benign. Thus the final dataset used in the experiments contains 5,560 malicious and 5,592 benign apps.

3.2 Generating Feature Vector

The feature set is the backbone of any machine learning/deep learning based Android malware detection system. Features extraction can be performed using static or dynamic analysis of Android apps [5,26]. From the malware designer perspective, malicious activities can be performed from any abstracted layer in the Android OS architecture[7]. However, Android malware detection model based on permission feature set can detect malicious activity performed through permission only. Thus feature set generated from a particular higher Android OS abstraction is bound to have limitations. On the other hand, any malicious activity designed on any abstracted level will have to execute on a set of opcodes to complete its desired effect. Thus we have used opcode frequency generated by static analysis as the feature vector to design Android malware detection system.

Android applications can be dissembled using Apktool[8] to generate its assembly code. The disassembled code consists of AndroidManifest.xml file, smali files, classes.dex files, images, and other application components. A *master opcode list* was generated by using a parser which lists the 256 Dalvik opcodes (represented in hexadecimal, ranging from 00 to FF) in each Android application. For example, hexadecimal values of opcodes *nop* and *move* are 00 and 01 respectively. The above list was also verified from the official Android website[9]. Finally, a different parser scanned through each of the Android applications and generated its opcode frequency vector. The final feature vector for the complete dataset is 11138×256 where a row denotes an Android app, and a column denotes the frequency of a particular opcode.

3.3 Evaluation Metrics

We have employed both unsupervised and supervised learning methods for building the Android malware detection system. Following are different evaluation metrics used to build detection models.

Methods/Metrics to Find the Optimal Number of Clusters: Clustering is an unsupervised learning method used to understand the pattern/structure of the data. In most clustering algorithm, the number of clusters should be provided by the programmer and finding it in the dataset is a very subjective and challenging task. Domain knowledge, metrics, visualization tools can be used

---

[7] https://developer.android.com/guide/platform.
[8] https://ibotpeaches.github.io/Apktool/.
[9] https://developer.android.com/reference/dalvik/bytecode/Opcodes.

to decide the optimal number of clusters, but there is no single thumb rule for it. We have used the Silhouette Score and Calinski-Harabasz Index to find an optimal number of clusters in clustering algorithms.

- **Sum of Square Error** is used to find the optimal number of clusters (k) in the k-means clustering algorithm. In this method, we calculated the Sum of Square Error (SSE) as a function of k which can be used to understand the compactness of the cluster(s). The value of k at an elbow-like bend in the plot can be considered as its optimal value. The mathematical representation of SSE is as follows:

$$SSE = \sum_{i=1}^{k} \sum_{x \in c_i} dist^2(x, c_i) \tag{1}$$

where k is number of clusters, c_i is the centroid of cluster i and x is all the points in cluster i

- **Silhouette Score** is used to measure the similarity of a point within the cluster (cohesion) compared to other clusters (separation). It can vary from $+1$ to -1 where a higher positive value indicates the given point is well inside the cluster boundary, zero value indicates that the point is on the cluster boundary, and a negative value indicates it is dissimilar to the assigned cluster. We have used Euclidean distance as the distance metric to measure the silhouette score.

$$s(i) = \frac{b(i) - a(i)}{max\{a(i), b(i)\}} \tag{2}$$

where $a(i)$ is the average distance between point i and all the points in the cluster (cohesion) and $b(i)$ is the average distance between point i and all the points in the neighbouring cluster(s) (separation)

- **Calinski-Harabasz Index** is the ratio of between-cluster covariance and within-cluster covariance.

$$CH - Index = \frac{SSE_B}{SSE_W} \times \frac{N - k}{k - 1} \tag{3}$$

where SSE_W is within-cluster covariance calculated by Eq. (1), SSE_B is the sum of SSE of all clusters minus SSE_W, k is the number of clusters, and N is the total number of data points.

Classification Algorithm Performance Metrics. To evaluate the performance of the Android malware detection models, we have used following metrics that are derived from the confusion matrix.

- **Accuracy** is the ratio of correct predictions (malware and benign) by the total predictions.

$$Accuracy = \frac{TP + TN}{TP + FP + TN + FN} \tag{4}$$

- **Recall (TPR)** measures how many actual malignant applications are classified as malware by the detection model.

$$TPR = \frac{TP}{TP + FN} \tag{5}$$

- **Specificity (TNR)** measures how many actual benign applications are classified as benign by the detection model.

$$TNR = \frac{TN}{TN + FP} \tag{6}$$

- **F-measure (F1)** is harmonic mean of recall and precision.

$$F1 = 2 \times \frac{recall \times precision}{recall + precision} \tag{7}$$

- **Area Under The Curve (AUC)** illustrates the ability of malware detection model to classify benign application as benign and malware application at malware. A Perfect classification model has an ideal AUC value of 1.

4   Experimental Analysis and Results

Firstly the opcode frequencies extracted from Android applications are embedded in the feature vector space. Analyzing the feature vector, we found that 44 opcodes out of 256 have never been used by any Android application (malicious or benign). Out of the above set, 26 opcodes are named as *unused_** and are reserved for future use by Android OS. Further analyzing the feature vector, we found that all the Android applications (malware and benign) are not of the same size. Thus the number of opcodes in each application will also not be the same. We propose the following Algorithm 1 for normalizing the feature vector. The algorithm first normalizes the opcodes based on Android application size and then based on their category (benign or malware). It also returns the k-prominent opcodes for further analysis to design Android malware detection models. Figure 1 shows top 15 prominent opcodes after preprocessing and sorted in descending order. Opcode *iget-object* has a maximum normalized frequency difference in malware and benign applications followed by *iget*, *const-string* and so on. It also signifies that the distribution of opcodes in malware and benign files are not the same. Some opcodes may be dominant in malicious Android applications, while others are more frequent in benign applications.

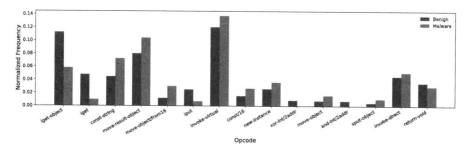

Fig. 1. Top 15 opcodes having maximum normalized frequency difference

Correlation is a statistical measure to indicate the relationship between two or more variables. Correlation analysis of Android malware dataset suggests that few opcode sets tend to occur more frequently in malicious apps. The top three opcode pairs in malicious apps having maximum correlations are {*monitor-enter & monitor-exit*}, {*add-double & sub-double*} and {*new-instance & invoke-direct*} with correlation values as 0.9993, 0.9846 and 0.9830 respectively. Similarly, co-correlation analysis of benign and malware apps separately indicates that the intersection of opcode pairs having high correlation values in both malicious and benign applications is negligible.

4.1   Feature Reduction

Since the feature vector consists of 256 opcodes with attribute type as continuous, thus the Android malware detection models built without any feature reduction is most likely to suffer from the curse of dimensionality. We used both categories of feature reduction methods: attribute sub-selection (viz. variance threshold) and new feature creation (viz. principal component analysis and autoencoders).

Variance Threshold (VT) is an unsupervised method used to remove noise and less relevant attributes from the dataset, thus removing opcodes having less prediction power. Figure 2 shows the top 30 opcodes having maximum variance in the complete dataset. Opcode *iget-object* has maximum variance followed by *invoke-virtual* and *move-result-object*. We removed opcodes having less prediction power, and thus the reduced feature vector from VT consists of top 30 opcodes having maximum variance.

Principal Component Analysis (PCA) is a data transformation technique that maps an input to a set of new orthogonal vectors. We performed PCA analysis on the original data and found that the number of principal components as 15 to be stable with different detection models. The Fig. 3 shows the two principal compeonts having the highest variance represented in x and y axis of the plot. The figure shows that most of the data points belonging to Android malware are restricted to one single region in the plot, while benign data points are distributed across the ranges of both the axes. Thus we can infer that malicious applications from a particular malware family will contain similar opcodes

---

Algorithm 1. Pseudocode for generating normalized features vector

---

Input: Pre-processed data

N_B: Number of benign applications

N_M: Number of malware applications

k: Total number of prominent opcodes required

n: Total number of opcodes in dataset

Output : List of sorted prominent opcodes

    for each file f **do**

        Compute sum of opcodes $\mathbf{Op_j}$ in file $\mathbf{f_i}$ and normalize it

        $f_i(Op_j) = f_i(Op_j)/(\sum_{j=1}^{n} f_i(Op_j))$

    end for

    for each opcode $\mathbf{Op_j}$ **do**

        Compute sum of frequencies of $\mathbf{Op_j}$ across all benign files $\mathbf{f_i}$ and normalize it to $\mathbf{F_B}(Op_j)$

        $F_B(Op_j) = (\sum_{i=1}^{N_B} f_i(Op_j))/N_B$

        Compute sum of frequencies of $\mathbf{Op_j}$ across all malware files $\mathbf{f_i}$ and normalize it to $\mathbf{F_M}(Op_j)$

        $F_M(Op_j) = (\sum_{i=1}^{N_M} f_i(Op_j))/N_M$

    end for

    for all opcodes $\mathbf{Op_j}$ **do**

        Find the difference of the normalized frequencies for each opcode $\mathbf{D(Op_j)}$

        $D(Op_j) =\mid F_B(Op_j) - F_M(Op_j) \mid$

    end for

    return k number of prominent opcodes with high $D(Op)$

---

with limited frequency ranges. In contrast, benign applications will be spread more exhaustively in the vector space.

Auto Encoder is an unsupervised learning technique based on deep neural networks used for dimensionality reduction. Autoencoder receives the data in the input layer and compresses it with encoding layers until the bottleneck layer. Further decoding layers in the network will uncompress the data to match the original data closely. Since the feature set consists of 256 attributes, the input and output layer in all the autoencoders contains 256 nodes. We have designed two different auto-encoders to produce two different data transformations on feature set:

- **1-layer Auto Encoder (AE-1L)** consists of the input layer, one encoding layer, and the output/decoding layer. The overall architecture of the AE-1L is 256-64-256
- **3-layer (stacked) Auto Encoder (AE-3)** consists of the input layer, three encoding layers of sizes 64, 32, 16 nodes consecutively, and three decoding layers of sizes 32, 64 and 256 nodes. The overall architecture of AE-3L is 256-64-32-16-32-64-256

All encoding and decoding layers of the two autoencoders are fully-connected and use the exponential linear unit (ELU) function for activation. ELU is used

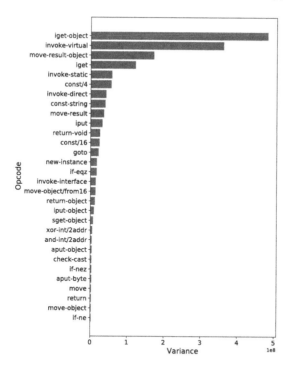

Fig. 2. Top 30 opcodes having maximum variance

over the rectified linear unit (ReLU) because it converges faster due to the smooth function. Since the autoencoders are prone to overfitting, dropout is used for better generalization. A drop probability of 0.4 was set to all hidden layers of AE-3 (layers with 32 and 64 nodes) except the bottleneck layer. All the autoencoders use Adam Optimizer with a learning rate of 0.001 and are trained over 100 epochs with a batch size of 32 samples. A validation set of 20% of the entire samples was separated to verify the results. As the goal is to reconstruct the input, Mean Squared Error (MSE) function was used to compare the loss between the original input and the produced output. During the AE training, the training and validation loss decreases steeply in the initial epochs since the autoencoder can perform reconstruction with a fast pace, after which further decrease in loss is prolonged because the bottleneck layer does not allow 100% reconstruction.

4.2   Baseline Malware Detection Models

We used three diverse categories of classification algorithms to build the Android malware detection system. The first set consists of classical machine learning classifiers viz. Decision Tree (DT), k-Nearest Neighbors (kNN) and Support Vector Machine (SVM) while the second set consists of ensemble classifier viz.

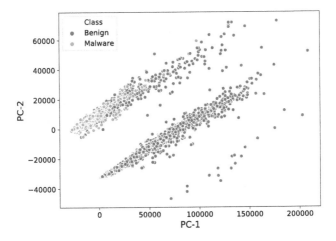

Fig. 3. PC-1 and PC-2 from PCA

Random Forest (RF), and Adaptive Boosting (AdaBoost). The third set uses deep learning to build three models based on deep neural network.

Malware Detection using Classical Machine Learning: DT is a tree-based classification algorithm used for predictive modelling. We used the GINI criterion for splitting the tree nodes with minimum samples required for the split set as two. The DT models were built without any restriction on tree depth or minimum applications needed in the leaf node. For the construction of kNN models, we considered five nearest neighbours and Euclidean distance was used to identify the neighbours. Also, equal weights were assigned to all the neighbours for voting. We train the SVM models using a linear kernel with penalty term C and tolerance for stopping criterion set to 1.0 and $1e-3$ respectively. Table 1 and Sect. 4.3 discuss the performance of the Android malware detection models built using the above classification algorithms with different feature reduction techniques based on different evaluation metrics.

Malware Detection Using Ensemble Learning: RF is an ensemble learning method which employs bagged DT. Our RF model uses an ensemble of 100 DTs, with the GINI index used as a criterion for determining best split. There was no constraint imposed on tree depth, the maximum number of leaf nodes in DT or number of samples required for a node split. Our AdaBoost model was an ensemble of 100 estimators, where the base estimator is a DT classifier with maximum depth as 1. Also, the learning rate from each model was set to 1. SAMME.R was used as the boosting algorithm. Performance of the ensemble learning models for Android malware detection are shown and discussed in Table 1 and Sect. 4.3 respectively.

Malware Detection Using Deep Neural Network: For classification of malicious Android applications, we train three different deep neural networks models with varying (shallow to deep network) architecture:

- **2-layer Deep Neural Network (DNN-2L)** contains one hidden layers with 64 nodes. The final architecture of DNN-2L is 256-64-1
- **4-layer Deep Neural Network (DNN-4L)** is a deeper network containing three hidden layers with 128, 32 and 8 nodes respectively. The final architecture of DNN-4L is 256-128-32-8-1
- **7-layer Deep Neural Network (DNN-7L)** contains six hidden layers with 128, 64, 32, 8, and 4 nodes. The final architecture of DNN-7L is 256-128-64-32-8-4-1

After each hidden layer in all the above networks, a dropout layer with probability as 0.4 has been added to prevent overfitting. The hidden layers use ELU as the activation function, while the output layer uses sigmoid activation (since the output is a probability for binary classification). Adam optimizer with the learning rate of 0.001 was used for training. Since it is a binary classification problem, the loss function used is binary cross-entropy. The differentiable nature of binary cross-entropy loss function will allow fast convergence. The entire dataset is split into 80:20 where 80% is used for training, and the remaining 20% is used for testing. The training set is further split to give a 20% validation split to analyze and tune the model learning during the training phase. The overall training is performed for 200 epochs with a batch size of 32. During training, the accuracy of the training and validation set was low during the initial epochs, but as the model starts to learn the accuracy increased in the future epochs. Detailed performance results of DNNs for malware detection are listed in Table 1 and discussed in Sect. 4.3.

4.3   Discussion

Table 1 illustrates the performance of different Android malware detection models based on different evaluation metrics.

In terms of Accuracy, RF outperforms all other machine learning and deep neural network models. It achieves the highest accuracy of 95.7% when trained on original data. RF achieved the second & third highest accuracy with VT & AE-1L data reduction technique.

As far as AUC is concerned, RF with any data reduction technique is more balanced & achieves more area under curve compared to any other classifier. RF (original data) attains AUC of 99.4, followed by RF (VT data), RF (AE-1L data), & RF (PCA data). High AUC score of RF models signifies that it can fit both malware and benign class properly without much variance.

Analyzing the recall, SVM achieves highest TPR of 98.7 with PCA data followed by SVM (VT data), DNN-7L (PCA data) and DNN-2L (PCA data). Also for all the above models, higher TPR was achieved at the cost of very low TNR. In other words, the above models form a decision boundary which is skewed and highly favours the positive class: thus classifying even benign applications as malicious, which makes malware detection system unreliable. The exact number of false alarms by SVM (PCA data) and SVM (VT data) were 2517 and 2203 respectively, which is very high for any real-time deployment. On the other hand,

Table 1. Performance of different Classification Algorithms combined Feature Reduction

Feature Reduction	No of features	Classification Algorithm	Accuracy	TPR	TNR	AUC	F1 Score	Train Time (sec)	Test Time (sec)
Original Data	256	DT[5]	93.0	94.7	91.4	93.1	93.0	6.65955	0.01028
VT[1]	30	DT	91.6	93.3	90.0	91.6	91.6	1.20814	0.00363
PCA[2]	15	DT	90.4	92.3	88.5	90.4	90.4	0.73475	**0.00268**
AE-1L[3]	64*	DT	91.4	93.3	89.6	91.4	91.5	3.18144	0.00551
AE-3L[4]	16*	DT	90.5	92.7	88.4	90.5	90.6	3.10379	0.00565
Original Data	256	kNN[6]	92.3	94.7	90.0	97.0	92.4	1.22648	24.39308
VT	30	kNN	91.1	94.2	88.1	96.3	91.2	0.12977	1.23292
PCA	15	kNN	90.5	93.7	87.5	95.9	90.7	**0.05033**	0.57151
AE-1L	64*	kNN	91.5	95.3	87.8	96.3	91.7	3.50612	20.80623
AE-3L	16*	kNN	89.9	93.2	86.7	95.7	90.1	3.97619	19.77041
Original Data	256	SVM[7]	84.5	96.3	73.1	93.3	86.0	108.1359	18.91573
VT	30	SVM	79.6	98.2	61.5	88.6	82.6	16.00776	2.14833
PCA	15	SVM	77.0	**98.7**	56.0	85.0	80.9	12.65536	1.17977
AE-1L	64*	SVM	82.5	96.0	69.4	92.6	84.4	119.1237	20.51435
AE-3L	16*	SVM	79.9	97.4	62.9	89.3	82.6	131.9112	22.92997
Original Data	256	RF[8]	**95.7**	96.4	**95.1**	**99.4**	**95.7**	21.4354	0.27449
VT	30	RF	94.5	96.0	94.3	99.1	94.5	14.54262	0.25277
PCA	15	RF	93.2	94.9	91.5	98.7	93.2	12.49487	0.2612
AE-1L	64*	RF	94.3	96.1	92.6	99.0	94.3	15.76513	0.27906
AE-3L	16*	RF	93.0	95.1	90.9	98.6	93.0	15.30469	0.2838
Original Data	256	AdaBoost[9]	92.9	94.2	91.6	98.2	92.8	65.8992	0.38113
VT	30	AdaBoost	90.3	93.8	86.8	96.3	90.5	16.54785	0.25632
PCA	15	AdaBoost	88.0	92.6	83.5	95.0	88.4	11.99837	0.2447
AE-1L	64*	AdaBoost	90.1	93.0	87.4	96.7	90.3	53.41497	0.37953
AE-3L	16*	AdaBoost	87.6	91.9	83.4	95.2	87.9	52.36362	0.37849
Original Data	256	DNN-2L[10]	91.7	95.5	87.9	91.7	91.9	408.0807	0.92617
VT	30	DNN-2L	86.6	96.6	76.8	86.7	87.7	392.182	1.49585
PCA	15	DNN-2L	79.4	97.6	61.6	79.6	82.4	418.8092	1.87103
AE-1L	64*	DNN-2L	89.8	92.9	86.8	89.9	90.0	409.074	1.06848
AE-3L	16*	DNN-2L	87.1	93.5	80.8	87.2	87.7	421.9584	1.21068
Original Data	256	DNN-4L[11]	93.7	93.4	94.0	93.7	93.7	561.4316	2.59779
VT	30	DNN-4L	89.5	92.5	86.5	89.5	89.7	542.6468	3.921
PCA	15	DNN-4L	84.9	96.9	73.2	85.0	86.4	531.3042	4.63093
AE-1L	64*	DNN-4L	91.9	92.1	91.8	91.9	91.9	536.8712	2.8647
AE-3L	16*	DNN-4L	89.6	93.7	85.5	89.6	89.9	561.4489	3.21776
Original Data	256	DNN-7L[12]	91.8	87.5	92.6	91.7	91.3	663.8196	5.68757
VT	30	DNN-7L	91.7	90.4	93.0	91.7	91.5	648.3339	8.08047
PCA	15	DNN-7L	83.6	97.9	68.6	83.8	85.7	714.5312	9.26997
AE-1L	64*	DNN-7L	91.6	89.5	93.6	91.5	91.3	697.7748	6.12618
AE-3L	16*	DNN-7L	90.3	92.5	88.2	90.3	90.4	730.9962	6.87906

[1] Variance Threshold [2] Principal Component Analysis [3] 1-layer Auto Encoder [4] 3-layer Auto Encoder [5] Decision Tree [6] k-Nearest Neighbour [7] Support Vector Machine [8] Random Forest [9] Adaptive Boosting [10] 2-layer Deep Neural Network [11] 4-layer Deep Neural Network [12] 7-layer Deep Neural Network

RF (original data) produces the best TNR of 95.1 followed by RF (VT data). A point to note here is RF (original data) archives less number of FP (280) and FN (201), making it more stable and reliable classifier. As expected SVM (PCA data) produces the worst TNR of 56.0 since it is overfitting the malware class.

Model building (training time) is a one-time activity. Thus after building the classification model once, it can iteratively be used for testing new Android applications. kNN (PCA data) and kNN (VT data) take the least time to train model since kNN classifier does not build a model as such. kNN only performs pre-processing during model training, and thus it takes more time during the testing phase as it is seen for kNN (PCA data) and kNN (VT data). Also, the performance of kNN becomes worse as numbers of dimensions are increased to original data because of the Euclidian distance calculation to find neighbours. Also, while comparing the training time, all deep neural networks have a higher training time than any machine learning model, which can be attributed to the multiple epochs over which these networks need to be trained.

For the testing time, tree-based classifiers like DT (PCA data) and DT (VT data) perform the best. Also, RF (VT data) and RF (PCA data) take 0.25 s and 0.26 s respectively for testing with an ensemble of 100 trees. In the above cases, PCA data and VT data are performing better because they have less number of features as compared to original data. Thus it is a tradeoff between accuracy and testing time.

4.4   Malware Detection Models Based on Classification Integrated with Clustering

As discussed in Sect. 4.3, many classifiers (namely SVM (original data), SVM (VT data), DNN-2L (VT data) etc.) were overfitting the malware class (vector space) which decreases the overall performance of the Android malware detection system. Now we plan to divide the vector space (11138 × 256) with clustering into smaller vector spaces (clusters). The idea is instead of building a highly complex malware detection model which may underfit/overfit a particular class, the vector space itself can be segregated into smaller vector spaces (clusters). Then different/same detection models can be trained on each of these smaller vector spaces (clusters), thus solving overall underfitting/overfitting problem. The above approach is intuitive as well because malicious Android applications come from a very restricted vector space often bounded by their malware family (refer Fig. 3). At the same time, there is no such limitation with the benign applications which are very diverse (refer Fig. 3). Thus we chose five different clustering algorithms (k-means, Agglomerative, BIRCH, DBSCAN, and GMM). The first 3 algorithms use a centre-based clustering approach while DBSCAN uses density measure, and GMM works on the probability distribution.

k-means follows the centre-based clustering approach with a cost function set to minimize SSE. However, it cannot find an optimal number of cluster (k) on its own. Thus we first used k-means clustering on the dataset to form clusters and then used the elbow method, Silhouette Score and Calinksi-Harabaz Score to find the optimal number of clusters. The elbow method analysis (refer Fig. 4) suggests that the optimal number of cluster(s) in the dataset is either 2 or 3. Also, the result of Silhouette Score and Calinksi-Harabaz Score shown in Table 2 concludes $k = 2$ as an optimal value. The highest Silhouette Score (0.74031) and Calinksi-Harabaz Score (27808.68) among all the clustering algorithms was achieved by k-means clustering algorithm with ($k = 2$). **Agglomerative clustering** with the bottom-up approach was used with Dendogram (refer Fig. 5), Silhouette Score and Calinksi-Harabaz Score to find the optimal number of clusters. We performed cluster analysis with cluster numbers as 2, 3, 4, 5 and achieved highest Silhouette Score (0.72839) and Calinksi-Harabaz Score (24025.74) when the number of clusters was set as 2 (refer Table 2). **BIRCH** is used to validate the scalability of the model, and it again follows the centre-based clustering approach. The highest Silhouette Score (0.72852) and Calinksi-Harabaz Score (24055.01) (refer Table 2) was yet again achieved at the number of clusters as 2 during cluster analysis with different cluster number (2, 3, 4, 5). **GMM and DBSCAN** performed poorly on the dataset with Silhouette Score and Calinksi Harabaz Score being the lowest among all the clustering algorithm at 0.20257 and 8117.87 with GMM (refer Table 2), and 0.55487 and 1348.71 with DBSCAN (refer Table 2) respectively.

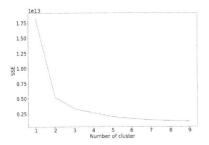

Fig. 4. Elbow Method (k-means Clustering)

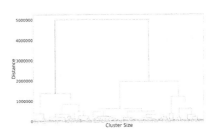

Fig. 5. Dendogram (Agglomerative Clustering)

Finally, we chose the k-means clustering algorithm (with $k = 2$) for cluster formation in the dataset since it has achieved the highest Silhouette Score and Calinksi-Harabaz Score among all the other algorithms (refer Table 2). After clustering the number of Android applications in Cluster-1 and Cluster-2 were 8, 344 and is 2, 794 respectively.

Table 2. Cluster formation using different Clustering Algorithms

Clustering Algorithm	No of Clusters	Silhouetee Score	Calinski Harabaz Score
k-means Clustering	2	0.74031	27808.68
	3	0.70380	24853.64
	4	0.61534	21623.26
	5	0.61141	22322.77
Agglomerative Clustering	2	0.72839	24025.74
	3	0.70970	20666.88
	4	0.55662	18818.29
	5	0.55554	19256.05
BIRCH Clustering	2	0.72852	24055.01
	3	0.70320	21479.21
	4	0.59214	20325.78
	5	0.58732	19735.05
GMM Clustering	2	0.20257	8117.87
	3	0.20257	2687.21
	4	0.11263	1634.45
	5	0.25938	5188.62
DBSCAN Clustering	5000 (eps)	0.55487	1348.71
	10000 (eps)	0.53745	3381.47
	15000 (eps)	0.67839	3638.12
	20000 (eps)	0.68565	4719.16

Table 3. Performance of Different Classifiers in Cluster-1

Feature Reduction	Classifier	Accuracy	TPR	TNR	AUC	F1 Score	Train Time (sec)	Test Time (sec)
Original Data	DT[1]	93.7	94.7	91.6	93.7	93.6	4.31299	**0.00936**
Original Data	kNN[2]	93.8	92.7	94.0	97.2	92.4	**0.84515**	18.99223
Original Data	SVM[3]	80.9	93.3	68.5	92.0	81.0	92.24813	17.99223
Original Data	RF[4]	**96.9**	96.2	**97.9**	**99.6**	**96.8**	16.26439	0.21686
Original Data	AdaBoost[5]	92.9	93.3	92.5	97.4	92.3	57.96454	0.25266
Original Data	DNN-2L[6]	92.1	89.5	94.7	92.1	91.6	332.88325	0.74821
Original Data	DNN-4L[7]	94.1	**96.3**	89.9	93.1	93.2	454.42803	1.97307
Original Data	DNN-7L[8]	93.7	91.0	96.4	93.7	93.5	583.60624	4.18910

[1] Decision Tree [2] k-Nearest Neighbour [3] Support Vector Machine [4] Random Forest [5] Adaptive Boosting [6] 2-layer Deep Neural Network [7] 4-layer Deep Neural Network [8] 7-layer Deep Neural Network

Cluster-1 Analysis: The Cluster-1 contains both malicious and benign applications. So we applied all the classifiers with similar parameters (Table 1) and achieved the results (refer to Table 3). Once again tree-based classifiers outperform all the classifiers. RF and DT have shown improvement in all metrics where RF outperforms DT. There has been 1.2% improvement in the accuracy and F1 score of RF from without the cluster approach. Other classifiers also performed better as compared to without the clustering approach.

Cluster-2 Analysis: Interestingly Cluster-2 had over 98% of benign applications with only 2% of malicious samples. On further analysis of malware applications in the cluster, we found that the majority of them belong to only two families (*Fatakr* and *Steek*). Thus it clearly shows instead of building a single complex classifier for the complete dataset, segregation of vector space can give better insights on the data and yield better results.

5   Conclusions and Future Work

Today Android mobile phones are growing exponentially, but traditional malware detection systems are failing to cope up with the volume, velocity, and sophistication of malware attacks performed on these devices. In this paper, we proposed to used machine learning and deep neural network integrated with clustering for detection of malicious Android applications. We conducted a comprehensive analysis with different feature reduction, classification and clustering techniques to propose effective and efficient Android malware detection models.

Our baseline experimental results for Android malware detection models show that RF built without feature reduction achieved the highest ROC (99.4), accuracy (95.7%), TNR (95.1), and F1 score (95.7). In fact, RF also performed better regarding the accuracy, ROC and F1 metric with any feature reduction method vis-à-vis other models with the same feature reduction method. Also, RF is more balanced (TPR $\sim$ TNR) and can fit both the malware and benign classes without much variance. Regarding training and testing time, tree-based classifiers viz. (RF) performed better than other classifiers, and is approximately 100 and 500 faster than DNN models respectively. Analyzing the other classifiers (viz. kNN, SVM), we found that they tend to over-fit malware class despite using cross-validation during model construction. A possible explanation is malware variants from a malware family tend to be similar to each other. Thus will be projected close to each other in the vector space while benign samples are well separated in the feature vector.

Our empirical results (clustering integrated with classification) show further improvement in AUC (99.6) and accuracy of RF (96.9%) in the cluster-1 and also direct identification of malware applications of the two families in another cluster. The experimental results shows that constructing a single highly complex detection model might overfit/underfit data and suffer from the curse of dimensionality. Thus first segregation of vector space (clusters) using clustering followed by classification can further improve the performance of detection models.

Another contribution of our study is the performance of DNN for Android malware detection. We designed autoencoders (AE-1L (shallow) and AE-3L (deep)) and DNN of different sizes (DNN-2L, DNN-4L, and DNN-7L). Surprisingly none of the combinations of autoencoder and DNN performed well.

One explanation could be a combination of complex feature reduction function, and sophisticated classifier leads to overfitting despite using drop out for generalization.

Further, it will be interesting to see the performance of other deep learning based feature reduction techniques like sparse, denoising, variational based autoencoders coupled with classification techniques like Hopfield Network, Sequence-to-sequence model etc.

References

1. Arp, D., Spreitzenbarth, M., Hubner, M., Gascon, H., Rieck, K.: Drebin: effective and explainable detection of android malware in your pocket. In: Network and Distributed System Security (NDSS) Symposium, vol. 14, pp. 23–26 (2014)
2. Buczak, A.L., Guven, E.: A survey of data mining and machine learning methods for cyber security intrusion detection. IEEE Commun. Surv. Tutor. **18**(2), 1153–1176 (2015)
3. Chau, M., Reith, R., (IDC-Corporate): Smartphone Market Share (2018). https://www.idc.com/promo/smartphone-market-share/os. Accessed May 2020
4. Clooke, R. :(GDATA) Cyber attacks on Android devices on the rise (2018). https://www.idc.com/promo/smartphone-market-share/os. Accessed May 2020
5. Egele, M., Scholte, T., Kirda, E., Kruegel, C.: A survey on automated dynamic malware-analysis techniques and tools. ACM Comput. Surv. (CSUR) **44**(2), 1–42 (2008)
6. Ganesh, M., Pednekar, P., Prabhuswamy, P., Nair, D.S., Park, Y., Jeon, H.: CNN-based android malware detection. In: International Conference on Software Security and Assurance (ICSSA), pp. 60–65. IEEE (2017)
7. Griffin, K., Schneider, S., Hu, X., Chiueh, T.: Automatic generation of string signatures for malware detection. In: Kirda, E., Jha, S., Balzarotti, D. (eds.) RAID 2009. LNCS, vol. 5758, pp. 101–120. Springer, Heidelberg (2009). https://doi.org/10.1007/978-3-642-04342-0_6
8. Henchiri, O., Japkowicz, N.: A feature selection and evaluation scheme for computer virus detection. In: 6th International Conference on Data Mining (ICDM'06), pp. 891–895. IEEE (2006)
9. Hou, S., Saas, A., Ye, Y., Chen, L.: DroidDelver: an android malware detection system using deep belief network based on API call blocks. In: Song, S., Tong, Y. (eds.) WAIM 2016. LNCS, vol. 9998, pp. 54–66. Springer, Cham (2016). https://doi.org/10.1007/978-3-319-47121-1_5
10. Kemp, S.:(WeAreSocial) Global Digital Report (2018). https://digitalreport.wearesocial.com/. Accessed May 2020
11. Li, W., Wang, Z., Cai, J., Cheng, S.: An android malware detection approach using weight-adjusted deep learning. In: International Conference on Computing, Networking and Communications (ICNC), pp. 437–441. IEEE (2018)
12. Lindorfer, M., Neugschwandtner, M., Weichselbaum, L., Fratantonio, Y., Van Der Veen, V., Platzer, C.: Andrubis-1,000,000 apps later: a view on current android malware behaviors. In: 3rd International Workshop on Building Analysis Datasets and Gathering Experience Returns for Security (BADGERS), pp. 3–17. IEEE (2014)
13. Peng, H., Long, F., Ding, C.: Feature selection based on mutual information: criteria of max-dependency, max-relevance, and min-redundancy. IEEE Trans. Pattern Anal. Mach. Intell. **8**, 1226–1238 (2005)

14. Rastogi, V., Chen, Y., Jiang, X.: Droidchameleon: evaluating android anti-malware against transformation attacks. In: 8th ACM SIGSAC Symposium on Information, Computer and Communications Security (ASIA CCS), pp. 329–334. ACM (2013)

15. Sarma, B.P., Li, N., Gates, C., Potharaju, R., Nita-Rotaru, C., Molloy, I.: Android permissions: a perspective combining risks and benefits. In: 17th ACM Symposium on Access Control Models and Technologies (SACMAT), pp. 13–22. ACM (2012)

16. Sewak, M., Sahay, S.K., Rathore, H.: An investigation of a deep learning based malware detection system. In: 13th International Conference on Availability, Reliability and Security (ARES), pp. 1–5 (2018)

17. Sewak, M., Sahay, S.K., Rathore, H.: DOOM: a novel adversarial-DRL-based opcode level metamorphic malware obfuscator for the enhancement of ids. In: Adjunct Proceedings of the 2020 ACM International Joint Conference on Pervasive and Ubiquitous Computing and Proceedings of the 2020 ACM International Symposium on Wearable Computers, pp. 131–134 (2020)

18. Sewak, M., Sahay, S.K., Rathore, H.: An overview of deep learning architecture of deep neural networks and autoencoders. J. Comput. Theor. Nanosci. **17**(1), 182–188 (2020)

19. Sharma, A., Sahay, S.K.: An investigation of the classifiers to detect android malicious apps. In: Mishra, D., Azar, A., Joshi, A. (eds.) Information and Communication Technology. AISC, vol. 625, pp. 207–217. Springer, Singapore (2018). https://doi.org/10.1007/978-981-10-5508-9_20

20. Sun, L., Li, Z., Yan, Q., Srisa-an, W., Pan, Y.: SIGPID: significant permission identification for android malware detection. In: 11th International Conference on Malicious and Unwanted Software (MALWARE), pp. 1–8. IEEE (2016)

21. Symantec: Internet Security Threat Report (ISTR), Volume 24, February 2019. https://www.symantec.com/content/dam/symantec/docs/reports/istr-24-2019-en.pdf. Accessed May 2020

22. Turner, A.:(BankMyCell) How many smartphones are in the world? (2020). https://www.bankmycell.com/blog/how-many-phones-are-in-the-world. Accessed May 2020

23. Wang, Z., Cai, J., Cheng, S., Li, W.: Droiddeeplearner: identifying android malware using deep learning. In: IEEE 37th Sarnoff Symposium, pp. 160–165. IEEE (2016)

24. Wu, D.J., Mao, C.H., Wei, T.E., Lee, H.M., Wu, K.P.: Droidmat: android malware detection through manifest and API calls tracing. In: Asia Joint Conference on Information Security (AsiaJCIS), pp. 62–69. IEEE (2012)

25. Xu, M., et al.: Toward engineering a secure android ecosystem: a survey of existing techniques. ACM Comput. Surv. (CSUR) **49**(2), 1–47 (2016)

26. Yan, P., Yan, Z.: A survey on dynamic mobile malware detection. Softw. Q. J. **26**(3), 891–919 (2018)

27. Yang, W., Xiao, X., Andow, B., Li, S., Xie, T., Enck, W.: Appcontext: differentiating malicious and benign mobile app behaviors using context. In: 37th International Conference on Software Engineering (ICSE), pp. 303–313. IEEE (2015)

28. Ye, Y., Li, T., Adjeroh, D., Iyengar, S.S.: A survey on malware detection using data mining techniques. ACM Comput. Surv. (CSUR) **50**(3), 41 (2017)

29. Zhou, Y., Jiang, X.: Dissecting android malware: characterization and evolution. In: IEEE Symposium on Security and Privacy (IEEE S&P), pp. 95–109. IEEE (2012)

Go2Edge - Edge Computing Networks, Systems and Services

Experimental Evaluation of RSA Algorithms for SDN-Programmable VCSEL-Based S-BVT in High-Capacity and Cost-Efficient Optical Metro Networks

Ricardo Martinez[1]($\boxtimes$), Ramon Casellas[1], Michela Svaluto Moreolo[1],
Josep Maria Fabrega[1], Ricard Vilalta[1], Raul Munoz[1], Laia Nadal[1],
Juan Pedro Fernández Palacios[2], Víctor López[2], David Larrabeiti[3], and Gabriel Otero[3]

[1] Centre Tecnològic de Telecomunicacions de Catalunya (CERCA/CTTC), Castelldefels, Spain
ricardo.martinez@cttc.es
[2] Telefónica I+D, GTCO, Madrid, Spain
[3] Universidad Carlos III, Madrid, Spain

Abstract. Future metro networks need to increase the transport capacity and improve the cost- and power-efficiency. These challenges are tackled by the EU-H2020 PASSION project exploiting dense photonic integration and cost-efficient optical technologies. Specifically, PASSION investigates a) modular sliceable bandwidth variable transceivers (S-BVTs) built upòn a set of both vertical cavity surface emitting lasers (VCSEL) and Coherent Receivers (CO-Rx); and b) hierarchical switching nodes in a flexigrid network. An SDN controller handles the network programmability where a key functionality is the path computation and resource selection to fulfil the connection requirements. This is conducted by the Routing and Spectrum Assignment (RSA) algorithms. The considered S-BVT transmitter imposes that each S-BVT VCSEL reaches up to 50 Gb/s. Thus, connections requesting higher bandwidth (e.g., 200 Gb/s) are accommodated over several optical flows. In this context, two RSA algorithms called *co-routed* (RSA-CR) and *inversed multiplexed* (RSA-IM) optical flows are proposed and compared. The RSA-CR enforces that all the connection's optical flows are routed over the same spatial path; the RSA-IM relaxes this allowing the optical flows being set up over different spatial routes. The experimental evaluation, made upon dynamic traffic, aims at comparing both RSA algorithms performance according to the blocked bandwidth ratio, the average used of S-BVT devices, and the average setup time.

Keywords: SDN · Flexi-grid metro networks · S-BVT

1 Introduction

The design of the metro networks is becoming crucial to deal with the requirements bound to the 5G services with respect to both huge transport capacity and very high dynamicity.

H. Gao et al. (Eds.): BROADNETS 2020, LNICST 355, pp. 131–142, 2021.
https://doi.org/10.1007/978-3-030-68737-3_8

In this context, as discussed in [1], 33% of the total transport capacity offered by the telecom operators will strictly remain within the metro networks. Thereby, such network segments need to be enhanced to support not only fully programable infrastructure, but also efficiently designed to lower operational and capital expenditures (e.g., cost, energy consumption, etc.) [2]. These challenges are being investigated within the EU H2020 PASSION project [5]. PASSION project aims at exploiting the advantages of programmable and photonic technologies over flexigrid networks [3] such as optical transceivers.

The automatic network configuration is attained by a centralized Software-Defined Networking (SDN) controller. This controller uses defined control interfaces (APIs) to interact with the control agents locally handling the programmability of every underlying network element and/or devices (i.e., optical switch and transceivers). To offer high transport capacity (i.e., Tb/s) at low cost and power within the metro networks, the PASSION project defines and deploys a modular sliceable bandwidth transceiver (S-BVT). This S-BVT leverages new appealing photonic technologies such as the vertical cavity surface emitting laser (VCSEL) at long wavelengths [4]. Moreover, the targeted metro network is formed by heterogenous optical switches providing both the transport as well as the aggregation functions of the optical flows. These optical switches are associated to a so-called Hierarchical Level (HL). As described in [5], four HLs are considered, namely: HL4, HL3 and HL2/1. Each of them defines specific switch characteristics such as the capability of either originate/terminate optical flows (i.e., add/drop operations) or enabling optical bypassing. In brief, HL4 and HL2/1 nodes border the access and core network segments, respectively; HL3 nodes are the transit optical switches interconnecting both HL4 and HL2/1 nodes. In this work, optical connections are always set up from HL4 to HL2/1 (an vice versa) traversing HL3 switches.

In the PASSION-designed S-BVTs, each constituting VCSEL element has a 20 GHz-bandwidth providing up to 50 Gb/s (r^{VCSEL}). Optical connections requests (*req*) may demand larger bandwidth (*b*) than r^{VCSEL}, e.g., 100, 200, or 400 Gb/s. This entails to allocate N (≥ 1) VCSELs (operating at different wavelengths) at the corresponding ingress S-BVT device to accommodate a *req*. Consequently, N different optical flows may need to be set up between the ingress and egress nodes. As an example, a *req* demanding 200 Gb/s requires allocating 4 different VCSELs at the ingress node, 4 Co-Rxs at the egress node, and 4 optical flows over the route interconnecting the ingress and the egress nodes. It is worth outlining that every individual optical flow occupies its own S-BVT VCSEL and Co-Rx at the ingress and egress nodes, as well as allocates a dedicated optical spectrum over the traversed path's links. Herein the occupied optical spectrum by an optical flow is referred to as Frequency Slot (FS).

The physical impairments accumulated over the optical signal while travelling from the source to the destination may end up with a received net data rata lower than r^{VCSEL}. To model this, in [5] it was defined three different received data rates for the same VCSEL associated to the so-called *operational modes* (OMs): *high, medium,* and *low.* Specifically, each OM determines different supported data rates depending on the maximum end-to-end path distance (km) and number of hops. Figure 1 lists for each defined VCSEL OM the data rate at the receiver as long as the maximum values for the route distance (i.e., aggregating the fiber length of all the traversed links) and the number of traversed optical switches (i.e., hops) are not exceeded.

VCSEL Mode (*OM*)	*r* (Gb/s)	Max. Distance (km); #Hops
High	50	30; 5
Medium	40	75; 9
Low	25	150; 15

Fig. 1. Defined VCSEL Operational Modes (OMs) describing the data rate (Gb/s), maximum path distance (km) and number of hops.

In [5], the authors presented and evaluated a Routing and Spectrum Assignment (RSA) algorithm which dynamically serves connection requests demanding different bandwidth (i.e., data rate) over the PASSION metro network solution (i.e., using the above HL nodes and the VCSELs' OMs). This RSA algorithm builds upon a modified K shortest path (K-SP) referred to as co-routed optical flows (RSA-CR). For a given *req*, the RSA-CR algorithm computes the necessary optical flows to fulfil the *req*'s bandwidth (i.e., *b*) considering the most convenient VCSEL's OM. For the sake of clarification, the most convenient OM means to foster selecting those paths enabling the VCSELs at the ingress nodes attaining the highest net data rates at the receiver. All the resulting optical flows from the RSA output are set up along the same spatial path (i.e., nodes and links) but occupying different FSs. The latter entails that each optical flow also occupies different S-BVT VCSELs and CO-Rxs. Bearing this in mind, herein we extend [5] proposing an RSA-CR algorithm variant. The new RSA algorithm leverages the *inverse multiplexing* capability within flexigrid optical networks [6]. That is, *req*'s optical flows can be routed over different spatial paths. The algorithm is referred to as RSA inverse multiplexed (RSA-IM) optical flows.

Both algorithms (RSA-CR and RSA-IM) are experimentally evaluated within the CTTC ADRENALINE testbed considering dynamic connection request with different bandwidth needs. The obtained results and comparison are realized using three performance metrics: the *blocked bandwidth ratio* (BBR), the average number of occupied S-BVTs VCSELs and CO-Rxs, and the average connection establishment (setup) time.

2 Targeted Optical Metro Network

Figure 2 depicts a candidate PASSION SDN-controlled flexi-grid optical metro network topology. All the *req*s arrive to the SDN controller from a Connection Request Application requests (via a RESTful API). The SDN controller is then in charge to compute the path and select the resources triggering the RSA algorithms. If the RSA succeeds, the selected resources are configured via dedicated control interfaces (RESTful API) as detailed in [5].

In the following, a description of the metro optical infrastructure involving the S-BVT and HL optical switches is provided. Next, it is also reported the key functions and operations handled by the SDN controller to attain the automatic configuration of the underlying transport network and devices when setting up connections.

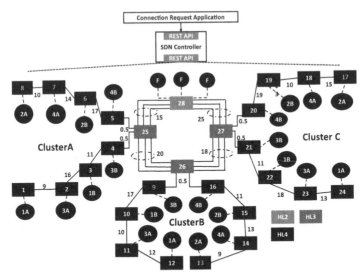

Fig. 2. Targeted SDN-controlled optical metro network.

2.1 Network Topology, S-BVTs and Optical Switches Features

The metro network topology is a star-ring infrastructure with three *clusters* (i.e., A, B and C). A cluster is made up of a pair of linear networks connected to a 4-node ring topology. Each linear network constitutes a *branch*. All the nodes are associated to a specific HL type as mentioned above. HL4 nodes (black squares in Fig. 2) deal with the access traffic aggregation. Additionally, HL4 node are equipped with an S-BVT. Formed by a single Module with 20 VCSELs. Thus, HL4 S-BVTs can provide a maximum capacity of 20 $\times r^{VCSEL}$, i.e., 1 Tb/s (if all the VCSELs operate at the *high* OM). Analogously, HL4 S-BVT Rxs are deployed with 20 CO-Rxs. Each S-BVT VCSEL is bound to a specific wavelength within the 191.900–195.875 THz spectral range. As a result, to support in a *cluster* all the frequencies in the targeted range, it is needed that each cluster *branch* uses 4 HL4 nodes. The wavelengths in the 4 S-BVTs for each individual *branch* are separated 50 GHz. The considered wavelength planning is detailed in Fig. 3. Clusters' S-BVTs are named as 1A, 1B, 2A,…, 4B. In the HL4 cluster (formed by 2 branches) the resulting wavelengths among all the S-BVTs' VCSELs are spectrally separated 25 GHz. HL4 optical switches are constructed upon Array Wavelength Grating (AWG) filter of 50 GHz.

The HL3 nodes form the ring topology being shown in Fig. 2 as red squares. These optical switches enable the interconnection between HL4 and HL2/1 nodes and are built on 25 GHz filters using Wavelength Selective Switches. HL3 nodes exclusively support the optical aggregation and bypass without originating/terminating optical flows, i.e. HL3 nodes do not have S-BVTs.

Finally, the HL2/1 node (blue squares in Fig. 2) are also made up of 25 GHz WSSs and interface the core network segment with 3 fully equipped S-BVTs. As detailed in Fig. 3, these fully equipped S-BVTs have 160 VCSELs and 160 CO-Rxs. That is, all the targeted spectral range is covered by one of these S-BVTs offering a transmission capacity of up to $160 \times r^{VCSEL}$, i.e., 8 Tb/s.

The modularity of the S-BVT designed within the PASSION project is attained thanks to a hierarchical architectural approach made up of a 3-tuple Module/subModule/VCSELs. Detailed description of the PASSION S-BVT can be found in [4]. A Module represents an *atomic* S-BVT element based on a photonic integrated chip. Taking advantage of the so-called modularity capability, different Modules (up to 4) could be arranged to provide S-BVT offering larger transport capacity depending on the bandwidth needs. Every Module integrates 4 subModules. A subModule is formed by 10 VCSELs each. Consequently, a S-BVT made up of a single Module is able to provide at the transmitter a data rate of up to: 4 (subModules) $\times$ 10 VCSELs $\times r^{VCSEL}$, i.e., 2 Tb/s. In the HL2/1 S-BVTs, observe that the S-BVTs have 4 Modules which offers a maximum transmission capacity of 8 Tb/s. At the S-BVT Receiver (Rx), CO-Rxs with tunable local oscillators are used.

S-BVT	#VCSELs & CO-Rxs	Supported Frequencies (THz)
1A	20	191.900, 192.100, 192.300, ..., 195.700
1B	20	192.000, 192.200, 192.400, ..., 195.800
2A	20	191.925, 192.125, 192.325, ..., 195.725
2B	20	192.025, 192.225, 192.425, ..., 195.825
3A	20	191.950, 192.150, 193.350, ..., 195.750
3B	20	192.050, 192.250, 192.450, ..., 195.850
4A	20	191.975, 192.175, 192.375, ..., 195.775
4B	20	192.075, 192.275, 192.475, ..., 195.875
Full (F)	160	191.900, 191.925, 191.950, ..., 195.875

Fig. 3. S-BVT with number of deployed VCSELs and CO-Rx and the supported wavelengths.

2.2 SDN Network Programmability

In [7], it is detailed the design and validation of the SDN controller to handle the programmability of the targeted metro transport network and devices (i.e., S-BVTs and HL optical switches). Such an SDN controller architecture tackles:

- the RESTful API to receive connection requests (*req*),
- the RESTful APIs to communicate with the network elements and devices agents enabling the (de-)/allocation of the optical resources.
- the functions supporting the operations of the SDN controller.

The SDN controller functions enable a) handling the optical connection lifecycle (i.e., establishment and removal); b) collecting updated resource information from the network element and agents; and c) executing the RSA algorithm to seek for a feasible path and optical resources fulfilling the *req* demands as well as attaining an efficient use of the overall network resources. The following focuses on describing the devised RSA-CR and RSA-IM algorithms upon processing a new *req*.

3   Routing and Spectrum Assignment (RSA) Algorithms

Each received connection request (i.e., *req*) specifies the source and destination end-points (i.e., *s* and *d*, respectively) along with the required bandwidth (i.e., *b*). Regardless of the executed RSA algorithm (RSA-CR or RSA-IM), the inputs are: i) the network topology (i.e., node connectivity, link distance, etc.) and the available optical spectrum over each link; ii) the available S-BVT VCSEL and Co-Rx resources at *s* and *d* end-points, respectively. A successful RSA computation provides the following output: i) the nodes and links to be traversed by each optical flow; ii) the selected S-BVT VCSELs at *s*; iii) the CO-Rxs (with their tuned local oscillators) at *d*; iv) the optical spectrum (i.e., FS) to be allocated for each required optical flow.

3.1   RSA Co-routed (RSA-CR) Optical Flows

This algorithm was proposed and evaluated in [5]. It is based on a modified K shortest path (K-SP) mechanism. The aim of the RSA-CR algorithm is to serve a *req* satisfying the spectral constraints and achieving an efficient use of all the network resources. The RSA-CR returns the first kth SP that accommodates the set of optical flows for a *req* over the same nodes and links. To this end, the RSA-CR algorithm operates in a two-step approach. In step 1, it is computed the K-SPs between *req*'s *s* and *d* nodes. Then, in Step 2, for each computed kth path, starting from the highest VCSEL OM (see Fig. 1), it is first checked whether that path fulfills the targeted OM's maximum distance and number of hops. If yes, then it is determined the number of required S-BVT VCSELs and optical flows to satisfy the *req*'s *b*, as well as the optical spectrum assignment for the optical flows. For the latter, observe that it is needed to consider: i) the available VCSELs optical carriers; ii) the unused optical spectrum through all the path links; and iii) optical flows are subject to the spectrum continuity and contiguity constraints. If either the OM's maximum distance or number of hops is not satisfied by the considered path, a lower VCSEL OM is explored and the spectrum assignment mechanism is checked. The RSA fails when no sufficient S-BVT resources are available at the endpoints or the spectrum constraints for the required optical flows cannot be fulfilled for any of the K-SPs.

Figure 4 (left) shows an example of the RSA-CR algorithm. Let us assume that a *req* of 100 Gb/s between nodes 9 and 28 arrives. Moreover, we consider that the high OM is feasible. This means that a path connecting node 9 and 28 (e.g., 9-26-25-28) does not exceed the maximum path distance and number hops determined by the *high* OM. Thus, the S-BVT VCSEL at the node 9 operates at the maximum data rate (r^{VCSEL}), i.e. 50 Gb/s. To fulfill the *req* bandwidth demand, two VCSELs need to be allocated at node 9 and two CO-Rxs at node 28. This does entail on setting up two individual optical flows referred to as X and Y. The flow X occupies the node 9 S-BVT VCSEL at the wavelength 192.050 THz; the flow Y allocates the VCSEL at the wavelength 192.250 THz. TheVCSEL's wavelengths for both X and Y flows identify the central frequency (n) of the respective FSs. The FS slot width (m) depends on the traversed HL optical switch and their filtering features. At node 9 (i.e., HL4), the FS of the flow X occupies $n = -168$ (ITU-T channel for 192.050 THz) and $m = 4$ (slot width of 50 GHz). For the flow Y, at the same node, the FS is $n = -136$ and $m = 4$. Nevertheless, at HL3 nodes (i.e., 26 and 25) and HL2/1 node (28) with 25GHz WSS filters, the FS for the flow X uses $n = -166$ and $m = 2$. Likewise, for the flow Y, the FS in those nodes is $n = -134$ and $m = 2$. Observe that according to the traversed HL node, the FS n and m may vary for a given flow. However, the optical spectrum transporting the effective data is invariant.

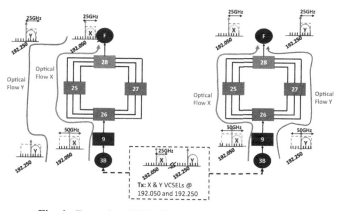

Fig. 4. Example of RSA-CR (*left*) and RSA-IM (*right*).

3.2 RSA Inverse Multiplexing (RSA-IM) Optical Flows

The RSA-IM algorithm is similar to the RSA-CR mechanism but rather than enforcing that all the optical flows are routed over the same spatial path, this is relaxed enabling to accommodate the optical flows over different nodes and links between s and d nodes. As in the RSA-CR algorithm, first it is computed the K-SPs. Then, starting from the highest VCSEL's OM, it is determined the number of VCSELs and optical flows to be allocated. If for the considered VCSEL's OM, no path fulfills the OM's maximum distance and number of hops are discarded, a lower VCSEL's OM is explored. Otherwise, it is created a subset of the K-SPs forming the pool of candidate paths satisfying the under-considered VCSEL's OM requirements. This candidate set of paths is then explored to accommodate the required optical flows. That is, for every optical flow, the algorithm iterates over the resulting candidate paths seeking for a feasible FS (i.e., subject to the available S-BVT VCSEL and the unused optical spectrum on every path). If the candidate paths cannot accommodate all the optical flows for *req*, the connection is blocked.

Figure 4 (right) shows the example for the RSA-IM algorithm. As in the previous example, a *req* of 100 Gb/s between nodes 9 and 28 needs to be set up; assuming high VCSEL's OM, X and Y optical flows are set up allocating the VCSEL wavelengths at 192.050 THz and 192.250 THz, respectively. X and Y flows are routed over different spatial paths, namely, X flow traverses the path formed by the node sequence 9-26-25-28, whilst Y flow is accommodated over the path 9-26-27-28. The aim of the RSA-IM algorithm when compared to the RSA-CR strategy is to favor fulfilling the spectrum contiguity and continuity constraint mostly within the subnetwork formed by the HL3 all-optical switches.

4   Experimental Evaluation

The performance evaluation of both RSA-CR and RSA-IM algorithms under dynamic connection requests is carried out at the CTTC ADRENALINE control plane [8]. The network topology shown in Fig. 2 is deployed over 28 Linux-based servers. Each server hosts an HLx node agent to emulate the optical flow establishment. Those servers hosting the HL4 agents (i.e., nodes 1 to 24) also provide the S-BVT device agents. The server for the node 28 agent co-locates three fully equipped S-BVT agents.

The connection requests are generated using Poisson process with an average inter-arrival time of 5 s. The duration of each connection (i.e., holding time, HT) is exponentially modeled. The HT mean is varied to attain multiple traffic loads. For each *req*, the *s* and *d* are randomly chosen to request a connection between HL4 nodes and (HL2/1), and viceversa. The *req*'s *b* is uniformly distributed as multiple of 50 Gb/s up to 200 Gb/s. 10k connection requests are generate for each data point. Links are formed by bidirectional optical fibers supporting 644 NCFs (spaced 6.25 GHz) covering the 191.900–195.875 THz spectrum range. The length of every link is labelled on each edge as depicted in Fig. 2. This information is needed to the adopted RSA algorithm to assess and select the most efficient VCSEL OM for a computed path. For different HT values, it is compared the performance attained when adopting either RSA-CR or RSA-IM algorithms. This comparison is realized also considering different K-SP values: 1, 3, 6 and 9. The performance metrics for such a RSA algorithm comparison are: i) the BBR; ii) the average number of used S-BVTs VCSELs and CO-Rxs; and iii) the average connection setup time. The BBR is defined as the attained ratio between the blocked bandwidth (accounting for the failed connections) and the total requested bandwidth. Thus, the lower the BBR, the better an RSA performs.

Figure 5 depicts the obtained BBR performance by both RSA-CR (left) and RSA-IM (right) for K = 1, 3 6 and 9 with respect to different HT. As expected for both RSA algorithms, as HT grows the BBR performance is worsened. Since more optical flows occupying resources (i.e., S-BVT VCSELs and CO-Rxs, links' NCFs) co-exist, this does complicate the RSA algorithm to find a feasible path and FS for the *req*'s optical flows. There are two RSA failing causes: i) not enough unused S-BVT VCSELs or CO-Rx at either *s* or *d*; ii) unable to ensure the spectrum constraints for all the *req*'s optical flows. For the second failure reason, since the S-BVT Tx VCSELs are associated to a given wavelength, this significantly narrows the set of feasible FSs when setting up an optical flow. That is, the S-BVT VCSELs not used at the *s* restricts the usable optical spectrum for the optical flows' FSs. Consequently, if one increases the K-SP number, larger spatial paths can be considered by the RSA algorithm. This leads to favor finding a kth path that supports a feasible FS fulfilling the spectrum constraints for each flow. Thereby, as K increases, the BBR enhances specially with respect to K = 1. This behavior is seen in both RSA algorithms. However, the improvement becomes less significant when passing from K = 3 to 6 and 9. The reason behind this is that increasing K may result on considering longer paths (in terms of hops and distance). Such long paths make the RSA algorithm to use the lowest OM for the S-BVT VCSELs. As a result, the number of required optical flows for a *req* is increased which yields on not only uses more S-BVT resources but also notably complicates satisfying the spectrum constraints for each optical flow.

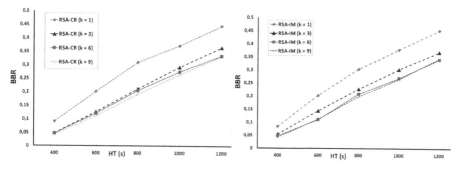

Fig. 5. BBR vs HT (K = 1, 3, 6 and 9); RSA-CR (left), RSA-IM (right).

Figure 6(a) compares the BBR performance attained by both RSA-CR and RSA-IM algorithms for both K = 1 and 9. We observe that both RSA algorithms perform similarly. Thus, the capability of the RSA-IM algorithm to route *req*'s optical flows over different paths with the purpose to better fulfil the spectrum constraints does not bring an improvement. The reason behind this is that the considered network infrastructure only enables route flexibility within the transit ring topology formed by nodes 25, 26, 27 and 28. This considerably narrows the route diversity that could be attained by the RSA-IM algorithm. In this regard, an interesting follow-up of this work is to explore how the network topology and node connectivity impacts on the performance of both RSA algorithms.

Figure 6(b) provides the average used S-BVT VCSELs and CO-Rxs for both different HT and K values attained by the considered RSA algorithms. As aforementioned, a higher K value leads to enhance the BBR performance, i.e. larger *reqs* can be successfully accommodated. Consequently, this does increase the number of average used S-BVT VCSELs and CO-Rxs. As an example, for K = 1 adopting the RSA-CR algorithm, the average used S-BVT VCSELs and CO-Rx are 10,2 for HT = 400 s. For a higher K (i.e., 9) and the same HT = 400 s, such an average utilization grows to 10,6. Moreover, as the traffic load becomes higher (HT = 1200 s), the average used S-BVT VCSELs and CO-Rxs do increase more significantly. Specifically, for the RSA-CR algorithm, the average utilization of the S-BVTs at HT = 1200 s ranges 16,1–16,2 at K = 1; whilst at K = 9, this average utilization metric reaches 19,2. Recall that as shown in Fig. 3, at the HL4 nodes the number of S-BVT VCSELs and CO-Rxs is 20. Thus, at K = 9 and HT = 1200 s most of the S-BVT resources are averagely occupied. Similar trend is accomplished when the RSA-IM algorithm is applied. In general, increasing the K value, allows the algorithm exploring larger number of candidate paths. Thereby, this provides higher spatial path flexibility which eases satisfying feasible *req's* optical flows fulfilling spectrum constraints. As a result, more concurrent connections co-exist within the network leading to increase the average used of S-BVT VCSEL and CO-Rx devices.

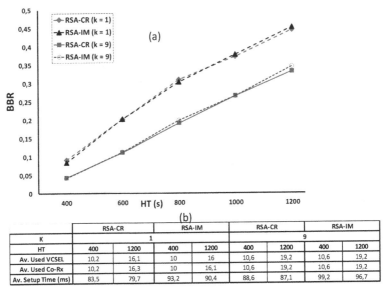

	RSA-CR		RSA-IM		RSA-CR		RSA-IM	
K	1				9			
HT	400	1200	400	1200	400	1200	400	1200
Av. Used VCSEL	10,2	16,1	10	16	10,6	19,2	10,6	19,2
Av. Used Co-Rx	10,2	16,3	10	16,1	10,6	19,2	10,6	19,2
Av. Setup Time (ms)	83,5	79,7	93,2	90,4	88,6	87,1	99,2	96,7

Fig. 6. (a) BBR performance comparing RSA-CR and RSA-IM (K = 1 and 9); (b) average used S-BVT VCSEL and Co-Rx and Average Setup Time for both RSA-CR and RSA-IM

The above improvement in both BBR performance and S-BVT resource utilization when increasing the K value (in RSA-CR and RSA-IM) are attained at the expenses of slightly increasing the average setup time as seen in Fig. 4(b). That is, the larger is the number of K pre-computed spatial paths, the higher the RSA computation time is. Additionally, in the RSA-IM algorithm, we observe that regardless of the HT, the average setup time is larger than those results attained by the RSA-CR algorithm. The reason of this is that in the RSA-IM algorithm for each *req's* optical flow, all the pre-computed K-SPs are checked. This, however, does not happen in the RSA-CR algorithm where for all *req's* optical flow only a single K-SP is checked for each iteration. Consequently, the RSA-IM algorithm tends to seek over more candidate K-SPs when computing each *req* resulting on a larger computational time, and in turn, higher average setup time.

5 Conclusions

The deployment of 5G technology fulfilling their requirements in terms of transport capacity, latency, etc. impacts significantly in the design of the upcoming metro network infrastructures. It is well-accepted that photonic technologies result an appealing enabler to deploy high-capacity, low-cost, and energy efficient metro networks. The EC-H2020 PASSION project investigates solutions on these metro network challenges via: i) SDN configurable and modular S-BVT devices leveraging VCSEL technologies; and ii) hierarchical flexi-grid optical networks. In [5] the RSA-CR algorithm was presented and evaluated to dynamically accommodate heterogenous data rate connections within the targeted metro network. Herein, this algorithm is extended through proposing the RSA-IM algorithm. The RSA-IM aims at relaxing the necessity of routing all optical flows of a given connection over the same spatial path. This may lead to better satisfy the optical flows' spectrum constraints. Both RSA algorithms are compared upon dynamic connection arrival varying the K value of the K-SP computation. We observe that both RSA algorithm attains similarly on the BBR metric. Thus, the BBR enhancement envisaged by the RSA-IM algorithm thanks to a better flexibility to route *req*'s optical flows over diverse spatial paths is not reflected. This may be caused by the considered metro network ring-star topology (showed in Fig. 2). One may realize that this topology lacks having significant path diversities to be exploited by the RSA-IM. Next studies will concentrate on assessing both algorithms over metro network topologies with higher nodal degree and network connectivity.

Acknowledgements. The research leading to these results has received funding from the EUH2020 PASSION Project (780326) and by Spanish MICINN AURORAS (RTI2018–099178-B-I00) project and Spanish Thematic Network Go2Edge (RED2018–102585-T).

References

1. CISCO White Paper: Cisco Visual Networking Index: Forecast and Trends, 2017–2022 White Paper, February 2019
2. Svaluto Moreolo, M., Fabrega, J.M., Nadal, L., Martínez, R., Casellas, R.: Synergy of photonic technologies and software-defined networking in the hyperconnectivity era. IEEE J. Lightwave Tech. **37**(16), 3902–3910 (2019)
3. EC H2020 PASSION Project. https://www.passion-project.eu/wpcontent/uploads/2018/01/PASSION-Project-Fact-Sheet.pdf
4. Paroli, P., Gatto, A., Boffi, P.: Long wavelength VCSELs exploitation for low-cost and low-power consumption metro and access network. In: Proceedings of 20th International Conference on Transparent Optical Networks (ICTON), July 2018
5. Martínez, R., et. al.: Experimental evaluation of an on-line RSA algorithm for SDN-controlled optical metro networks with VCSEL-based S-BVTs. In: Proceedings of IFIP/IEEE Optical Network Design and Modelling (ONDM), May 2020
6. Jinno, M., Takara, H., Kozicki, B., Tsukishima, Y., Sone, Y., Matsuoka, S.: Spectrum-efficient and Scalable elastic optical path network: architecture, benefits, and enabling technologies. IEEE Commun. Mag. **47**, 66–73 (2009)

7. Martínez, R., et. al.: Design and deployment of an SDN programmable optical metro network with VCSEL-based S-BVTs. In: Proceedings of International Conference on Transparent Optical Networks (ICTON 2020), July 2020
8. Muñoz, R., et. al.: The ADRENALINE testbed: an SDN/NFV packet/optical transport network and edge/core cloud platform for end-to-end 5G and IoT services. In: Proceedings of European Conference on Networks and Communications (EuCNC), June 2017

Implementing a Blockchain-Based Security System Applied to IoT

Martí Miquel Martínez[✉], Eva Marín-Tordera, Xavi Masip-Bruin,
Sergio Sánchez-López, and Jordi García

Advanced Network Architectures Lab (CRAAX), Technical University of Catalunya (UPC),
Barcelona, Spain
marti.miquel@upc.edu, {eva,xmasip,sergio,jordig}@ac.upc.edu

Abstract. Several discussions regarding IoT devices and Blockchain came out recently. On one hand, IoT devices have been widely adopted by a notable set of Internet services driven by their capacity to cover several needs (for example, monitoring a manufacturing process, guiding an autonomous car, or tracking a train). On the other hand, Blockchain technology has been considered by several companies to support some critical functionalities, such as security provisioning or data protection. Nowadays, many challenges on both technologies remain yet unsolved, in spite of the unstoppable and ever-growing interest both technologies are attracting. Actually, a substantial push to them both comes from their agnosticism, i.e., many scenarios, particularly those considered as smart, are considered as proper candidates for their deployment, for example smart transportation, smart manufacturing or smart cities, just to name a few. This paper focuses on the latter, proposing a preliminary architecture using both technologies intended to provide security and robustness in Smart Cities. Several Blockchain strategies are analysed in the paper to identify unequivocally every device that belongs to the proposed architecture, also describing the operation of the chosen Blockchain to meet the security requirements. In summary, in this paper, an architecture able to resist certain attacks and proven to be useful to the previous mentioned examples is designed and implemented.

Keywords: IoT · Cybersecurity · Blockchain

1 Introduction

Nowadays ICT systems are able to supervise itself, process information and perform other smart and tedious operations throughout ubiquitous, affordable and small IoT devices. The acronym stands for Internet of Things, encompassing anything connected to the Internet. There are plenty of use cases where IoT becomes relevant, from a simple environment sensing to the deployment of real actions, such as sending messages, issuing warnings, deploying smart decision making process, etc., all to be applied to a large set of domains, including manufacturing processes in the Industry 4.0, autonomous vehicles control, control systems in smart cities, e-health services, etc.

© ICST Institute for Computer Sciences, Social Informatics and Telecommunications Engineering 2021
Published by Springer Nature Switzerland AG 2021. All Rights Reserved
H. Gao et al. (Eds.): BROADNETS 2020, LNICST 355, pp. 143–153, 2021.
https://doi.org/10.1007/978-3-030-68737-3_9

For instance, in an Industry 4.0 context, a factory might deploy several IoT devices responsible for monitoring PLCs (Programmable logic controller) or even for carrying out relevant actions, such as shutting down specific systems or powering them up. Moreover, workers from outside the factory might have the possibility to execute code remotely, thus easing a dynamic management of the whole infrastructure. In a Smart City scenario, data from sensors along the city should be able to be read, having the ability to send commands to actuators deployed in the city remotely and securely. In both scenarios, the information is forwarded throughout the existing telecom infrastructure, leading to security concerns, mainly motivated by the inherent IoT dynamics and heterogeneity.

Needless to say, many threats are expected to pop up in the data transmission process, mainly coming from external attackers but also from internal issues (media transmission issues, errors, etc.), both of them potentially affecting any part of the entire system. Therefore, it is mandatory to secure the whole supply chain.

In these hostile scenarios, a certain level of protection is required in order not to leak or tweak the data from and to unknown actors. In consequence, manufacturers, companies and city managers need, in essence, tools and solutions aimed to prevent these hazardous actions to happen, thus providing security in every step within the pipeline. However, many challenges arise when facing nearly complete security provisioning to every transaction involving whoever and whatever is accessing IoT devices.

Indeed, a long supply chain presents vulnerabilities driven by weak points where attackers might want to sneak in. Identifying such weak points along with the impact the potential vulnerabilities may have on the whole ICT system, is a highly appealing research field, demanding for novel AI-assisted estimation techniques intended to proactively eliminate or mitigate the potential attacks effects.

Two main strategies may be applied when dealing with ICT systems security: i) encrypting data, so nobody different than the recipient and the sender can understand the data, making sure it is not manipulated, and; ii) verifying the peer's identities. In fact, every node should be supervised so system administrators are aware of their status and whether they are being attacked or not. The aftermath of an attack may have highly negative effects, turning into serious monetary (blackmail, downtime, etc.) and even physical damages, when considering an industrial scenario.

The solution proposed in this paper deals with the two strategies highlighted above. Regarding the data encryption, we plan to use the classic TLS (Transport Layer Security) protocol to encrypt and decrypt data. However, to deal with the identity management, although it could also guarantee a vague identification, supported by the SSL Certificate, it only proves that the server is who is supposed to be, but no information about the client identity is provided. Hence, in order to fill this gap, we propose to use Blockchain for identity management, distributing every node's information and making it accessible for every participant.

This paper is structured as follows: Sect. 2 reviews the state of the art related to securing IoT, Sect. 3 presents the proposed architecture, Sect. 4 validate it and Sect. 5 concludes the paper.

2 State of the Art

In this section, we review previous work addressing new approaches for securing IoT. A survey with problems, challenges and proposed solutions for securing IoT can be found in [1]. Aligned to what we stated in the introduction, [1] highlights the fact that existing security technologies are not enough for securing the vast amount of heterogeneous and decentralized devices included in IoT, especially when these traditional approaches are based on centralized architectures. The problems arising in these centralized architectures are usually related to scalability, but also due to the dynamicity and volatility of IoT devices.

In this scenario, different authors have proposed the use of a Blockchain network. In [1] there is a revision of the benefits of using Blockchain in IoT; the main challenges found in the reviewed approaches are, on one hand the need for distributing the security architecture, and specifically the identity management and access control, and on the other hand, take into account the constrained capacity of IoT devices for implementing security features, what turns into the fact that IoT devices cannot store large ledgers. One of the existing approaches is presented in [2], where authors propose a Blockchain network for access control, which is composed by nodes actively working in the transaction process (validating it by mining). However, due to the IoT constraints (CPU and memory), the IoT devices do not belong to this network and then do not store the ledger, but they are clients of the Blockchain nodes. When an IoT device creates a transaction, the transaction is forwarded to the Blockchain network for processing and storing. Although, as in our case, the access control for IoT devices is proposed to be done by means of Blockchain, the article is only a guidance about using Blockchain to make a more secure IoT, and there is neither a deeply description of the architecture nor an implementation.

The work presented in [3] also proposes a decentralized access control architecture for IoT, where the access control information is stored and distributed using Blockchain. Similarly to [1], authors in [3] propose not to store the Blockchain (ledger) in IoT devices, but define a new type of Blockchain node, so-called Management Hub Node, that acts on behalf of IoT devices and that can be connected to several IoT devices, requesting the access to the network for these IoT devices. Additionally, in this paper authors propose the use of a single smart contract. In this smart contract, they are defined all the operations allowed in the access control system; and only a new proposed entity called manager is allowed to access and update the smart contract, for example for defining new access policies.

In a similar approach in order to overcome the difficulty to store and process the Blockchain by IoT devices, in [4] authors propose to cluster devices. A node from each cluster is selected as the cluster head, so-called Overlay Block Managers (OBMs), and will serve as manager of the Blockchain; to ensure scalability, transactions and blocks are broadcast only to the OBMs. In addition, authors also incorporate a number of optimizations specially tuned for IoT devices, such as a distributed time-based consensus algorithm, a distributed trust method, a distributed throughput management strategy and the separation of the transaction traffic from the data flow. Similar to this approach, in this paper we also propose a clear separation of IoT data and transaction data.

The main difference between our proposal and the reviewed proposals [2, 3] and [4] resides on where the Blockchain is physically implemented. Indeed, unlike these reviewed proposals where OBMs or management hubs nodes (responsible for processing and storing the Blockchain) are non-specialized devices executing also other processes or tasks, in our proposal the Blockchain nodes (peers) are implemented at fog devices only executing Blockchain related tasks. This approach is due to the high CPU and storage consumption of Blockchain tasks, including consensus algorithms.

The work presented in [5], despite not being the main objective proposes to secure IoT communication between IoT network and big databases by means of blockchain. The main difference with our proposal is, on one hand the use of the blockchain to store IoT data, and on the other hand the use of two levels of blockchain, one to pre-process and create the block (sidechain) and the blockchain network.

Finally, other approaches may be found in the literature aimed at securing IoT not based on Blockchain. One of these proposals, coming from the H2020 ANASTACIA project [6], presented in [7], focusses on the ability of software-based network mechanisms to protect IoT systems against security threats, providing automated and self-configurable SDN/NFV-based security mechanisms. The proposed security framework not only addresses the security of IoT devices, but also includes other functionalities, such as reconfiguring the system to disallow access to a certain sensor when detecting an attack.

3 Secure Fog to Cloud Architecture Based on Blockchain (SF2C-BC)

3.1 Scenario

Two different scenarios are envisaged, despite having similarities, Industry 4.0 & Smart-cities. In the first one, there exists a hierarchy responsible for segregating tasks and assigning them to each pyramid level. For example, simple actuators (machines) which work directly with the goods, are the lowest pyramid level (Fig. 1) whereas software designed to supervise hundreds of factories remotely represents the highest level. Devices which are part of level 0 only perform their work as ordered by higher levels, hence they are not capable of making decisions based on outside or external events. In the upper layers we find control systems which manage the equipment in lower layers. In this scenario, it could be a good idea to deploy IoT distributed devices in those factories to take measurements (level 0), act according to the control systems in level 1, and finally affect other devices situated at level 0. As mentioned in the Introduction, if these IoT devices are to be controlled remotely, security measures are needed to forward information from IoT devices to the higher layers and vice-versa.

In the second scenario, Smart cities could take different measurements, such as environment, traffic, status of buildings (lift, garbage etc.), and then forward the collected data to control systems managing the city. For instance, afterwards, traffic would be limited in certain time schedules to prevent pollution from rising, also narrowing down city congestion. In the same way, bus stops could show information regarding the on-going bus routes, possible delays, bus occupation and more. Security concerns emerge

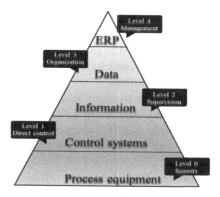

Fig. 1. Automation pyramid

due to the massive information being sent through communication networks, that would represent a Smart city, some of which could be sensitive.

3.2 Secure Fog to Cloud Blockchain (SF2C-BC) Solution

In both scenarios and with current management systems, IoT devices are present but not always reachable from everywhere (at least using traditional Internet connections point-to-point). For example, in previous Fig. 1, management systems at level 4 couldn't direct access to IoT devices at level 0. Therefore, reachability, security & identification are keywords that will be addressed later on in this paper in order to assert system's proper functionality.

Nowadays there exist numerous architecture paradigms that offer connectivity, reliability and more features such as Cloud or Fog-to-cloud (F2C) [8]. Referring to the earlier mentioned architectures, there are two main necessities: nearly immediate response (action-reaction) and persistent data (stored indefinitely). In case an action happens, such as a machine just broke or is malfunctioning, an action must be performed to repair it or even turn it off; it is time critical. What is more, perhaps for the company, knowing the conditions in which the machine was operating could result in useful information not to letting it happen again.

Considering the need of nearly immediate response, cloud is discarded. Therefore, the solution proposed is based on F2C, with devices at different layers including the entire cloud continuum, that is Edge, Fog and Cloud. However, the F2C architecture must be extended to guarantee a secure connectivity between all devices. In our proposal, Secure Fog to Cloud Blockchain (SF2C-BC), we deploy a VPN (Virtual Private Network) to assure the data encryption and propose Blockchain for identity and access control, see Fig. 2.

The tree layers are considered, Cloud (Data centres), Fog (Nodes), and Edge (Devices), so while large computation is carried out in the cloud, other simpler tasks stay between Fog and Edge. However, knowing that third party attackers may keep trying to sniff traffic for illegal purposes, VPN will be used to provide secure communication between the devices in different layers. One of the main reasons for choosing VPN is to mitigate the inability of maintaining public IPs for every IoT device (needed so they become reachable from everywhere) – specially nowadays where IPv6 is not yet world-wide adopted [9]. Also, VPN provides ACL (Access Control List) in part as a result of PKI (Public Key Infrastructure) infrastructure, letting revoke certificates whenever desired therefore banning future connections.

At this point, we can prohibit clients from accessing; however, there is no any record for IoT devices information. Thus, using a decentralized immutable database like Blockchain will persist nodes known IP addresses, IDs, roles, characteristics etc. The immutability property is crucial for having the awareness that data is untouchable, every transaction will be persisted. Every device's modification or addition of a new one leads into a Blockchain transaction. Blockchain peers will be distributed among the city (or factories) in specialized devices at the Fog layer.

The proposed Blockchain is Hyperledger Fabric, due to its modularity. One advantage is that the main consensus algorithm proposed is byzantine-failure resilient (RBFT), which hugely helps rejecting malicious requests from legit nodes. Only every IoT device info will be saved into the blockchain, whereas data generated by IoT devices situated at the edge will be persistently stored in the cloud, with large storage capacity, thus being perfect for this task.

VPN Centre, a powerful server which could be replicated as shown in Fig. 2 will be placed, for instance in the smart city scenario, in a public facility with a public IP; all devices will be able to reach out to it from anywhere. Its main purpose is to interconnect Fog & Edge devices within themselves. Throughout the VPN, Fog and Edge devices are not only able to communicate between themselves but also with the Blockchain nodes.

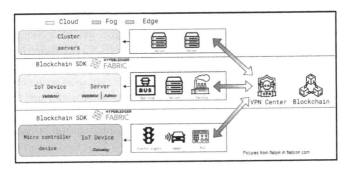

Fig. 2. SF2C-BC

Let's assume that we want to know the weather in a specific area within the city. To do so, IoT devices at the Edge layer which are situated in that area and have weather measurement capabilities will begin to take them. Then, they prepare a JSON-RPC payload with the gathered information, own unique identity and signed digest. At this point, they only prove that in fact they own a pair of public & private keys but anything else. There is a need to verify this payload against Blockchain records, and check whether that node is still able to send requests. Consequently, some devices situated at the Fog layer (validators) will proxy those requests, validate the signing chain and later on act accordingly (sending data to the cloud & reaching to other EDGE devices if needed to), see Fig. 3.

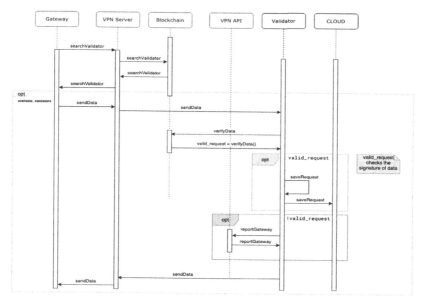

Fig. 3. Message passing

If the checks fail, VPN Centre will have a record of that and obviously there won't be any further actions. The earlier mentioned message passing is depictured in Fig. 3.

Every device in Fog – Edge layer depicted in Fig. 2 through different colours will have either one of these roles:

i)   Gateway: IoT device belonging to the Edge which only takes measurements or performs actions.
ii) Validator: Device belonging to Fog which validates gateways petitions by using asymmetric RSA signing.
iii) Administrator: Reserved for future use, able to perform any action to the system.

Cloud will be responsible for persisting data indefinitely for future processing, whereas devices situated at Fog layer will temporarily save them in RAM (Random Access Memory) for nearly immediate access. To summarize, we'll have data replicated because it will be in certain time lapses both in Cloud and Fog, with the advantage of being able to save data and carrying out tasks really quickly.

Nevertheless, every device at Fog and Edge layers will be identified by a unique UUID (Universal Unique Identifier), along with these attributes:

• Node_Type: Validator | Gateway | Administrator
• Virtual_IP: IP static address assigned by the VPN Centre

- Banned: Boolean regarding ban status
- Banned_timestamp: Timestamp from the moment in which the node is banned.
- RSA_Public_Key: Public RSA key in PEM format.

4 Validation

We can safely assume that in order to check the performance of the proposed solution, we'll have to run testing in different conditions for scalability purposes. To this end, we'll need these devices:

1. Sensor & microcontroller (Edge)
2. IoT device with "gateway" role (Edge)
3. IoT device with "validator" role (Validator)
4. VPN Centre in one Fog node
5. Blockchain distributed in two specialised Fog nodes
6. Server intended for Cloud

In the testbed, there'll be a real IoT device, sensor and validator whereas other components will be simulated using virtualization technologies such as Docker and Virtual Machines, see Fig. 4. The first test consists of proving that the architecture works for the simplest use case: report weather in a smart city coming from a sensor. As a proof of concept, one city will be tested along its scalability.

In essence Fig. 4 represents the scenario of two smart cities, with their own servers to interconnect Fog and Edge devices. Although only one of the scenarios is represented, the main idea can be extended for the Industry 4.0 scenario, where instead of two smart cities we can assume two factories; installed sensors in machinery monitor their operation. As a proof of concept, one city will be tested along with its scalability.

The blockchain is placed near the VPN Centre, distributed into two peers, allowing the interaction through Fabric SDK's smart-contracts. They intend to do it by running what they call chain-code (available in different programming languages); every device that has to either read or write new transactions to the blockchain, will have to invoke RPC (Remote Procedure Call) methods. Also, they'll sign the petitions with their private RSA key, leading to non-repudiation of origin.

Figure 5 depicts the internal structure of testbed's Fabric; end-users such as IoT devices belong to the red area, blue area are peer nodes and finally in grey the CA servers which issue credentials using PKI (Public Key Infrastructure).

4.1 Tests

We carry out two tests: one to check the basic functionality of the system and the second for testing the scalability:

- Basic functionality including: 1 sensor, 1 gateway, 1 validator, 1 VPN Centre, 1 Cloud and 2 Blockchain peers:

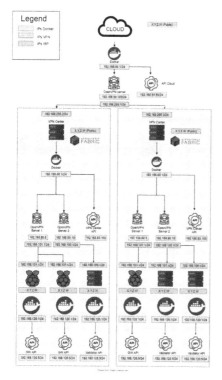

Fig. 4. Two smart-cities architecture

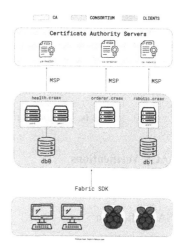

Fig. 5. Internal Blockchain architecture

- **Input**: Sensor sends a valid JSON RPC payload (weather measurements) with a valid signed digest.
- **Expected output**: Transaction success, cloud has a copy of this data stored.
- **Transaction success** means that the validator is able to verify the signature of the payload's digest correctly, and the requester is not banned in the Blockchain, some of the transactions are shown in Fig. 6.
- Scalability test including the following devices with the same input, expected output and transaction success, see Table 1.

Table 1. Amount of used devices

Device	Quantity	Device	Quantity
Real sensor	1	Simulated Gateway	19
Simulated sensor	19	Simulated Validator	20
Real Gateway	1	VPN Centre	1
Blockchain peer	2	Cloud	1

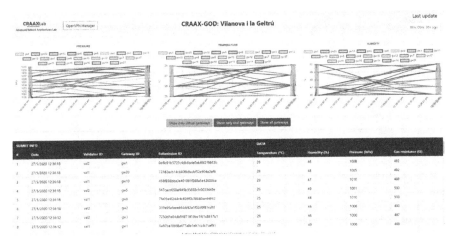

Fig. 6. Dashboard representing various successful requests

4.2 ACL Verifications

In this section, we will test that ACLs are correctly applied by two type of verifications:

- RSA verification

Firstly, the chosen validator extracts the signed digest from the JSON-RPC payload in every request, taking the unique ID given by the request and obtains the corresponding public RSA key from the Blockchain. Afterwards, it verifies that in fact that message was signed by whomever that had a private key from which the public key derived from. If the result is incorrect, notify VPN Centre and reply with a negative response to the gateway, considering the petition non-legit. Figure 7 shows the warnings due to non-legit petitions.

Warning ID	Submitter	Offender	Date	Reason	Delete
9ac6a25J-99a4-4384-a793-ea299d227f5c	val1	192.168.1.102 -> gw1	Mon, 09 Nov 2020 09:05:56 GMT	Public key verification failed	Delete
f79a9bd5-0d26-446d-962a-88da6b0efa4a	val2	192.168.1.102 -> gw1	Mon, 09 Nov 2020 09:05:45 GMT	Public key verification failed	Delete
870fa378-7972-4605-82cb-7153124cf01d	val2	192.168.1.102 -> gw1	Mon, 09 Nov 2020 09:05:37 GMT	Public key verification failed	Delete

Fig. 7. Petitions from non-verified devices

- Blockchain banned device

Firstly, extract the signed digest from the JSON-RPC payload in every request. Take the unique ID given by the request and check with the Blockchain whether the device is banned. If it is, notify the VPN Centre and reply with a negative response to the gateway, considering the petition non-legit, see Fig. 8.

Fig. 8. Petitions from banned devices

5 Conclusions

In this paper, we have ensured that despite having security concerns in any of the two envisaged ICT scenarios (industry 4.0 and smart cities), an architecture capable of withholding impersonations (attacks) has been designed, nevertheless only the smart city scenario has been implemented and validated. What is more, we've tested numerous devices in the Fog & Edge layers to simulate a more real scenario, sending requests at a high rate in a random fashion, and validating the results in terms of ACL verifications and delay. It has been verified that Blockchain can help in these cases as long as information doesn't require to be updated frequently; obtaining information from each IoT device within the Blockchain is not a transaction, rather a read operation. Only modifications and additions are considered transactions leading to propagated updates.

Acknowledgements. This work was partially supported by the Spanish Ministry of Economy and Competitiveness, under contract RTI2018-094532-B-I00 (MINECO/FEDER) and the Spanish Thematic Network under contract RED2018-102585-T.

References

1. Hassija, V., Chamola, V., Saxena, V., et al.: A survey on IoT security: application areas, security threats, and solution architectures. IEEE Access **7**, 82721–82743 (2019)
2. Singh, M., Singh, A., Kim, S.: Blockchain: a game changer for securing IoT data. In: IEEE World Forum Internet Things, WF-IoT 2018 - Proceedings 2018-January, pp. 51–55 (2018)
3. Novo, O.: Blockchain meets IoT: an architecture for scalable access management in IoT. IEEE Internet Things J. **5**, 1184–1195 (2018)
4. Dorri, A., Kanhere, S., Jurdak, R., Gauravaram, P.: LSB: a lightweight scalable blockchain for IoT security and anonymity. J. Parallel Distrib. Comput. **134**, 180–197 (2019)
5. Casado-Vara, R., Chamoso, P., De la Prieta, F., Prieto, J.: Non-linear adaptive closed loop control system for improved efficiency in IoT-blockchain management. Information Fusion **49**, 227–239 (2019)
6. ANASTACIA Project. https://www.anastacia-h2020.eu/
7. Molina Zarca, A., Bernal Bernabe, J., Farris, I., et al.: Enhancing IoT security through network softwarization and virtual security appliances. Int. J. Netw. Manag. **28**, 1–8 (2018)
8. Masip-Bruin, X., Marín-Tordera, E., Tashakor, G., Jukan, A., Ren, G.: Foggy clouds and cloudy fogs: a real need for coordinated management of fog-to-cloud computing systems. IEEE Wireless Commun. **2**, 9–20 (2012)
9. IPv6 – Google. https://www.google.com/intl/en/ipv6/statistics.html

Joint Core and Spectrum Allocation in Dynamic Optical Networks with ROADMs with No Line Changes

I. Viloria, R. J. Durán$^{(\boxtimes)}$ ⓘ, I. de Miguel ⓘ, L. Ruiz ⓘ, N. Merayo ⓘ, J. C. Aguado ⓘ, P. Fernández ⓘ, R. M. Lorenzo ⓘ, and E. J. Abril ⓘ

Optical Communications Group, Universidad de Valladolid, Paseo de Belén, 15, 47011 Valladolid, Spain
rduran@tel.uva.es

Abstract. Future metro networks will connect many multiaccess edge computing resources (MEC) working in a coordinating fashion to provide users with cloud computing capabilities with very low latency. That highly distributed computing architecture has to be connected by a network that provides high bandwidth and flexibility. Elastic optical networks (EONs) are currently the best option to perform that task. In a next step of optical network evolution, EONs can increase the bandwidth that they provide by using multicore fibers (MCF). When dynamic optical circuits are established in these networks, the routing, core and spectrum assignment (RCSA) problem must be solved. In this paper, two algorithms are presented in order to solve the RCSA problem considering continuity constraints in both the spectrum and the core (as we consider a cost-effective metro network architecture based on ROADMs without line changes). One of these versions explores the full spectrum of all cores in order to grant the best solution when solving the RCSA problem. The results of a simulation study show that exploring all the cores when solving the RCSA problem can reduce the blocking ratio of those networks and, therefore, increase its performance at the expense of a slight increment of the computing time required to provide a solution.

Keywords: RCSA · Routing · Spectrum assignment · Core assignment · Multicore fibers · Elastic optical networks

1 Introduction

The explosion of paradigms like the Internet of Things (IoT), Tactile Internet or Industry 4.0 are inducing an evolution of communication infrastructures. The new application and services as well as the number of connected devices impose stringent requirements that current networks cannot satisfy [1]. 5G is a promising technology for that evolution, as it supports a high number of connected devices and enables high-capacity and low latency communications [2]. At the same time, the offshoring of computing and storage capacity from data centres (DCs) to the edge of the network thanks to Multi-access Edge

© ICST Institute for Computer Sciences, Social Informatics and Telecommunications Engineering 2021
Published by Springer Nature Switzerland AG 2021. All Rights Reserved
H. Gao et al. (Eds.): BROADNETS 2020, LNICST 355, pp. 154–162, 2021.
https://doi.org/10.1007/978-3-030-68737-3_10

Computing (MEC) or fog computing technologies puts processes closer to the end-user helping to reduce the latency, one of the most stringent key performance parameters of 5G [3].

While the fronthaul of this architecture is based on wireless technologies, the back-haul will be based on fiber networks as they offer high bandwidth, dynamicity, scalability and reliability [4]. Current wavelength-routed optical networks (WRON) use wavelength division multiplexing (WDM) not only to increase the bandwidth but also for routing purposes when establishing lightpaths (i.e., optical circuits between network nodes not necessarily adjacent in the physical network) [5]. Lightpaths can be established and released on-demand improving the flexibility of WRONs. However, as current WRONs use ITU-T fixed channels to establish the lightpaths, they waste network capacity as they cannot accommodate traffic in the most effective way. In order to deal with such a problem, elastic optical network architectures were proposed. Elastic (or flexible) optical networks (EONs), thanks to the use of techniques like OFDM or Nyquist-WDM [6, 7], enable the allocation of a variable portion of spectrum to each optical connection according to its requirements. In these networks, when a lightpath request arrives (with information about the demanded bandwidth in addition to source and destination nodes), the control plane must determine the sequence of fibers (route) and a portion of spectrum in order to establish the lightpath. This problem is known as the routing and spectrum allocation (RSA) problem [8] and can be solved by a central entity (e.g., path computation element, PCE).

The next step in the evolution of EONs is the use of multicore fibers (MCFs), which expand the network capacity by using space division multiplexing, at the expense of increasing the crosstalk between cores. When EONs are equipped with these fibers, the RSA problem is transformed into the Routing, Core and Spectrum Assignment (RCSA) problem adding a new degree of complexity to the RSA problem [9]. In the literature, there are some proposals to solve the RCSA problem [9–14]. In most of them, even when they consider the spectrum continuity constraint (i.e., there are not wavelength converters in the network and the lightpath must use the same spectrum in the complete route), they do not consider core continuity constraints when solving the RCSA problem. However, in [14], it is shown that using an architecture based on ROADMs without line changes (therefore, imposing the core continuity constraint) is much more economic at the expense of a little performance reduction.

In this paper, we propose two methods to solve the RCSA problem in a dynamic network scenario in which lightpaths are established and released on real time. In this kind of scenarios, the main goal is to establish all the connections requested by end users, but, as that is not always possible due to limited network resources, the objective is to reduce the ratio of non-established (or blocked) lightpath requests. We have considered that all lightpath establishment requests are solved by a PCE and assumed a metro network architecture connecting MEC resources using ROADMs without line changes [14]. Hence, our proposals consider continuity constraints in both the spectrum and the core assigned to the lightpath. In contrast to the RCSA method used in [14], which is based on first-fit when solving the spectrum assignment, in our work, the spectrum slot that better fits the connection request capacity is selected. Moreover, we show that solving the core and spectrum assignment jointly, improves the performance, as it minimizes the blocking probability of the requests.

2 Algorithms for Solving the Dynamic RCSA Problem

Solving the RCSA problem in dynamic networks with centralized control is the extension of the RSA problem in elastic networks when they operate in networks equipped with MCFs. Users demand the establishment and release of lightpaths on real time. In their requests, users indicate the source and destination node of the lightpath as well as the required bandwidth of the optical circuit. In centralized architectures, a central element, like a PCE, has to assign resources to establish the lightpath, i.e., find a route, a core in each fiber of the route and a portion of the spectrum. If there are enough idle resources, the lightpath is established, and it is rejected otherwise [7]. The connection will not be permanently established but it will be torn down at some point in the future, i.e., lightpaths have a limited duration.

Most of works in flexible networks consider that the spectrum is divided into frequency slots, i.e., narrow spectrum segments of a given width in GHz, all of them with the same bandwidth. When a lightpath request arrives at the PCE, the RCSA algorithm will assign as many available slots as needed to allocate all the bandwidth required by the user in a superchannel. If no waveband conversion is used, the same portion of spectrum must be reserved in all the fibers of the route. It is important to note that a guard-band is reserved between two consecutive demands in the spectrum to avoid interference between them. One of the metrics to evaluate the performance of the method that solve the dynamic RCSA problems (assuming that all requests demand the same capacity) is the blocking ratio, i.e., the portion of the connections which cannot be established due to lack of resources.

Some works from literature solve the problem of determining the modulation level of the lightpath when solving the RCSA problem, resulting in the RMCSA (Routing, Modulation, Core and Spectrum Assignment) problem. Determining the modulation level is clearly affected by physical impairments. Some papers deal with that problem, adding a constraint in the modulation level used by the lightpath depending on its length. Other studies also take into account the crosstalk between signals traveling in different cores when solving the RCSA problem in networks equipped with MCFs [9–13]. When the inter-core distance is high enough, the crosstalk is negligible [9]. Inter-core crosstalk is also influenced by the length of fiber link (the higher link length, the higher the impairment caused).

In this study, we have focused on solving the RCSA in future metro networks (backhaul of 5G networks equipped with MEC resources) where the distance will be short enough to use the best modulation available (i.e., with the highest spectral efficiency) and the influence of inter-core crosstalk is also limited. Moreover, it is also expected that the number of cores in a MCF installed in a metro network will not be very high and, therefore, the inter-core distance will be high enough to avoid considering the physical impairments in such a scenario. Furthermore, we envision a metro network architecture equipped with ROADM without line changes [14]. In such architecture, the RCSA problem has to be solved considering both core continuity and spectrum continuity constraints.

In our proposal, routing is solved using pre-calculated k-shortest paths in a graph where each network node is represented as a vertex and each MCF as an edge. Then, each time that a lightpath request arrives at the PCE, it will use the information from the TED (Traffic Engineering Database) to build the joint spectrum availability vector (JSAV) of each of the fiber cores of each route. Figure 1 shows the construction of the JSAV of the route a → b → c → d using core 1. Let us assume that only that path (and that core) is considered as a candidate for establishing the connection in this example. As it can be seen in that figure, there are two idle spectrum slices to establish new lightpaths: from slot 4 to 7 (4 slots) and from slot 11 to 12 (2 slots). If a connection request arrives at the network and requires two spectral slots (including guard-bands), it can be placed in both gaps. However, if a first-fit strategy for spectrum assignment is used, that is, if the first available gap is selected for allocating this request (for instance, using slots 4 and 5), the resulting spectrum will then have two gaps of two slots. Therefore, if a new lightpath request arrives in that moment demanding three or four slots, it will be blocked (since there are no available gaps of that size, and no more candidate paths in this example). In contrast, if slots 11 and 12 had been selected to allocate the first request, the new request would have also been successfully allocated. Our RCSA methods follow this idea and they look for the gap that better fits the request (a gap with equal size to the request, or the smaller between those with more slots than required). Therefore, instead of employing a first-fit strategy for spectrum assignment as in [14], a best gap strategy is used.

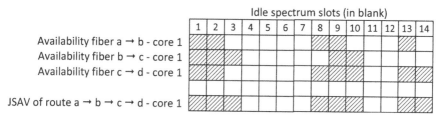

Fig. 1. Construction of the JSAV of route a → b → c → d in core 1.

Regarding the selection of the cores, some studies use the first-fit technique [11, 14], i.e., the first core with spectrum availability is selected. Other studies also follow first-fit method, but take into account the inter-core crosstalk [10, 12, 13]. However, apart from [14], all of them consider an architecture with line changes and, therefore, they do not impose the core continuity constraint.

However, the use of MCF can be better exploited if the selection of the core and the assignment of spectrum is done jointly, with the aim of finding the best gap by considering the spectrum availability of all the cores. Figure 2 shows an example of these two strategies: (i) using first-fit for core assignment and best gap for spectrum allocation, and (ii) searching for the best gap along all cores for a joint allocation of core and spectrum. Suppose that a user requires the establishment of a lightpath demanding three spectral slots (including guard-bands). Figure 2 shows the JSAVs of route a → b → c → d using core 1 and core 2. If first-fit is used for core assignment, the method will assign the gap 4 to 6 in core 1 for that connection, thus leaving an isolated idle slot in slot 7. However, the second method, finds the gap that better fits the request along all the cores, which is placed in slots 6–8 in core 2.

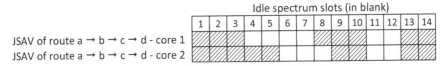

Fig. 2. Example JSAV of route a → b → c → d in core 1 and core 2.

In summary, in [14], a first-fit method is used for core selection, and also for spectrum allocation. In contrast, in this paper we propose and analyze two methods. The first one uses a first-fit approach for selecting the core, and a best gap method for spectrum allocation (Algorithm 1 and first-fit core assignment in the figures). The second method looks for the best gap along all the cores, thus solves the core and spectrum allocation subproblems jointly (Algorithm 2 and best core assignment in figures).

Algorithm 1: first-fit core assignment Heuristic

1:   **Procedure** first-fit_core_assignment(*network_state, source_node, destination_node, bandwidth_required*)

2:       *bandwidth_required* ← *bandwidth_required* + *guard_bands*

3:       *number_slots_required* ← determine_number_slots_required(*source_node, destination_node, bandwidth_required*)

4:       *transmitters_assigned_to_lightpath* ← assign_transmitters(*source_node, number_slots_required*)

5:       *receivers_assigned_to_lightpath* ← assign_receivers(*destination_node, number_slots_required*)

6:       **if** *transmitters_assigned_to_lightpath* ≠ ∅ **and** *receivers_assigned_to_lightpath* ≠ ∅ **then**

7:           **for each** *path* **in** k-shortest-paths(*source_node, destination_node)* **do**

8:               **for each** *core* **in** *cores_per_MCF* **do**

9:                   *JSAV* ← build_JSAV(*path, core*)

10:                  *slots_assigned_to_lightpath* ← best_gap_spectrum_allocation(*path, JSAV, number_slots_required*)

11:                  **if** *slots_assigned_to_lightpath* = ∅ **then**

12:                      **continue**   # Not enough contiguous slots found on JSAV (jump to line 8)

13:                  **end if**

14:                  establish_lightpath(*path, core, slots_assigned_to_lightpath, transmitters_assigned_to_lightpath, receivers_assigned_to_lightpath*)

15:                  **go to** end procedure

16:              **end for**

17:          **end for**

18:      **end if**

19:      reject_lightpath()

20: **end procedure**

Algorithm 2: best-fit core assignment Heuristic

1: **Procedure** best_core_assignment(*network_state, source_node, destination_node,*
                                        bandwidth_required)
2:      *bandwidth_required* ← *bandwidth_required + guard_bands*
3:      *number_slots_required* ← determine_number_slots_required(*source_node,*
                                        destination_node, bandwidth_required)
4:      *transmitters_assigned_to_lightpath* ← assign_transmitters(*source_node,*
                                        number_slots_required)
5:      *receivers_assigned_to_lightpath* ← assign_receivers(*destination_node,*
                                        number_slots_required)
6:      **if** *transmitters_assigned_to_lightpath* ≠ ∅ **and**
            receivers_assigned_to_lightpath ≠ ∅ **then**
7:          **for each** *path* **in** k-shortest-paths(*source_node, destination_node*) **do**
8:              *combined_JSAV* ← ∅
9:              **for each** *core* **in** *cores_per_MCF* **do**
10:                 *combined_JSAV* ← *combined_JSAV* ∪ build_JSAV(*path, core*)
11:             **end for**
12:             *core_and_slots_assigned_to_lightpath* ← best_gap_spectrum_alloca-
                                        tion(*path, combined_JSAV, number_slots_required*)
13:             **if** *core_and_slots_assigned_to_lightpath* = ∅ **then**
14:                 **continue**   # Not enough contiguous slots found on JSAV (jump to line 7)
15:             **end if**
16:             establish_lightpath(*path, core_and_slots_assigned_to_lightpath,*
                                        transmitters_assigned_to_lightpath, receivers_assigned_to_lightpath)
17:             **go to** end procedure
18:         **end for**
19:     **end if**
20:     reject_lightpath()
21: **end procedure**

3 Simulation Study

3.1 Simulation Scenario

In order to evaluate the performance of the algorithms, we have implemented a simulator of EONs using OMNeT++ [13]. As we want to test our proposal in a mesh metro network, the physical network topology used for this study is the 14-node NSFNet (a very well-known mesh topology but adapting its distances to the range of metro networks). Each cable between two network nodes is assumed to consist of two MCFs (one for each direction). Each MCF has two cores. The available capacity in each core is 4 THz and no physical impairments are considered. Four different slot sizes have been considered: 12.5 GHz (like most EONs proposals) and 50 GHz (the classical slot size uses in WRONs). The guard-band width is 10 GHz.

Lightpath requests arrive at the network following a Poisson process and the source-destination nodes pairs of each request are randomly selected using a uniform distribution. The demanded bandwidth of each lightpath is selected randomly following a uniform distribution between 1 GHz and 300 GHz, and the holding time of a connection is obtained by means of an exponential distribution. The number of paths explored with the *k*-shortest paths method was set to 2 routes per node pair. All the results are shown with 95% confidence intervals (although in most cases they are smaller than the size of the symbols employed in the following figures).

3.2 Simulation Results

Figure 3 shows the blocking ratio of lightpaths depending on the load, the size of the slots and the method followed to assign the core: first-fit or best core. Results from Fig. 3 shows that the blocking ratio of the network increases with the load. Moreover, independently of the method followed to assign the core, using a smaller slot size improves the network utilization and increases its performance by reducing the blocking ratio. Finally, Fig. 3 also shows that thank to the joint allocation of spectrum and core (best core assignment), the blocking ratio of the network is reduced when compared to the method that uses first-fit for core assignment.

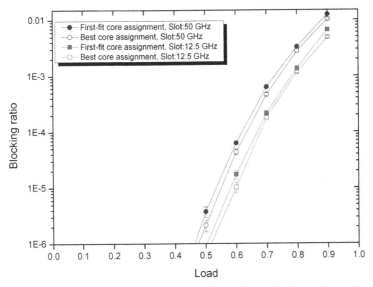

Fig. 3. Blocking probability of connection request depending on the load when using (i) first-fit for core assignment and best gap for spectrum assignment, and (ii) joint core and spectrum allocation (best core), with two slot sizes: 12.5 GHz and 50 GHz.

One of the main concerns of exploring the full spectrum of all the cores (required for the joint core and spectrum allocation) is the computing time required to obtain a solution. In dynamic networks, this time is critical as connections should be served on real time. Even when the best core method can be easily parallelized, thus reducing its computing time, for the sake of comparison, no parallelization has been used in our tests. Figure 4 shows the computing time with the different versions of the RCSA algorithm.

Figure 4 shows that when the slot size decreases, the computing time required to solve the RCSA problem increases, as there is a higher number of slots that must be explored to provide the solution. When comparing the computing time of the two versions of the RCSA algorithm, the first-fit version is the one that has a lower computing time, as it sequentially explores the spectrum of the cores, but when a solution is found in one core, no other cores are evaluated. On the contrary, the joint allocation of core and spectrum explores the spectrum of all the cores to find the best gap along all the cores. However, the computing time of both versions is very similar for low and middle loads where, according to Fig. 3, the blocking ratio is below 10^{-3}. In any case, the computing time of all the tests are under 30, ms and that is a low value compared with the time required to physically establish (configuring the involved resources) and to activate the lightpaths.

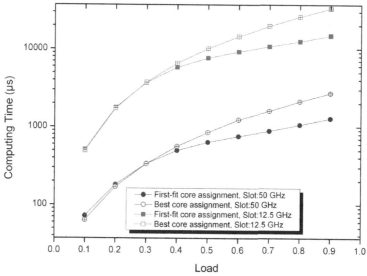

Fig. 4. Computing time that (i) first-fit for core assignment and best gap for spectrum assignment, and (ii) joint core and spectrum allocation (best core), take to solve a connection request depending on the load and using with two slot sizes: 12.5 GHz and 50 GHz.

4 Conclusions

In this paper, we have presented two algorithms for solving the routing, core and spectrum assignment for a metro elastic optical network equipped with multicore fiber and ROADM without line change. That cost-effective architecture provides the bandwidth and flexibility required for the backhaul of 5G networks equipped with MEC resources. Lightpath requests and releases are assumed to arrive at the network on-real time and a PCE is in charge of searching the solution of the RCSA problem using the information in the TED. Both versions use k-shortest paths for solving the routing problem and find the spectrum gap that better fits the lightpath request. However, they differ in the way in which cores are assigned. First-fit sequentially explores each core and it stops when finding a possible solution while the joint allocation explores the spectrum of all the cores to find the best available gap. Simulation results show that the blocking ratio is reduced when using the joint allocation at the expense of slightly increasing the computing time required to find a solution. In any case, the computing time of both versions is low enough to use them in the described architecture. This work establishes the first step for more complex studies in which networks with higher number of cores will also be explored.

Acknowledgment. The research leading to these results has been supported in part by Spanish Ministry of Economy and Competitiveness through the project ONOFRE-2 (TEC2017–84423-C3-1-P) and the research network Go2Edge (RED2018–102585-T) and the European Regional Development Fund (ERDF) through the project DISRUPTIVE of the cooperation programme Interreg V-A Spain-Portugal (POCTEP) 2014–2020.

References

1. Mayoral, A., et al.: Cascading of tenant SDN and cloud controllers for 5G network slicing using transport API and openstack API. In: Proceedings of OFC17, M2H.3 (2017)
2. Maternia, M., et al.: 5G PPP use cases and performance evaluation models. In: 5G-PPP, Techical Report (2016)
3. Patel, M., et al.: Mobile-edge computing introductory technical white paper. In: Mobile-Edge Computing (MEC) Industry Initiative (2014)
4. Wong, E., et al.: Predictive resource allocation for tactile internet capable passive optical LANs. J. Lightwave Technol. **35**(13), 2629–2641 (2017)
5. Mukherjee, B.: Optical Communication Networks. McGraw-Hill, New York (1997)
6. Christodoulopoulos, K., et al.: Elastic bandwidth allocation in flexible OFDM-based optical networks. J. Lightwave Technol. **29**(9), 1354–1366 (2011)
7. Christodoulopoulos, K., Tomkos, I., Varvarigos, E.A.: Routing and spectrum allocation in OFDM-based optical networks with elastic bandwidth allocation. In Proceedings of IEEE GLOBECOM 2010 (2010)
8. Durán, R.J., et al.: Performance comparison of methods to solve the routing and spectrum allocation problem. In: Proceedings of ICTON 2012 (2012)
9. Tode, H., Hirota, Y.: Routing, spectrum, and core and/or mode assignment on space-division multiplexing optical networks [invited]. IEEE/OSA J. Opt. Commun. Netw. **9**(1), A99–A113 (2017)
10. Muhammad, A.: Routing, spectrum and core allocation in Flexgrid SDM networks with multi-core fibers. In: ONDM 2014 (2014)
11. Yang, M., Zhang, Y., Wu, Q.: Routing, spectrum, and core assignment in SDM-EONS with MCF: node-arc ILP/MILP methods and an efficient XT-aware heuristic algorithm. IEEE/OSA J. Opt. Commun. Netw. **10**(3), 195–208 (2018)
12. Savva, G., et al.: Physical layer-aware routing, spectrum, and core allocation in spectrally-spatially flexible optical networks with multicore fibers. In: Proceedings of IEEE ICC 2018 (2018)
13. Chen, Y., et al.: Crosstalk-aware routing, spectrum, and core assignment in space division multiplexing networks with bi-directional multi-core fibers. In. Proceedings of APC 2018 (2018)
14. Rumipamba-Zambrano, R., et al.: Space continuity constraint in dynamic flex-grid/SDM optical core networks: an evaluation with spatial and spectral super-channels. Comput. Commun. **126**, 38–49 (2018)

Comparison of Efficient Planning and Optimization Methods of Last Mile Delivery Resources

J. A. Maestro[(⊠)], S. Rodriguez, R. Casado, J. Prieto, and J. M. Corchado

BISITE Research Group, Universidad de Salamanca, Espejo 2, 37007 Salamanca, Spain
{josemaestro,srg,rober,javierp,corchado}@usal.com

Abstract. A review of recent Last Mile Delivery optimization proposals is presented. The proposals are classified according to the criteria of collaboration, ranging from optimization of a single route to the integration of multiple carriers. An alternative proposal is presented, based also on collaboration, but which does not involve either integration into a single organization or sharing of its resources. Each carrier is represented as a Virtual Organization of Agents (VO). A global optimizer, also a VO, oversees the search for deliveries that can be better delivered by another carrier and new routes are calculated based on a win-win approach. This approach has the advantages of being easily configurable by integrating or removing the VO of each carrier, highly distributable using a cloud infrastructure, easily scalable both for physical areas and computational resources using the cloud infrastructure in case more computational power is needed. It also allows the sharing of the least amount of information possible among carriers, so that they only know about the deliveries that they are losing or gaining.

Keywords: Multi-Agent Systems · Last mile delivery · Planning optimization · Cloud computing

1 Introduction

Last Mile Delivery (LMD) is increasing in importance due to several reasons, such as the growing population in cities and the progressive increase in deliveries associated with e-commerce [1, 2]. Urban freight distribution, while necessary to maintain the supply of goods in cities, support economic development and increase customer satisfaction, has some drawbacks. The more common side effects mentioned in literature include: congestion, air pollution, greenhouse gas (GHG) emissions, traffic accidents, noise, etc. [2–4]. As freight delivery in urban areas can be up to 15–20% of the vehicle traffic [2], an optimization in this field can contribute to increase the sustainability of the service as well as to a significant reduction of its side effects.

Several attempts have been proposed to try to reduce the economic cost of the LMD, usually by reducing the length of the route in a few ways. These approaches range from crowdsourcing, to integrating several carriers to share resources, among others. For

© ICST Institute for Computer Sciences, Social Informatics and Telecommunications Engineering 2021
Published by Springer Nature Switzerland AG 2021. All Rights Reserved
H. Gao et al. (Eds.): BROADNETS 2020, LNICST 355, pp. 163–173, 2021.
https://doi.org/10.1007/978-3-030-68737-3_11

example, the crowdsourcing approach seeks to reduce the number of stops on a route or even eliminate the route altogether by replacing carriers with ordinary people. The opposite approach attempts to reduce cost by sharing the resources of several carriers and behaving as if they were one.

The rest of this paper is organized as follows: the following section contains a review of the different alternatives that can be found in recent publications. This is followed by our own approach, a solution based on agents and collaboration. Discussion and final remarks end the paper.

2 Optimization in Last Mile Delivery

The optimization of last mile delivery has been approached from several points of view. The proposed solutions range from the simple use of optimization methods to group the recipients and the delivery route(s) to the integration of several carriers in a city and the search for a common and global solution for the whole set of deliveries. Intermediate solutions include various kinds of cost reduction by sharing resources, using alternative forms of delivery, using alternative vehicles, incorporating additional infrastructure, or sharing resources among several carriers. [5] includes a good description of the LMD problem, which can be summarized as: several carriers compete with each other in the city and this results in a fragmented market and a lack of coordination and therefore to low vehicle load factor, excessive vehicle movement, a high cost for the overall delivery system and environmental side effects. Authors enumerate a set of problems associated with the LMD problem, namely: (*i*) pick-up and delivery points often located in areas of restricted access, far from large distribution centers, with scattered demand groups and with some access restrictions such as time windows for delivery; (*ii*) congestion, (*iii*) limitations on the use of the vehicle fleet; and (*iv*) with a dynamic interaction among many interests and services, polices and interventions. [5] also proposes four areas to achieve collaboration between the different actors in urban freight delivery: (*a*) eco-friendly collaborative delivery, (*b*) synchronization & multi-objective planning, (*c*) multi-party coordination and (*d*) data harmonization & analytics. Most of the proposed solutions can be classified in one or more of these areas. However, focusing especially on collaboration among carriers, the literature reviewed can be classified according to the degree of collaboration they seek to achieve in three main groups, namely: (*I*) single-route optimization, (*II*) increasing the vehicle load factor, and (*III*) joint optimization of multiple carriers. A graphic description of the possible options could be represented as in Fig. 1.

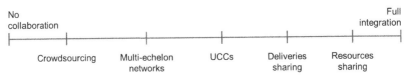

Fig. 1. Different kinds of collaboration among carriers arranged progressively.

2.1 Single-Route Cost Reduction

Some approaches are based on optimizing a single route or maybe several routes for the same carrier. The approaches chosen include several options as the final objective, the cost reduction, can be achieved in several ways. For instance, by asking others to make the delivery or by using existing public transportation.

Crowdsourced and Mixed Delivery. Several authors have proposed using any kind of 'crowdsourced' delivery. Crowdsourced delivery–also known as crowd-shipping– is described in [6] as the crowdsourcing of the delivery task to a set of individuals who deliver parcels along their routes while using the empty space in their cars or luggage. In this case, a win-win relationship can be obtained: better customer experience is achieved, and the crowd individuals get some additional income. At the same time, some side effects can be reduced, such as reducing the urban traffic, or a lower environmental footprint.

In [7] it is proposed to use this approach for food delivery using motorbikes. [8] also describes how to use a crowdsourcing model in a two-echelon distribution network: first, a truck transports the parcels from a depot to the city center, then, at an arranged location(s), parcels are transferred for crowdsourced delivery to their final recipients. [9] goes one step further and extends the problem to a network of crowdsourced drivers that can transfer parcels to each other at agreed locations to avoid long detours for the drivers. This allows for a more flexible assignment of drivers and parcels. [6] includes not only crowdsourced drivers but also pedestrians and cyclist. [10] proposes to mix some professional drivers with crowdsourced ones who deliver parcels from a shop on their way to their own destination. Moreover, time can be introduced as a new variable of the solution: in [9] is proposed to wait to allow the possibility for a store to group deliveries received online, which will be delivered by the customers who are present in the store. Obviously, time windows for delivery and some deadlines must be considered.

In [11] the usage of an online platform –without carrier– to receive pick-up orders, accept the task and compute the route is considered. If a crowdsourced driver is not available, an external carrier is contacted to do the job.

Use of Alternative Means of Transport. Several authors have proposed the use of public transport, such as buses, trams, or taxis, as a means of obtaining savings and reducing side effects. For instance, in [4] it is proposed to mix the usual methods of public transport available such as bus, trams or subway together with e-bikes as they are eco-friendly and can be transported on public transport. A similar idea is presented in [12] where it is proposed to use bus stations as small distribution hubs and bus lines as the transport network. The use of taxis has also been proposed to reduce the cost of parcel transportation by sharing the cost of the ride with passengers [13].

2.2 Increased Vehicle Load Factor Through Consolidation

Some proposals include the use of additional infrastructure other than the carrier(s) main repository or intermediate or auxiliary infrastructure. The usual objective is to reduce the distance that parcels travel by using an intermediate hub for subsequent distribution or to avoid additional trips because the parcel cannot be delivered to the recipient.

Multi-Echelon Networks. A distribution network using only one level can be ineffi-cient, as the origin of the trip, the depot, can imply long trips to the recipients and this led to long trips. The existence of time windows for delivery can also lead to reduced vehicle load factor [14]. This can be mitigated using a network of satellite hubs which can be used to consolidate and deconsolidate the deliveries, allow using smaller and less pollutant vehicles, better fitted for dense traffic. [14] includes an updated review of the relevant literature about this topic. This kind of distribution networks is designed to include ancillary depots or satellites, maybe interconnected among them, located in the city in areas where there is a dense concentration of recipients. The use of this kind of networks is proposed in [8, 14, 15] and [17].

Urban Consolidation Centers (UCC). As a way of balancing interests among carriers, receivers, citizens and public administrators, the use of UCCs has been proposed in some cities. A UCC is a hub, usually located within city limits and easily accessible. The UCC is a consolidation center and the objective are to increase the load factor of the delivery fleet and reduce the distance traveled [3]. The use of a UCC appears to have an economic impact on last mile delivery, however. Cost analyses of the UCCs can be found in [3, 17]. Because of this economic impact, it is stated in [18] that the main decision for a courier is whether to let the UCC deliver a parcel or make a direct delivery to the recipients.

Success of the UCC may depend on some constraints which are out of the control of the carriers. [2] mention some incentives to use a UCC: (*i*) mandatory usage of eco-friendly vehicles for last leg delivery; (*ii*) restrictions on access the city center such as time windows for delivery or depending on the kind of vehicle; (*iii*) pollution charges. For example, [3] describes the UCC in the city of Antwerp, Belgium. The city suffers from traffic congestion, so it has been stated time windows for freight delivery and a Low Emissions Zone (LEZ) in the city. The UCC is used by 4 carrier companies, can benefit from several kinds of freight arrivals, such as trucks or ships, and delivers to the city area, the port, and the outskirts. As the UCC is run by the public postal company, it has enough budget and no other subsidies are needed. Nevertheless, the authors estimate that it needs to increase daily deliveries from 75 to 336 to reach financial equilibrium.

Other authors provide simulations on the viability of the introduction of a UCC in some cities. For example, [1] considers introducing a UCC in the city of Frankfurt am Main (Germany), and [2] in the city of Austin, Texas (USA). The latter considers using electric vehicles (vans) and e-bikes for delivery and also, the renewal of the existing fleet of polluting vans for newer and less polluting ones. Both present several scenarios and estimate the impact of the proposed changes.

Both approaches, the multi-echelon network and the UCC, can be combined when designing the distribution network, as proposed in [14] and [15]. The latter also includes a collaboration approach and proposes sharing both UCC and satellites among several carrier enterprises to reduce the infrastructure costs.

2.3 Joint Optimization of Multiple Carriers

[19] classifies the possible collaboration between urban freight delivery enterprises into 3 interaction levels:

1. Transactional: coordination and standardization of administrative practices and exchange techniques.
2. Informational: exchange of business information, for instance, sales forecasts, stock levels or scheduled delivery dates.
3. Decisional, which can be divided into 3 kinds of collaboration at different planning horizons of logistics and transportation activities: (*i*) Operational planning (everyday operations that can be coordinated or shared such as freight transportation or cross-docking); (*ii*) Tactical planning (middle-term planning stage, which includes operations such as forecasting, shipping, inventory, production management, quality control); (*iii*) Strategic planning (long-term planning decision such as network design, facility location, finance, and production planning).

Local/Global Route Optimization by Collaboration. A curious form of collaboration is proposed in [20]. Assuming that stores send new orders based on stock management, the delivery process will produce some inefficiencies such as vehicles not being fully loaded. To reduce this problem, it is proposed that carriers ask stores on the route already set to anticipate their orders, so that the load factor of the vehicles increase, and the overall process becomes more efficient. Therefore, stores collaborate to increase efficiency in the delivery process, which allows them to reduce the total cost of delivery and travel less distance to serve the same load. Stores anticipating their orders receive a discount on the cost of the delivered freight.

Other possible form of collaboration is proposed in [21]. The routes are built by a set of collaborating agents, in a Multi-Agent System. Each agent represents a carrier and contains its own goals. However, the agents collaborate to optimize all the routes, including having one carrier deliver parcels from another carrier if this is the best computed solution. If so, the carrier should visit, in this order, both the other carrier's depot and the recipient, to make the delivery.

Resources Sharing. [19] describes a possible solution through collaboration in which three different carriers coordinate and collaborates to increase vehicle load factor and reduce delivery costs. In this proposal, the solution is achieved by transferring part of the freight to be delivered from two of the carriers to the other one because the better location of its depot and the possible routes from it allow them to optimize costs. A reduction in the number of trips and travelled distance is obtained and therefore, the corresponding savings in delivery cost. This approach consists mainly of coordinating the three carriers as if they were one, sharing parcels, vehicles and therefore drivers, as necessary.

[15] describes the case of the city of Quongqing (China), where two carriers joined in an alliance. The proposed solution includes the design of a multi-echelon network and a set of Collection Points (CP). A cost reduction in the number of vehicles from 37 to 20 at best, compared to maintaining two independent carriers, is reported.

Table 1 shows a classification of the proposals considered in the review. Proposals are classified according the kind of collaboration they propose, the kind of problem being solved (B2C or B2B), and the kind of solution they propose: agent-based, machine learning, heuristics, exact solution using mainly linear programming.

Table 1. Classification of the proposals considered in the review.

	Single Route		Load factor		Carrier integration	
	Crowd-based	Public transport	Multi-echelon	UCCs	Collaboration	Integration
Proposal	[6–11]	[4, 12, 13]	[8, 14–16]	[1–3, 14, 15, 17, 18]	[20, 21]	[15, 19]
B2C	[6–11]	[4, 12, 13]	[8, 14, 16]	[14]		[15, 19]
B2B			[15, 16]	[1, 15, 18]	[20]	
Agents	[6]	[4]	[16]	[1, 18]	[20, 21]	
M.L.	[7]	[13]		[18]		
Heuristics	[8–10]	[13]	[8, 14, 15]	[15, 18]	[21]	[15, 19]
Exact	[8, 11]	[12]	[8, 14]		[21]	[19]

2.4 Criticisms of the Proposed Approaches

Single Route Cost Reduction. Although this type of optimization can achieve a reduction in costs by reducing stops on a route, it cannot allow for an overall optimization of routes, since the reduction is not based on increasing the vehicle load factor but on reducing the number of parcels delivered by the carrier. It is assumed that some reduction of the route for the carrier can be achieved by making some of the deliveries by occasional drivers, or other form of collective courier. Furthermore, as pointed out in [11], on the one hand, the crowd-based approach to delivery is scalable, but on the other hand, the quality obtained by a fleet of professional drivers can be higher.

Increasing the Load Factor Through Consolidation. Some authors have mentioned the drawbacks of the UCCs. For instance, [1] mention that the cost associated with the UCC makes it unattractive to carriers, and [2] summarizes four reasons for the failure of the UCCs, namely: (*i*) lack of planning, (*ii*) too ambitious forecasts, (*iii*) dependence on local authorities for subsidies and too high operating costs, and (*iv*) some wrong decisions such as the location of the UCC or the kind of vehicles in the fleet. In addition, regarding the cost associated with the establishment of the UCC, it has been proposed to be established by a large company, to avoid dependence on public subsidies [3].

Progressive Integration of Carriers. Some proposals, being theoretically interesting, are difficult to be practical. For instance, proposals such as [19] or [16] basically involve uniting carriers to work as one. However, some practical problems need to be addressed, for instance, in [19] part of the freight is transferred from two of the carriers to a third one, because its depot allows for better routes, if the depot can store the extra freight, if it can manage the extra freight or if there are enough bays for the extra delivery vehicles or not is not taken into account.

3 Alternative Proposal

The idea of consolidating deliveries to increase the load factor of delivery vehicles as a way to improve the delivery process that underlie the UCC is attractive, although the drawbacks, mainly the operational cost of introducing new delivery infrastructure can make the idea unsuitable for all cities. However, a cost reduction can be achieved by collaboration without the drawbacks of establishing a new UCC and avoiding the integration of several carriers into one. The idea of a virtual UCC was already proposed in [5] based on an auction mechanism in which carriers offer some deliveries and other carriers bid for them.

As an alternative, focused more on a collaboration approach, it is proposed to perform a general optimization of the routes. The proposed process consists mainly of sending the routes already built to a common shared optimizer. This central element will try to improve the group of routes, in a win-win basis. The optimizer will seek out stops on the route that can be delivered by another carrier at a lower cost, based on a distance/cost travelled criterion. Some basic assumptions must be made: first, the routes are at least partially overlapped, and second, the individual routes are already optimized for delivery.

To obtain a robust, flexible, configurable and extendable solution, the use of an agent-based approach is proposed, and more precisely a Virtual Organization (VO) of Agents [22–24] which is a paradigm for managing collaboration between Multi-Agent Systems (MAS). A MAS is formed by a group of agents, which have some characteristics such as: sociability, autonomy, and proactivity [25]. The agents will pursue their own goals or the global goal, and behaviors such as goal delegation or collaboration among several agents to achieve a goal can be present [26]. One of the key features of a MAS is its ability to reorganize and adapt to changes in the environment. VOs go one step further, agents and MAS arranged in organizations needs to coordinate resources and services across the organizational boundaries to achieve their goal [23]. Thus, VOs allow to organize groups of agents and MAS, not necessarily homogeneous, and so that they can achieve their goals through collaboration.

An agent-based solution has some advantages to deal with complex problems, such as the capacity of distribution in computers and organizations, the ability to deal with complex communication, independence in the behavior of the agents, etc. Some proposals already mentioned include agent technology in the solution, such as [4, 6] or [16]. The agent technology will provide the solution with a great versatility and the ability to be distributed and even easily scalable. Examples of the use of the MAS approach and challenges related to it can be found in [25].

3.1 Organizational Design

Each carrier and the common shared optimizer will be organized as VOs of agents. To optimize the routes, there are agents for performing each of the task needed, such as: recovering the stops for each route from local systems, planning an optimized route, with the help of some other agents for obtaining the street map, the information about cut-off or worksite streets from local authorities, weather forecast, urban traffic information (if available), etc. Some other agents can be available e.g. an agent for learning the real route the drivers do, because of the weather, an accident, knowledge about parking, etc. for further route optimization. Also, there will be agents to manage the communication with the common shared optimizer. These agents will oversee sending the locally optimized routes, provide any other information necessary and receive the globally optimized routes.

The common optimizer will also consist of several agents capable of developing complex tasks such as: identify possible stops on a route that can be changed to other carrier-route based on optimization criteria, performs their own route optimization process, and hence, those auxiliary agents for obtaining the street map, the state of the city streets, the forecast and traffic information, will also be present. The agent being able to manage the communication should also be included.

To ease the MAS design and the scalability of the solution, each VO representing a carrier will communicate with the optimizer VO through the communication agent. A graphical representation is depicted in Fig. 2. The internal structure of agents in each VO fits well with the federation organization described in [22, 25] and [26]. The common optimizer will prevent carriers from exchanging unnecessary information and undesirable behaviors in the agents in the VO of any carrier. The common optimizer would be a single point of failure as its main drawback.

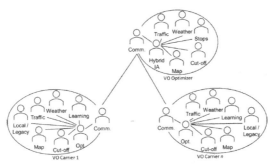

Fig. 2. Virtual Organizations of agents for the route optimization solution.

The usage of VOs proposed will allow the system to add or remove carriers (VOs) easily and thus, to adapt to changes in the environment. This also will allow to change the scope of the solution easily. For cities small enough, a single optimizer would be sufficient, bigger cities may need to replicate the solution for neighborhoods for instance, but the adaptability of this kind of systems help to manage these situations.

Cloud deployment provides the solution with flexibility, general availability and the ability to change the scope and computing requirements. A carrier (its VO) can easily be added or removed since only the global optimizer needs to be contacted via its communication agent and the necessary information exchanged, while the VO can be kept in the company's own cloud. Computing resources can be adapted as necessary to meet requirements due to the number of carriers using the service.

3.2   A Hybrid AI-Based Solution

The proposed solution is based on Artificial Intelligence (AI) to globally optimize routes. To control the computational cost of the process, an exact global solution is discarded. Our solution is divided into two parts. First, a heuristic is proposed to select the stops that can be changed to another route. Those stops on a route closer to a stop on another route are candidates to be changed. In case of an exchange of stops, a transfer point, the place where both drivers must meet, and where the freight is exchanged, must also be added to both routes. Although, this is not necessarily a synchronous event. Locations for a possible asynchronous transfer include the carrier's depot, parcel lockers, stores, etc. Once the transfer point has been selected for the exchange of parcels, parcels that could be interchangeable and that are at stops on the route prior to the exchange point should be reconsidered if their exchange is still feasible or has become unfeasible due to the cost of the detour. Second, as both routes must be modified, a hybrid approach is proposed [27], so that an expert system and route optimization algorithms will calculate the new routes. The chosen optimization algorithm will be based on the characteristics of the route, for instance the number of stops or the existence of restrictions on the route. Thus, it is possible to choose the best possible option, even an exact solution, depending on the optimization algorithm that is best suited for each route. Many of the current proposed solutions to LMD rely on some AI algorithm, for instance, a heuristic solution such as in [8, 9] or [14], or based on Machine Learning such as in [7, 13] as a way to avoid the computational cost of obtaining an exact solution.

Given that the new solution should improve the existing one, two constraints should be included: (*i*) a transferred stop from a route allows the carrier who lose the stop not to worsen its cost function, and (*ii*) the set of routes reduces the overall cost. Thus, both local and global optimization is considered. This also allows some preferences to be included in the corresponding agents, such as: is it necessary to make a profit to accept the changes in a route? Is it enough if the new route is not worse than the original one? Is it enough to make an overall profit to accept the proposed changes?

4   Discussion and Final Remarks

A review of recent proposals for LMD is presented. The different proposals have been classified based on how the collaboration is approached. Those proposals closer to crowd-sourcing try to reduce stops on the route or even the route itself. This option, however, does not allow for any further optimization as no other stakeholders are included. The load factor increase approach may need to include expensive extra facilities that may hinder the economic viability of this solution. Other approaches based on collaboration between carriers have also some drawbacks. Full integration of carriers can be cost-effective for companies, but competition among carriers disappeared. A proposal for route optimization based on collaboration has been included. The proposal seeks to reduce inefficiencies in the delivery process due to the distance to some stops, which perhaps may be better served by other carrier. This approach seeks local optimization for each carrier and, at the same time, global optimization for the overall LMD system. To achieve this, the solution is divided into two stages: first, stops on the route are identified that can be served more efficiently on another route. Then, as any route can lose some stops and gain others, a new optimization process is developed using a hybrid solution based on an expert system and several optimization algorithms.

Acknowledgements. This work has been developed as part of "Virtual-Ledgers-Tecnologías DLT/Blockchain y Cripto-IOT sobre organizaciones virtuales de agentes ligeros y su aplicación en la eficiencia en el transporte de última milla", ID SA267P18, project financed by Junta Castilla y León, Consejería de Educación, and FEDER funds.

References

1. Elbert, R., Friedrich, C.: Simulation-based evaluation of urban consolidation centers considering urban access regulations. In: Proceedings of the 2018 Winter Simulation Conference, pp. 2827–2838, Gothenburg, Sweden. IEEE (2018)
2. Simoni, M.D., Bujanovic, P., Boyles, S.D., Kutanoglu, E.: Urban consolidation solutions for parcel delivery considering location, fleet and route choice. Case Stud. Transp. Policy **6**, 112–124 (2018). https://doi.org/10.1016/j.cstp.2017.11.002
3. Kin, B., Verlinde, S., Lier, T.V., Macharis, C.: Is there life after subsidy for an urban consolidation centre? an investigation of the total costs and benefits of a privately-initiated concept. Trans. Res. Procedia **12**, 357–369 (2016)
4. Chatterjee, R., Greulich, C., Edelkamp, S.: Optimizing last mile delivery using public transport with multi-agent based control. In: IEEE 41st Conference on Local Computer Networks Workshops, pp. 205–212 (2016). https://doi.org/10.1109/lcnw.2016.40
5. Souza, R.D., Goh, M., Lau, H.-C., Ng, W.-S., Tan, P.-S.: Collaborative urban logistics – synchronizing the last mile. a Singapore research perspective. Procedia Soc. Behav. Sci. **125**, 422–431 (2014). https://doi.org/10.1016/j.sbspro.2014.01.1485
6. Chen, P., Chankov, S.: Crowdsourced delivery for last-mile distribution: an agent-based modelling and simulation approach. In: Proceedings of the 2017 IEEE International Conference on Industrial Engineering and Engineering Management (IEEM), pp. 1271–1275 (2017). https://doi.org/10.1109/ieem.2017.8290097
7. Habault, G., Taniguchi, Y., Yamanaka, N.: Delivery management system based on vehicles monitoring and a machine-learning mechanism. In: IEEE 88th Vehicular Technology Conference, pp. 1–5 (2018). https://doi.org/10.1109/vtcfall.2018.8690619
8. Kafle, N., Zou, B., Lin, J.: Design and modeling of a crowdsource-enabled system for urban parcel relay and delivery. Transp. Res. Part B Methodol. **99**, 62–82 (2017). https://doi.org/10.1016/j.trb.2016.12.022
9. Chen, W., Mes, M., Schutten, M.: Multi-hop driver-parcel matching problem with time windows. Flex. Serv. Manuf. J. **30**(3), 517–553 (2018)
10. Archetti, C., Savelsbergh, M., Speranza, M.G.: The vehicle routing problem with occasional drivers. Eur. J. Oper. Res. **254**(2), 472–480 (2016). https://doi.org/10.1016/j.ejor.2016.03.049
11. Arslan, A., Agatz, N.A., Kroon, L., Zuidwijk, R.A.: Crowdsourced delivery: a dynamic pickup and delivery problem with ad-hoc drivers. ERIM Report Series Reference, Erasmus University, Rotterdam School of Management (2016). https://doi.org/10.2139/ssrn.2726731
12. Pimentel, C., Alvelos, F.: Integrated urban freight logistics combining passenger and freight flows –mathematical model proposal. Transp. Res. Procedia **30**, 80–89 (2018)
13. Li, B., Krushinsky, D., Woensel, T.V., Reijers, H.A.: The share-a-ride problem with stochastic travel times and stochastic delivery locations. Transp. Res. Part C Emerg. Technol. **67**, 95–108 (2016). https://doi.org/10.1016/j.trc.2016.01.014
14. Janjevic, M., Winkenbach, M., Merchán, D.: Integrating collection-and-delivery points in the strategic design of urban last-mile e-commerce distribution networks. Transp. Res. Part E **131**, 37–67 (2019). https://doi.org/10.1016/j.tre.2019.09.001
15. Zhou, L., Baldacci, R., Vigo, D., Wang, X.: A multi-depot two-echelon vehicle routing problem with delivery options arising in the last mile distribution. Eur. J. Oper. Res. **265**(2), 765–778 (2018). https://doi.org/10.1016/j.ejor.2017.08.011
16. Martins-Turner, K., Nagel, K.: How driving multiple tours affects the results of last mile delivery vehicle routing problems. Procedia Comput. Sci. **151**, 840–845 (2019). https://doi.org/10.1016/j.procs.2019.04.115
17. Janjevic, M., Ndiaye, A.: Investigating the theoretical cost-relationships of urban consolidation centres for their users. Transp. Res. Part A **102**, 98–118 (2017). https://doi.org/10.1016/j.tra.2016.10.027

18. Firdausiyah, N., Taniguchi, E., Qureshi, A.: Modeling city logistics using adaptive dynamic programming based multi-agent simulation. Transp. Res. Part E **125**, 74–96 (2019). https://doi.org/10.1016/j.tre.2019.02.011
19. Muñoz-Villamizar, A., Montoya-Torres, J.R., Vega-Mejía, C.A.: Non-collaborative versus collaborative last-mile delivery in urban systems with stochastic demands. Procedia CIRP **30**, 263–268 (2015). https://doi.org/10.1016/j.procir.2015.02.147
20. Anand, N., Duin, R.V., Tavasszy, L.: Ontology-based multi-agent system for urban freight transportation. Int. J. Urban Sci. **18**(2), 133–153 (2014). https://doi.org/10.1080/12265934.2014.920696
21. Hasan, M., Niyogi, R.: A meta-heuristic based multi-agent approach for last mile delivery problem. In: Proceedings of the 22nd International Conference on Enterprise Information Systems (ICEIS 2020), vol. 1, pp. 498–505 (2020). SCITEPRESS – Science and Technology Publications, Lda. https://doi.org/10.5220/0009349004980505
22. Rodriguez, S., Julián, V., Bajo, J., Carrascosa, C., Botti, V., Corchado, J.M.: Agent-based virtual organization architecture. Eng. Appl. Artif. Intell. **24**(5), 895–910 (2011). https://doi.org/10.1016/j.engappai.2011.02.003
23. Argente, E., Botti, V., Carrascosa, C., Giret, A., Julian, V., Rebollo, M.: An abstract architecture for virtual organizations: the THOMAS approach. Knowl. Inf. Syst. **29**, 379–403 (2011). https://doi.org/10.1007/s10115-010-0349-1
24. Rodríguez, S., et al.: Trends on the development of adaptive virtual organizations. In: de Leon, F., de Carvalho, A.P., Rodríguez-González, S., De Paz Santana, J.F., Rodríguez, J.M.C. (eds.) Distributed Computing and Artificial Intelligence. AISC, vol. 79, pp. 113–121. Springer, Heidelberg (1998). https://doi.org/10.1007/978-3-642-14883-5_15
25. Dorri, A., Kanhere, S.S., Jurdak, R.: Multi-agent systems: a survey. IEEE Access **6**, 28573–28593 (2018). https://doi.org/10.1109/access.2018.2831228
26. Abbas, H.A., Shaheen, S.I., Amin, M.H.: Organization of multi agent systems an overview. Int. J. Intell. Inf. Syst. **4**(3), 46–57 (2015). https://doi.org/10.11648/j.ijiis.20150403.11
27. Borrajo, M.L., Baruque, B., Corchado, E., Bajo, J., Corchado, J.M.: Hybrid neural intelligent system to predict business failure in small-to-medium-size enterprises. Int. J. Neural Syst. **21**(4), 277–296 (2011)

Decision Making Under Uncertainty for the Deployment of Future Networks in IoT Scenarios

Néstor Alzate Mejía[1,2] (ID), Germán Santos Boada[2(✉)] (ID),
and José Roberto de Almeida Amazonas[2,3] (ID)

[1] Cooperative University of Colombia, Santiago de Cali, Colombia
[2] Universitat Politècnica de Catalunya, Barcelona, Spain
nestor.alzate@upc.edu, {german,amazonas}@ac.upc.edu
[3] Escola Politécnica of the University of São Paulo, São Paulo, Brazil

Abstract. The main characteristic of various emerging communication network paradigms in the dimensioning, control and deployment of future networks is the fact that they are human-centric, entailing closely-knit interactions between telematics and human activities. Considering the effect of user behavior, whose dynamics are difficult to model, new uncertainties are introduced in these systems, bringing about network resource management challenges. Within this context, this study seeks to review different decision-making computational methods in conditions of uncertainty for Internet of Things scenarios such as smart spaces, and industry 4.0, through a systematic literature review. According to our research results, a new paradigm for computationally capturing and modeling human behavior context must be developed with the purpose of improving resource management.

Keywords: Uncertainty · Resource management · Decision making

1 Introduction

Different approaches to Data Communications Networks (DCN) have evolved gradually in tandem with technological advances. However, these changes entail new network resource management challenges, which must be overcome to meet the objectives from emerging approaches.

Consequently, in relation to traditional DCN management, performance is examined with regards to quantitative technical data, such as package delivery

This work has been partially supported by the Spanish Ministry of Economy and Competitiveness under contract TEC2017-90034-C2-1-R (ALLIANCE project) that receives funding from FEDER. Moreover, it has been partially supported by the Spanish Thematic Network under contract RED2018-102585-T (Go2Edge) and by the aid granted by the Sinfoni project INV2733 of the Cooperative University of Colombia.

H. Gao et al. (Eds.): BROADNETS 2020, LNICST 355, pp. 174–184, 2021.
https://doi.org/10.1007/978-3-030-68737-3_12

delays, the number of packages that were not delivered to their destination, transmission speeds between origins and destinations, among others. Based on this focus, data is provided by electronic devices such as sensors, and mobile and network equipment.

Further, another burgeoning DCN-related concept is a human-centric network (HCN), which proposes the optimization of both services and network applications by centering their decisions on the wellbeing of individuals. To accomplish this, network performance is assessed by considering both traditional quantitative and qualitative data. Qualitative data generated by individuals, either directly through opinions posted on web pages or social media or through interactions between individuals and their devices, which log human activities on several platforms.

This growing and closely knit interaction between individuals and their online activity-tracking devices has changed the roles played by individuals from passive to active in terms of DCNs [9,11]. In this new role, human activities determine network usage behaviors. Therefore, the uncertainty produced by individuals through their perceived experiences influences DCN performance to a greater extent.

Diverse studies have approached these novel phenomena from a wide range of perspectives. For example, [12] studied diverse machine-learning techniques that may be implemented to support decision making and knowledge extraction, grounded on feedback from Internet of Things (IoT) paradigms and cyber-physical systems when combined through cloud and fog computing. Within the Industry 4.0 context, [22] developed a system implementation architecture that interacts between human agents and machines in the manufacturing sector. This proposed method included five levels with different types of challenges to overcome. With regards to smart spaces, in their work, [7] proposed an online framework, rooted on a logical Markovian network, for developing voice-driven home automation systems aimed at improving comfort and autonomy at home, thus addressing uncertainty based on context awareness. In their study on Self-Organized Networks, [16] discussed a decision-making framework supported by various machine-learning algorithms that could manage fifth-generation mobile network resources. Their novel approach was to use software-defined networks (SDN) and network function virtualization (NFV) as decision-making technologies. However, they do not consider qualitative data.

Therefore, HCN features can be used in application domains for concepts such as IoT, Industry 4.0 and smart spaces. For these concepts, inherent interactions between individuals and machines suggest that computational methods can be combined with other disciplines to improve the modeling of this phenomenon.

2   Computational Methods for Decision Making Under Uncertainty

Decision making involves selecting of the best option from a specific set to solve a given problem in the best possible manner. An agent is an entity that makes decisions according to its interaction with the environment. Agents can be persons, robots, and even entities implemented through software [19]. This research study centers on computational decision-making systems, especially those that accept designs with a significant degree of process automation and that are able to handle uncertainty. A classification of the most significant methods described in the literature is listed in Fig. 1.

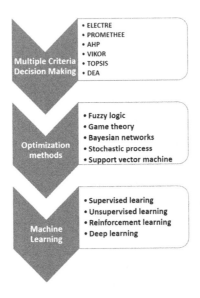

Fig. 1. Classification of computational methods for decision making.

2.1 Multiple Criteria Decision Making

In decision making, a set of alternatives is usually assessed by various criteria, with different weights according to their relevance to the issue at hand [4]. The problem lies in how to assign appropriate weights to each criterion. To address this situation, several Multiple Criteria Decision-Making (MCDM) tools have been extensively studied [2,13]. Therefore, there are different MCDM methods which may be classified depending on the academic currents from the European, American, and other schools.

The European school uses the following methods:

– Elimination and Choice Expressing Reality (ELECTRE): it is used to eliminate non-viable solution alternatives. This method is usually combined with another MCDM method to minimize execution times, as in the following studies: [10,28,35].

- Preference Ranking Organization Method for Enrichment of Evaluations (PROMETHEE): this method is founded on mathematical and psychological methods used to develop an external classification for various alternatives, thus helping agents to choose the option that best serves its purpose as per its own understanding of the issue. This method has been assessed in several fields, such as for infrastructure construction [15], the electric power sector [1,32], and engineering decision making [29], among others.

The North American school proposes the following method:

- Analytic Hierarchy Process (AHP): this method is structured to manage complex decisions based on appraisals and assessments, combining physical and psychological elements which are usually conflicting. In studies such as [25], this is evident because decision making is tackled under uncertainty or based on subjective product recommendations from consumers [21].

From different origins we can name:

- Multicriteria Optimization and Compromise Solution (VIKOR): is a method for determining the best possible solution, especially when dealing with conflicting options or with different units of measurement. In fact, there are several proposals for this method. For example, one is to combine this method with other techniques [27] to develop a method for assessing feelings in social media, for group decision-making processes [24] or for evaluating airline service quality [26].
- Technique for Order of Preference by Similarity to Ideal Solution (TOPSIS): this method seeks to find an alternative solution with the shortest and longest Euclidean distance from the optimum positive solution and the optimum negative solution, respectively. These solutions are mostly addressed in studies where this method is supplemented by additional algorithms, as shown in [5,8,33].
- Data Envelopment Analysis (DEA): it is a methodology created to assess the relative efficiencies of comparable entity sets by solving a series of mathematical programming models [18].

3   Internet of Things Application Domain

Internet of Things is a paradigm that arises from the possibilities foreseen by the communications technologies that emerged in the 1990s, such as Radio-Frequency Identification (RFID). Kevin Ashton initially introduced the term IoT at a presentation in 1999 [3]. From then onwards, organizations such as the International Telecommunications Union (ITU), the Institute of Electrical and Electronic Engineers (IEEE), the European Telecommunications Standards Institute (ETSI), and the Internet Engineering Task Force (IETF), among others, have worked on its standardization. However, they have not reached a unique definition for IoT yet. In our view, an accurate definition is provided by an EU-funded project known as Coordination and Support Action for Global RFID-Related Activities and Standardization (CASAGRAS), which defines it as "A global network infrastructure, linking physical and virtual objects through the exploitation of data capture and communication capabilities. This infrastructure includes existing and evolving Internet and network developments. It will offer specific object-identification, sensor and connection capability as the basis for the development of independent cooperative services and applications. These will be characterized by a high degree of autonomous data capture, event transfer, network connectivity, and interoperability" [17].

3.1   Mobile Wireless Sensor Network

A Mobile Wireless Sensor Network (MWSN) evidences a case of uncertainty within an IoT network, as shown in Fig. 2. The MWSN resources are limited, especially in terms of processing capacity and power independence. In this scenario, multiple mobile wireless sensors installed on drones intercommunicate without requiring the infrastructure of a physical network to monitor and identify intruders in specific neighborhood areas. Figure 2(A) provides a late-night example, at hours when it is unlikely that people will be out in the streets. Nevertheless, a sensor finds an intruder and, based on the conditions at that moment, the only possible route is resolved: sending an alert to the control station. However, because the sensors are moving, various situations may happen that might render the chosen route unfeasible, such as one or more sensors being outside coverage range or hardware failures. Figure 2(B) displays how one of the drones is left offline because the multiple signals detected exceeds its maximum processing capacity. This is driven by an event that forces sector residents to leave in mass, such as when catastrophic, astronomical, or other events occur. This shows the value of making context-based decisions because uncertainty is likely to disappear.

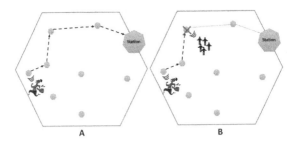

Fig. 2. IoT scenario with uncertainty problems.

3.2   Smart Spaces

Gartner, a consulting and IT research company, believed that smart spaces were one of the ten strategic technological trends in 2019. Gartner defined smart spaces as "a physical or digital environment in which humans and technology-enabled systems interact in increasingly open, connected, coordinated and intelligent ecosystems" [6].

Figure 3 denotes a scenario of a home focused on the care and wellbeing of an ill person, who requires monitoring of her activities and vital signs. Because her health may be affected by changes in light, temperature, humidity, and noise, these variables will also have to be controlled. This particular scenario depicts a house furnished with all types of sensors and portable devices used for controlling the environment and alerting a nearby hospital if needed. The idea is to provide immediate assistance by sending an ambulance. In addition, her social media are also monitored to supplement the data and, in some cases, to provide additional context to the data extracted from the sensor. Nevertheless, situations may occur in which uncertainty does not allow for a clear decision or wherein it may lead to incorrect decisions. For example, if the person decides to take a nap on the floor, it may appear that the patient has fainted or suffered an accident, depending on when the images or videos taken are seen. If a person is watching a horror movie, their pulse may be disturbed, but if the video is not able to determine what activity the person is doing, the data from portable devices may cause a false alarm. This example would show that context awareness is a significant matter when managing uncertainty in decision making.

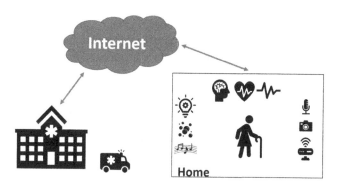

Fig. 3. Smart space scenario with uncertainty

3.3   Industry 4.0

To examine the impact of uncertainty on Industry 4.0, let us review the scenario of a call center providing customer services for a mobile phone company. The main goal of these service companies is to provide timely attention to as many customers as feasible. Therefore, the average time of user calls is a significant factor that must be controlled because network resources are limited, whether in terms of telephone lines or bandwidth. To streamline these resources, among other technological measures adopted, the call center has a Customer Relationship Management (CRM) system to profile users and record, monitor, track, and predict events. System data are registered after receiving user consent, whether from social media, information from cell phones, or through other means. The information recorded in the CRM system supports processing requests received by various means such as telephone calls, social media, chats, or email in a more efficient manner. Nevertheless, if this information is not properly contextualized, the opposite effect can be created, thus actually increasing the time spent in responding to a request and using more network infrastructure resources. The following example presents a case where people uncertainty affects resource usage for the proposed scenario. Let us assume that some users have been selected to answer a loyalty survey, which has an estimated maximum timeframe. Based on these criteria, users were selected if they had stated that they were highly satisfied with the service. In addition, users had to be young, assuming that they handle new technologies better; belong to a high socioeconomic status; reside in an urban population; and have completed minimum academic levels. Nevertheless, when the call center agent places the corresponding calls, some respondents who meet all the criteria exhibit conditions or situations that significantly increase the time required to complete the survey. For example, some may have some cognitive disorder, or answer the call while performing some other activity that they continue doing concurrently as they provide their responses, such as playing video games, or some may even have some mild hearing, vision, or speech impairments. Hence, as it can be observed that Industry 4.0 features offer, in a prospective vision, deep changes and transformations, especially in terms of the workforce, social inequality, and new business model developments. The application of such technological concepts also creates new challenges faced by communications networks to support services proposed by this fourth revolution, thus proving the need for developing computational methods to solve uncertainty problems related to human beings. Therefore, several proposals have been found to solve this kind of technical problems, and they all have SDN in common. SDN are emerging communications networks that separate the control plane from the data plane to allow for interoperability, programmability, and flexibility [20] to co-exist as features. In addition, all of the studies found address the technical problems of Industry 4.0 from several SDN-compatible focuses. For example, network virtualization [23], Ethernet network metrics [34], cloud manufacturing [30], cybersecurity [14], or resource allocation and information exchange for IoT [31].

4   Open Problems and Future Research Directions

The increased interweaving of networks and systems with human activities creates new development possibilities within several contexts. However, this brings about several challenges in the triad assessed in this work, such as the integration of decision making under uncertainty, network resource management, and HCN. At this stage, we describe the main open research problems arising within this context, classified as presented in Fig. 4.

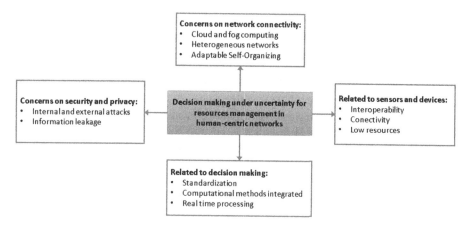

Fig. 4. Open problem categories

We identify, at least, the following future research directions:

- IoT massification and the deployment of the 5G network will cause high network densification, which brings about the need to examine new routing protocols that may support constant changes in user contexts. This means that these protocols may use context information whenever moment priorities change, employing the required resources to meet new objectives.
- The large level of ubiquity and information exchange among users and systems will facilitate security threats sustained by artificial intelligence. Therefore, there is an urgent need to set up policies and measures to protect personal information.
- HCNs can potentially generate large amounts of data due to the integration and interconnection of individuals and machines as part of their network infrastructure. The availability of data generated by people and machines brings about an opportunity to compile context awareness. In this light, a new information technology paradigm must be proposed to consider the rationality and irrationality of human behavior when managing the resources of underlying infrastructures. For instance, to suppress the data uncertainty that humans add to emerging networks, the structuralist nature of psychoanalysis can be researched to model human uncertainty.

5   Conclusions

In foresight, human-centric networks are destined to transform how we live our daily lives. Nevertheless, the intensive use that may be given to HCN may generate high traffic rates that will have an impact on DCN resources. However, the solution may be related to the data that generate this traffic. In this study, we presented a comprehensive review of several decision-making computational methods like MCDM, optimization algorithms, and machine learning proposed for dimensioning, control and deployment of future networks. These methods have been separately and jointly assessed in different fields, such as telecommunications, energy, transportation, health, business decisions, problems under uncertainty, complex systems, and for improving decision-making processes. However, various decision-making method combinations are clearly yet to be explored, especially those related to machine learning methods. In addition, we believe that a new multidisciplinary computational paradigm must be developed to address several uncertainty factors. Although it is beyond the scope of this review, information security is relevant issue due to the implications and the scope that may be feasible when processing private personal information. Therefore, we think that a strong emphasis should be placed on methods aimed at limiting potential abuses with personal data as, otherwise, the emerging concept of HCNs would lose all credibility. Finally, based on a review of emerging concepts, such as smart spaces and Industry 4.0, the lack of standardization is clearly evidenced, even in the heterogeneity of their definitions.

References

1. Almeida, A.T.d., Morais, D.C., Alencar, L.H., Clemente, T.R.N., Krym, E.M., Barboza, C.Z.: A multicriteria decision model for technology readiness assessment for energy based on PROMETHEE method with surrogate weights. In: 2014 IEEE International Conference on Industrial Engineering and Engineering Management, pp. 64–68 (2014)
2. Asadabadi, M.R.: The stratified multi-criteria decision-making method. Knowl.-Based Syst. **162**, 115–123 (2018)
3. Ashton K.: That 'Internet of Things' thing in the real world, things matter more than ideas. RFID J. (2009)
4. Cables, E., Lamata, M., Verdegay, J.: RIM-reference ideal method in multicriteria decision making. Inf. Sci. **337–338**, 1–10 (2016)
5. Cables, E.H., Lamata, M.T., Verdegay, J.L.: Ideal reference method with linguistic labels: a comparison with LTOPSIS. In: Bello, R., Falcon, R., Verdegay, J.L. (eds.) Uncertainty Management with Fuzzy and Rough Sets. SFSC, vol. 377, pp. 115–126. Springer, Cham (2019). https://doi.org/10.1007/978-3-030-10463-4_6
6. Cearley, D., Burke, B., Furlonger, D., Kandaswamy, R., Litan, A.: Top 10 Strategic Technology Trends for 2019. Technical report, March 2019, Gartner (2019)
7. Chahuara, P., Portet, F., Vacher, M.: Context-aware decision making under uncertainty for voice-based control of smart home. Expert Syst. Appl. **75**, 63–79 (2017)
8. Chen, S.M., Cheng, S.H., Lan, T.C.: A new multicriteria decision making method based on the topsis method and similarity measures between intuitionistic fuzzy sets. In: 2016 International Conference on Machine Learning and Cybernetics (ICMLC), vol. 2, pp. 692–696. IEEE, July 2016
9. Conti, M., Passarella, A., Das, S.K.: The Internet of People (IoP): a new wave in pervasive mobile computing. Pervasive Mob. Comput. **41**, 1–27 (2017)
10. Dammak, F., Baccour, L., Ayed, A.B., Alimi, A.M.: ELECTRE method using interval-valued intuitionistic fuzzy sets and possibility theory for multi-criteria decision making problem resolution. In: IEEE International Conference on Fuzzy Systems, pp. 1–6. IEEE, July 2017

11. Dix, A.: Human-computer interaction, foundations and new paradigms. J. Vis. Lang. Comput. **42**, 122–134 (2016)
12. Fei, X., et al.: CPS data streams analytics based on machine learning for cloud and fog computing: a survey. Future Gen. Comput. Syst. **90**, 435–450 (2019)
13. Ferrara, M., Rasouli, S., Khademi, M., Salimi, M.: A robust optimization model for a decision-making problem: an application for stock market. Oper. Res. Perspect. **4**, 136–141 (2017)
14. Fraile, F., Flores, J.L., Poler, R., Saiz, E.: Software-defined networking to improve cybersecurity in manufacturing oriented interoperability ecosystems. In: Popplewell, K., Thoben, K.-D., Knothe, T., Poler, R. (eds.) Enterprise Interoperability VIII. PIC, vol. 9, pp. 31–41. Springer, Cham (2019). https://doi.org/10.1007/978-3-030-13693-2_3
15. Gervasio, H., Da Silva, L.S.: A probabilistic decision-making approach for the sustainable assessment of infrastructures. Expert Syst. Appl. **39**(8), 7121–7131 (2012)
16. Jiang, W., Strufe, M., Schotten, H.D.: A SON decision-making framework for intelligent management in 5G mobile networks. In: 2017 3rd IEEE International Conference on Computer and Communications (ICCC), pp. 1158–1162. IEEE, December 2017
17. Ken, S.A.F. et al.: RFID and the inclusive model for the Internet of Things (2009)
18. Khezrimotlagh, D., Chen, Y.: Data envelopment analysis. In: International Series in Operations Research and Management Science, vol. 269, pp. 217–234. Springer, Dordrecht (2018)
19. Kochenderfer, M.J., et al.: Decision Making Under Uncertainty: Theory and Application. MIT Lincoln Laboratory Series (2015)
20. Kreutz, D., Ramos, F.M.V., Veríssimo, P.E., Rothenberg, C.E., Azodolmolky, S., Uhlig, S.: Software-defined networking: a comprehensive survey. Proc. IEEE **103**(1), 14–76 (2015)
21. Kumar, G.: A multi-criteria decision making approach for recommending a product using sentiment analysis. In: 2018 12th International Conference on Research Challenges in Information Science (RCIS), pp. 1–6. IEEE, May 2018
22. Lee, J., Bagheri, B., Kao, H.A.: A cyber-physical systems architecture for industry 4.0-based manufacturing systems. Manuf. Lett. **3**, 18–23 (2015)
23. Ma, Y.W., Chen, Y.C., Chen, J.L.: SDN-enabled network virtualization for industry 4.0 based on IoTs and cloud computing. In: 2017 19th International Conference on Advanced Communication Technology (ICACT), pp. 199–202. IEEE (2017)
24. Morente-Molinera, J.A., Kou, G., Samuylov, K., Ureña, R., Herrera-Viedma, E.: Carrying out consensual group decision making processes under social networks using sentiment analysis over comparative expressions. Knowl.-Based Syst. **165**, 335–345 (2019)
25. Mousavi, S.M., Gitinavard, H., Siadat, A.: A new hesitant fuzzy analytical hierarchy process method for decision-making problems under uncertainty. In: 2014 IEEE International Conference on Industrial Engineering and Engineering Management, pp. 622–626 (2014)
26. Perçin, S.: Evaluating airline service quality using a combined fuzzy decision-making approach. J. Air Transp. Manag. **68**, 48–60 (2018)
27. Qin, J., Liu, X., Pedrycz, W.: An extended VIKOR method based on prospect theory for multiple attribute decision making under interval type-2 fuzzy environment. Knowl.-Based Syst. **86**, 116–130 (2015)

28. Chen, S., Liu, J., Wang, H., Augusto, J.C.: An evidential reasoning based approach for decision making with partially ordered preference under uncertainty. In: 2013 International Conference on Machine Learning and Cybernetics, vol. 04, pp. 1712–1717. IEEE, July 2013

29. Smet, Y.D.: About the computation of robust PROMETHEE II rankings: empirical evidence. In: 2016 IEEE International Conference on Industrial Engineering and Engineering Management (IEEM), pp. 1116–1120 (2016)

30. Thames, L., Schaefer, D.: Software-defined cloud manufacturing for industry 4.0. Procedia CIRP **52**, 12–17 (2016)

31. Wan, J., et al.: Software-defined industrial Internet of Things in the context of industry 4.0. IEEE Sens. J. **16**(20), 1–1 (2016)

32. Wei, L., Yuan, Z., Yan, Y., Hou, J., Qin, T.: Evaluation of energy saving and emission reduction effect in thermal power plants based on entropy weight and PROMETHEE method. In: 2016 Chinese Control and Decision Conference (CCDC), pp. 143–146 (2016)

33. Yu, B., Cai, M., Li, Q.: A λ-rough set model and its applications with TOPSIS method to decision making. Knowl.-Based Syst. **165**, 420–431 (2019)

34. Zeng, P., Wang, Z., Jia, Z., Kong, L., Li, D., Jin, X.: Time-slotted software-defined industrial ethernet for real-time quality of service in industry 4.0. Future Gen. Comput. Syst. **99**, 1–10 (2019)

35. Zhang, P., Yao, H., Qiu, C., Liu, Y.: Virtual network embedding using node multiple metrics based on simplified ELECTRE method. IEEE Access **6**, 37314–37327 (2018)

An Initial Approach to a Multi-access Edge Computing Reference Architecture Implementation Using Kubernetes

Ignacio D. Martínez-Casanueva$^{(\boxtimes)}$ ⓘ, Luis Bellido ⓘ, Carlos M. Lentisco ⓘ, and David Fernández ⓘ

Departamento de Ingeniería de Sistemas Telemáticos, Universidad Politécnica de Madrid, 28040 Madrid, Spain
i.dominguezm@alumnos.upm.com

Abstract. The increasing demand of data and real-time analysis has given rise to edge computing, providing benefits such as low latency, efficient bandwidth usage, fine-grained location tracking, or task offloading. Edge computing based on containers brings additional benefits, facilitating the development and deployment of scalable applications adapting to changing market demands. But in order to enable edge computing in the telco industry, it is important that current standardization efforts are followed by software platforms implementing those standards. This paper proposes an approach to the design and implementation of an edge computing platform based on Kubernetes and Helm providing functional blocks and APIs as defined by ETSI in the Multi-Access Edge Computing (MEC) reference architecture. Although this proposal is still at a work-in-progress state, this paper describes the design and implementation of an open-source proof-of-concept scenario focusing on the lifecycle management of cloud native MEC applications. The resulting prototype shows the feasibility of this approach, that can be adequate to create a lightweight MEC demonstration platform for university laboratories and experimentation.

Keywords: Edge computing · Application virtualization · Platform virtualization

1 Introduction

Edge computing technologies, by moving cloud computing resources closer to the end users, bring many benefits such as low latency, efficient bandwidth usage, fine-grained location tracking, or task offloading. Edge computing based on containers rather than on virtual machines will help develop and deploy scalable applications that can adapt dynamically to meet changing market demands. But besides the computing resources to run applications, edge computing relies on management and orchestration services to manage the application lifecycle and orchestrate different services.

H. Gao et al. (Eds.): BROADNETS 2020, LNICST 355, pp. 185–193, 2021.
https://doi.org/10.1007/978-3-030-68737-3_13

ETSI has already began the standardization work for Multi-access Edge Computing (MEC). This paper presents an initial approach to implementing the MEC reference architecture defined by ETSI, using a container-based computing infrastructure. We focus on the Kubernetes platform because it provides scaling, scheduling and fault-tolerance features that can be leveraged to address the lifecycle management of cloud native MEC applications. But platforms providing edge computing management and orchestration services for container-based edge computing, such as Akraino or Airship, are still not aligned with the ETSI standards.

The objective of this work is to analyze how Kubernetes can support MEC services following a clean slate approach, in which first the ETSI standards are analyzed, to then map the reference architecture to a design based on Kubernetes and supported by other open-source components. In the long term, we think this approach can result in a reference platform that can be simpler to deploy than the current edge computing platforms for university laboratories and experimentation.

The remainder of the paper is organized as follows. Section 2 provides an overview of the MEC reference architecture, an introduction of Kubernetes and Helm as container management tools, and a discussion of related work. Section 3 describes the HelmMEC proposal, a middleware that allows the deployment of containerized MEC applications on Kubernetes following the ETSI standard specifications. Section 4 provides a description of a proof-of-concept showing the feasibility of this proposal. Finally, conclusions are summarized in Sect. 5.

2 Background

In this section, ETSI standardization of the Multi-Access Edge Computing (MEC) paradigm is first introduced along with the MEC reference architecture. Then, the new concept of cloud native applications is presented as an approach that can be embraced to build applications within the scope of MEC. Then, the main technologies used as a basis of the proposal are introduced: Kubernetes as a container management solution and Helm as a package manager for cloud native applications. Finally, a brief discussion of related work is provided.

2.1 Multi-access Edge Computing (MEC)

Edge computing is a new paradigm that moves cloud resources closer to the end users. Due to the proximity of the consumers to the applications, the edge computing technology brings many benefits such as low latency, an efficient bandwidth usage, fine-grained location tracking, or task offloading [1]. ETSI standardized the Multi-access Edge Computing (MEC) term and it is currently working on providing specifications of a reference architecture and the different APIs used by its components. ETSI ISG MEC defines a reference architecture [2] for MEC systems as depicted in Fig. 1, with two levels: MEC system level and MEC host level.

The MEC system level is composed of the following functional blocks: Operations Support System (OSS), MEC Orchestrator (MEO) and User Application Life Cycle Management Proxy (UALCMP). The MEO is the core component in the MEC system

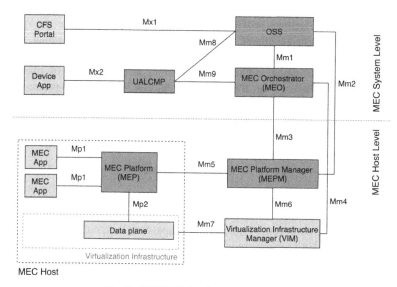

Fig. 1. ETSI MEC reference architecture

since it is responsible for keeping track of the provisioned MEC hosts, the available resources as well as MEC services. The MEO is also responsible for the management of MEC application packages, and the scheduling, relocation, and instantiation/termination of MEC applications deployed across the controlled MEC hosts. Customers or external device applications can interact with the MEO through the OSS, which is responsible for granting and forwarding requests to the MEO. Eventually, MEO forwards these requests to the MEPM, which realizes them by interacting with the target MEP and the VIM.

The MEC host level is composed of: MEC Platform Manager (MEPM), Virtualization Infrastructure Manager (VIM) and MEC host. The MEC host contains a virtualization infrastructure that supports the instantiation of MEC applications. These MEC applications are registered and configured by the MEC Platform (MEP) with the purpose of exposing and/or consuming services. The MEC applications may interact with each other and external users via a configurable data plane on the MEC host.

2.2 Cloud Native Applications

Due to the benefits that MEC provides, MEC technology opens an ecosystem for new and innovative applications that need to quickly adapt to changing market demands. In this respect, ETSI promotes the use of DevOps practices to deliver applications for MEC [3]. Development of cloud native applications has risen as one of the approaches followed by DevOps engineers.

Cloud native [4, 5] is a set of modern cloud techniques which aim at building scalable, dynamic applications than can quickly adapt to changing demands. Cloud native applications embrace microservices-based architectures rather than the common monolithic approach. The separation into independent services facilitates the development of applications as each microservice can evolve at a different pace. The package isolation

and portability that containers provide makes them the perfect choice for virtualization as developers can just focus on implementing the business logic rather worrying
about the underlying infrastructure. But building and deploying complex containerized
applications requires container orchestration, which can be provided by open source
orchestrators such as Docker Swarm [6] or Kubernetes (K8s) [7]. In this paper, we focus
on the Kubernetes platform because it provides scaling, scheduling or fault-tolerance
features that can be leveraged to address the lifecycle management of cloud native MEC
applications.

2.3 Helm

Helm [8] is an open source project that enables application package management for
cloud native applications that run on Kubernetes. Helm bundles the different Kubernetes
resources of an application (e.g., Pods, ConfigMaps, Services, etc.) into a Helm chart.
Helm charts are stored in a separate repository, and each chart may have different versions
available.

Using Helm, application lifecycle management is made possible by registering
releases of Helm charts in the Kubernetes datastore. Thus, when a user triggers a basic
management task from Helm, e.g., *instantiate*, Helm combines the previous, current,
and desired states of the application and applies changes in Kubernetes accordingly.
Helm operates with the Helm client which realizes charts as one-time operations against
Kubernetes. Upon issuing an operation over a given chart, the Helm client computes
changes and makes sure the resulting requests of resources to the Kubernetes API are
accepted. But, once this operation is finished, the Helm client no longer intervenes in
the lifecycle management of the chart.

Flux Helm Operator [9] is an open source project that provides an implementation
of a Kubernetes operator [10] for Helm. This project extends Kubernetes by defining the
Helm chart as a new Custom Resource Definition (CRD) and implements an operator
that runs Helm logic while watching for changes on Helm chart objects. Therefore, Flux
Helm Operator can be used as the basis of an application lifecycle management solution
for MEC applications based on Helm charts.

2.4 Related Work

Several open source platforms have been developed to provide the benefits of MEC
computing technologies in different industrial and entertainment areas. Akraino [11] is
an open source project of the Linux Foundation that implements MEC by using both
OpenStack and Kubernetes as a VIM. Airship [12] is a project originally conceived for
automatically deploying cloud infrastructures such as OpenStack. By means of Helm
charts, Airship automates the installation of OpenStack services such as Neutron or
Nova. But Airship can also be used to deploy MEC applications. However, the technical
documentation provided by these open source projects does not specify how the MEPM
and the MEO functions can be implemented in practice. This paper provides an initial
approach to implementing these functions using Helm and Kubernetes.

ETSI has focused for some time in an alternative approach to provide MEC. ETSI
has analyzed how the management and orchestration frameworks for MEC and for NFV,

which share many similarities, can be integrated into a unified MECinNFV architecture [13]. From this perspective, MEC applications can be deployed as VNFs over existing NFV platforms such as Open Source Mano (OSM) [14]. However, it is still not possible to deploy a MEC application over an NFV platform as it is defined in the standards. MEC applications are defined in a different manner than virtual network functions and the functions performed by the MEO and the MEPM differ from the functions that the NFVO and the VNFM entities can carry out. Taking into account these limitations, Schiller et al. developed a generic VNFM based on JuJu, that can also play the role of the MEPM [15]. However, in this paper we discuss how Kubernetes can work not only as a VIM, but also as the core of the MEPM. Section 3 explains that Kubernetes natively provides lifecycle management, scheduling, fault, or configuration features that make it an intent-driven orchestrator that meets the needs of the MEPM.

3 Cloud Native MEC Applications Managed by Helm

Kubernetes main limitation for working as a MEPM block is that it is not aware of the concept of a MEC application. Besides, identifying what exactly is a MEC application becomes cumbersome due to Kubernetes's nature. Hence, to fulfill the desired role of the MEPM, an additional functional block that translates from MEC application management to Kubernetes resource management is required. Helm offers this functionality by mapping Helm charts with MEC applications. Flux Helm Operator project provides a mechanism that can be utilized to manage the lifecycle of a MEC application while defining it in a declarative way through Kubernetes. As a result, Helm Operator works as a generic MEPM for MEC applications that are declared as Helm charts.

The declaration of MEC applications in Kubernetes provides the means for an implementation of the MEPM's interfaces specified by ETSI in the reference architecture (see Fig. 2). ETSI GS MEC 010 [16] provides REST API specifications for the Mm1 and Mm3 reference points. The Mm1.AppPkgm and Mm3.AppPkgm APIs focus on MEC application package management whereas Mm1.AppLcm and Mm3.AppLcm focus on MEC application lifecycle management. Additionally, ETSI defines Mm3.AppLccn APIs at the MEPM for notifying the MEO about changes on the status of an application instance that are related to lifecycle management operations. In this paper we propose an implementation of the MEPM via a new layer that supports Mm3.AppPkgm, Mm3.AppLcm and Mm3.AppLccn APIs. This layer receives the name of HelmMEC.

3.1 HelmMEC

Figure 3 shows an overview of the proposed MEPM design, including the K8s Control Plane and the three main components of HelmMEC: HelmMEC proxy, Flux Helm Operator, and NoSQL database.

The HelmMEC proxy is a web server that implements the standardized REST APIs at the Mm3 reference point. It is responsible for handling requests through the Mm3 reference point and translating them into interactions with the K8s Control Plane via the K8s API.

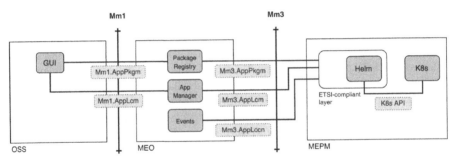

Fig. 2. REST APIs specified by ETSI for Mm1 and Mm3 reference points

The HelmMEC proxy uses a NoSQL database to store all the information related to MEC application instances. This information is necessary to run operations to create, delete, instantiate, and terminate MEC application instances. Each application instance has an appDId that is used by the HelmMEC proxy to identify which application package, i.e., Helm chart, is used by the application. The MEC application package information is managed at the MEO where the package appDId is associated with Helm chart-specific details.

The Helm Operator is the core component of HelmMEC as it provides the functionalities of a generic manager of Helm-based applications. Helm Operator achieves this by adding the HelmRelease CRD in Kubernetes, which will allow a declarative management of Helm-based applications via K8s API. The HelmMEC proxy interacts with the Helm Operator by configuring HelmRelease resources in Kubernetes. These configurations are the result of translating requests coming from the Mm3 REST APIs.

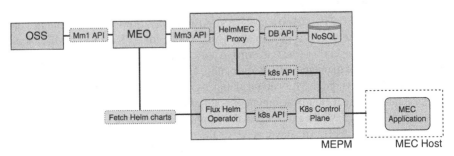

Fig. 3. HelmMEC internal components

As a result, the OSS can request lifecycle management operations on MEC application instances that will eventually trigger configurations in the Helm Operator. For example, in the case of instantiating a MEC application instance: the HelmMEC proxy creates a new HelmRelease in Kubernetes out from the package information of the application; the Helm Operator fetches the corresponding Helm chart information from the MEO, and ultimately orders Kubernetes the creation of the resources that compose the MEC application.

4 Proof-of-Concept Validation

In this section we introduce the prototype that has been developed to validate HelmMEC. The Virtual Network over linuX (VNX) [17] virtualization tool has been used to simulate a scenario that resembles a MEC system as depicted in Fig. 4. The installation and configuration of all the components has been automated with Ansible playbooks. The code of the prototype is available in our GitHub repository [18].

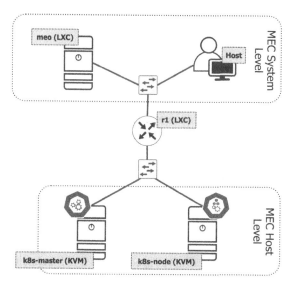

Fig. 4. MEC system prototype based on Kubernetes

At the MEC host level, a Kubernetes cluster is provisioned on two KVM virtual machines running Ubuntu 18.04 LTS image. The K8s cluster is configured using open source project Kubespray [19]. Kubespray is a collection of Ansible playbooks that enable installing production-ready Kubernetes clusters that can be easily customized with a variety of configuration parameters specified from Ansible. The HelmMEC components run as containerized services on the Kubernetes cluster. The HelmMEC proxy is based on a web server programmed with FastAPI framework [20] that partially implements the Mm3.AppLcm interface. An instance of MongoDB is deployed as the NoSQL database that stores application instance-related information. Flux Helm Operator runs as another Kubernetes service following Flux's guidelines.

An emulated gateway router (r1) provides connectivity between the MEC host level and the MEC system level. The router has been implemented by setting up a Linux Container (LXC) that runs Ubuntu 18.04 LTS. In addition, the BGP daemon BIRD [21] has been configured to BGP-peer with the Kubernetes cluster, thus enabling dynamic routing to services running in Kubernetes.

At the top of Fig. 4, the MEC system level components are displayed. This level contains the MEO which is deployed as a Linux Container (LXC) that runs an Ubuntu 18.04 image. The MEO is configured with a web server programmed using FastAPI web framework [20]. This web server acts as a MEC application package manager that partially implements the Mm1.AppPkgm interface. It relies on MongoDB as its NoSQL database for storing application package-related information. Additionally, the user's host machine is attached to the same network as the MEO, enabling users to interact with the MEC system as the OSS component.

As a result, the prototype allows users to request the MEO to onboard new Helm charts as MEC application packages, as well as directly request the MEPM to instantiate MEC applications from a chosen Helm chart.

5   Conclusions

We presented the HelmMEC middleware that leverages Kubernetes and Helm to realize MEPM functions. Helm provides package management features that fit the needs for cloud native MEC applications. By running Helm as a Kubernetes Operator, a promotion of generic applications as first-class objects in Kubernetes is achieved. This enables benefiting from Kubernetes lifecycle management capabilities for whole generic applications. HelmMEC proposal is aligned with ETSI reference architecture for MEC. The declarative definition of applications through Kubernetes, facilitates the integration with ETSI-specified APIs for the MEPM functional block.

The proof-of-concept presented in this work shows the feasibility of implementing a MEC system aligned with the reference architecture that is based on Kubernetes playing the roles of VIM and MEPM.

As a future work, the prototype will be extended to implement the remaining APIs for the reference points Mm1 and Mm3 as specified by ETSI. In addition, an elaborated association between MEC application packages and Helm charts should be addressed. The prototype will be a key element of initial experiments to support MEC based services on campus networks in the context of our research group projects.

Acknowledgement. This work was supported in part by the Spanish Ministry of Science and Innovation in the context of the ECTICS project (PID2019-105257RB-C21) and by the Spanish Ministry of Science, Innovation and Universities in the context of the Go2Edge project (RED2018–102585-T).

References

1. Hu, Y.C., Patel, M., Sabella, D., Sprecher, N., Young, V.: Mobile edge computing - a key technology towards 5G. https://www.etsi.org/images/files/ETSIWhitePapers/etsi_wp11_mec_a_key_technology_towards_5g.pdf. Accessed 30 Sept 2020
2. ETSI: Multi-access Edge Computing (MEC); Framework and Reference Architecture. ETSI GS MEC 003 V1.1.1 (2019)
3. Sabella, D., et al.: Developing software for multi-access edge computing. https://www.etsi.org/images/files/ETSIWhitePapers/etsi_wp20ed2_MEC_SoftwareDevelopment.pdf. Accessed 30 Sept 2020
4. Microsoft - Defining Cloud Native. https://docs.microsoft.com/en-us/dotnet/architecture/cloud-native/definition. Accessed 22 Sept 2020

5. Richardson, A.: What is cloud native and why does it exist? https://www.cncf.io/webinars/what-is-cloud-native-and-why-does-it-exist/. Accessed 24 Sept 2020
6. Docker Swarm mode overview. https://docs.docker.com/engine/swarm. Accessed 22 Sept 2020
7. Production-Grade Container Orchestration – Kubernetes. https://kubernetes.io. Accessed 08 June 2020
8. Helm. https://helm.sh/. Accessed 08 June 2020
9. Flux Helm Operator. https://docs.fluxcd.io/projects/helm-operator/en/stable/. Accessed 08 June 2020
10. Operator pattern – Kubernetes. https://kubernetes.io/docs/concepts/extend-kubernetes/operator/. Accessed 08 June 2020
11. Akraino. https://www.lfedge.org/projects/akraino. Accessed 22 Sept 2020
12. Airship: Automated OpenStack Deployment for Open Source Infrastructure. https://www.airshipit.org. Accessed 22 Sept 2020
13. ETSI: Mobile Edge Computing (MEC); Deployment of Mobile Edge Computing in an NFV environment. ETSI GR MEC 017 V1.1.1 (2018)
14. Open Source Mano. https://osm.etsi.org. Accessed 22 Sept 2020
15. Schiller, E., Nikaein, N., Kalogeiton, E., Gasparyan, M., Braun, T.: CDS-MEC: NFV/SDN-based Application Management for MEC in 5G Systems. Comput. Networks. **135**, 96–107 (2018). https://doi.org/10.1016/j.comnet.2018.02.013
16. ETSI: Multi-access Edge Computing (MEC); MEC Management; Part 2: Application lifecycle, rules and requirements management. ETSI GS MEC 010-2 V2.1.1 (2019)
17. Virtual Networks over linuX (VNX). https://web.dit.upm.es/vnxwiki/index.php/Main_Page. Accessed 08 June 2020
18. vnx-mec-k8s: VNX scenario that deploys a K8s-based MEC system. https://github.com/giros-dit/vnx-mec-k8s. Accessed 17 Sept 2020
19. Kubespray - Deploy a Production Ready Kubernetes Cluster. https://kubespray.io. Accessed 17 Sept 2020
20. FastAPI framework, high performance, easy to learn, fast to code, ready for production. https://fastapi.tiangolo.com. Accessed 21 Sept 2020
21. The BIRD Internet Routing Daemon Project. https://bird.network.cz. Accessed 22 Sept 2020

Author Index

Printed in the United States
By Bookmasters